ARE YOU PAID WHAT YOU'RE WORTH?

Michael O'Malley

ARE YOU PAID WHAT YOU'RE WORTH?

The Complete Guide to Calculating and
Negotiating the Salary, Benefits, Bonus,
and Raise You Deserve

BROADWAY BOOKS
NEW YORK

BROADWAY

Broadway Books titles may be purchased for business or promotional use or for special sales. For information, please write to: Special Markets Department, Bantam Doubleday Dell Publishing Group, Inc., 1540 Broadway, New York, NY 10036.

BROADWAY BOOKS and its logo, a letter B bisected on the diagonal, are trademarks of Broadway Books, a division of Bantam Doubleday Dell Publishing Group, Inc.

LIBRARY OF CONGRESS CATALOGING-IN-PUBLICATION DATA

O'Malley, Michael, 1954–
Are you paid what you're worth? : the complete guide to calculating and negotiating the salary, benefits, bonus, and raise you deserve / by Michael O'Malley. — 1st ed.
p.   cm.
Includes index.
ISBN 0-7679-0131-2
1. Wages.   2. Merit pay.   3. Negotiation in business.   I. Title.
HD4906.O47   1998
650.14—dc21   97-47523
                              CIP

FIRST EDITION

Designed by Kathryn Parise

98 99 00 01 02 10 9 8 7 6 5 4 3 2 1

To Stephanie, Kathryn, and Ryan—all the reward I need—
and to Don, Peg, and Nina
for their many years of encouragement and support.

Special thanks to Suzanne Oaks and John Thornton
for making this project possible and to Marlene Brask
for her behind-the-scenes artistry.

Contents

Introduction

When I ask employees to tell me something about their company's compensation plans, they usually respond with a shrug and something like this:

> "I didn't know we had a plan."
> "I know what I get paid, and that's about it."
> "I think there is something written on that somewhere."
> "To be honest, I couldn't tell you how it works."
> "Whatever it is, it doesn't pay enough."

The truth is, despite how much every single one of us cares about our earnings, most employees have only superficial knowledge of their compensation plans. And much of what we assume is often incorrect because our opinions arise from the one kernel of truth we possess—our own pay. But without knowing how these compensation systems work, you may be denying yourself the opportunity to get paid what you're worth or to increase your compensation to its maximum at your level of employment.

The purpose of *Are You Paid What You're Worth?* is to expose the secrets of the confusing compensation plans in the workplace so you will know how to improve your chances for greater earnings. Given the secrecy that surrounds compensation and the subterfuge of compensation jargon, discussing salary with an employer is like playing a game of cards that requires one person, the employee, to display his or her hand while the other party, the employer, conceals its. How could you ever win? It is impossible to play the compensation game effectively unless the rules are understood and the basic compensation facts are known.

In order to positively influence the amount you earn, you must understand how pay is determined within organizations and how to judge whether the amount of pay you receive is fair and competitive. In this book, I'll show you what companies actually do when determining your pay. This is not an economic or theoretical treatise on labor: Little attempt is made to explain the rationale for wages. Instead, I want to simply and clearly explain how employees in most corporate positions within most functional disciplines, professions, and industries—from the shop floor to the executive suites—are compensated and what procedures are used to set that compensation.

Are You Paid What You're Worth? explores the criteria companies use to set pay and allows you to use a personal version of these criteria to arrive at an accurate assessment of your own market value. All you need to do is answer a few simple questions and, based on your responses, calculate a dollar figure that represents your "competitive worth." Further, these estimates of market worth will take into account the size of the company for which you work (or for which you anticipate working), the type of industry in which you are employed, the functional area of your job (e.g., finance), and your company's location.

You will also be given the chance to realistically assess—for good or ill!—your unique value to your company. Companies do a poor job at this—at measuring the unique capabilities of a person—and it is the source of considerable frustration among employees. Let me give you an example that illustrates the point. Jan R. is an employee who feels underappreciated and underpaid. She looks for another job and finds one, comparable to the one she now has with one exception: she is offered 15% more money. She informs her company of her new job prospects and her company immediately makes a counteroffer.

What does this story say? It says that Jan's company wasn't attuned to her value and when confronted with certain facts was forced to admit that it wasn't paying Jan her full worth. The company, in all likelihood, would not have come to this realization without first being slammed in the head by a two-by-four. Companies tend to treat employees as an amorphous mass with respect to pay (i.e., each person in the same job class is pretty much treated the same way), while employees view themselves, not surprisingly, as individuals with uncommon qualities who generally are worth more than the going rate for the job.

Using a diagnostic test found in Chapter 4, you can score yourself on the degree to which you are indispensable to your company and the extent to which you make significant contributions. In turn, you will use this information to modify your general market worth to reflect the special talents and abilities you possess. Be warned, though: The result may not be flattering! You may discover that you are overpaid and not underpaid.

If you find that you are underpaid, as I suspect you will (who has ever concluded that he or she is overpaid?), that doesn't necessarily mean that your specific company will pay you for these attributes, but it *is* likely that some company will. In this sense, this exercise will provide you with an index of how much money you could probably fetch on the open market. This information is vital if you ever change jobs and would like to get a quick fix on your market potential.

As you can see from this brief introduction, there is ample opportunity within this book for you to see just how you measure up on pay. Throughout the book, you will be asked to contrast your pay with several subjective and objective standards to gauge the reasonableness and adequacy of your compensation, and you also will be given various references for evaluating your compensation such as model salary grades (adjusted by company size).

But you will have to work to maximize your pay and implement strategies for enhancing your compensation. One important caution is to never get too comfortable and complacent. Don't make the fatal mistake of believing that you will somehow be taken care of by a mythical compensation system that is impartial and exact in dispensing rewards when, in fact, it is neither. No matter how hard a company strives for perfect justice, it is never attained. Deliberate, active participation on your part is required in order to improve your chances of due recognition and increased pay.

When a company looks at its employees, it sees a sea of people like bobbers in the ocean and throws them just enough money to keep them afloat. Some employees stand out as shiny objects and get what they deserve. Most employees, however, have to wave for attention, "Hey, over here, over here." Take Laura R., a diligent, standout clerk, who went unnoticed for years. Laura developed new filing systems, new data entry procedures and spreadsheet templates, new methods of tracking and ordering office supplies, and introduced many other administrative efficiencies into her department. Her reward? Average annual increases of between 3% and 4%—until, that is, this unassuming clerk began to wave and the company began to notice her many achievements. Her reward? A promotion and a 10% pay adjustment.

In addition to strategies that will help you increase how much you're paid, this book will show you how to negotiate starting salaries and salary increases; how to get a promotion; how to position yourself for greater bonus opportunities; how to develop an airtight, high-level job description; how to maximize performance ratings; what benefits to look for before accepting an employment offer, etc. There is also considerable advice regarding the many economic decisions you will face during your work life, such as: "Should I accept lower base pay in exchange for greater stock?" "Should I accept an intracompany transfer to another business unit?" "How much should I ask for as a sign-on bonus?"

We'll also be discussing financial incentives on top of your salary— short- and long-term bonus plans, including gain sharing and stock options. You'll be able to review the usual eligibility criteria for getting into these plans and the amount of money (as a percent of base salary) that you can expect to receive from these plans. Most important, in keeping with the theme of this book, you are told what you can do to benefit more from these plans: how to get into them in the first place and what you can do to increase the likelihood and size of payouts.

This book addresses the compensation of employees in most positions, but there are jobs that require special handling or fall outside the for-profit corporate world, jobs to which special rules or restrictions apply. I'll discuss many of these positions—most notably, the almost 10% of the population who are "self-employed"—and how they can benefit from knowledge of how similar people are "valued" in the marketplace. I'll examine the opportunities and earnings of people who choose to work for themselves. Corporate employees who are seriously considering going it alone will find the information and salary data within this section of the book to be useful.

A good portion of employees work for nonprofits. The rationale for pay in these organizations mirrors that of for-profit companies, but there are financial and regulatory limitations that affect the amounts of compensation available and the ways in which compensation can be distributed. We will discuss these. Federal and state workers also have their own compensation system; most of what is described in this book applies equally to these employees.

Even within the corporate structure, a few groups are "different." Salespeople have their own compensation systems, and you'll see the range of earnings of various salespeople at different organizational levels, as well as learn how salespeople are paid (e.g., commissions).

Proximity to power (e.g., the financier's boat captain, the pilots on private jets, the corporate gardener), although formally not one of the criteria used for determining pay, clearly attracts compensation dollars. Compensation professionals have difficulty dealing with these positions because they don't fit neatly with other jobs in the compensation structure. That is because pay has to be augmented by a multiple of power (described in the book). And then there are the powerful themselves: the CEOs and the executives who report to them. There is clearly executive privilege with respect to pay, and the substance of this privilege is reviewed.

Companies are always experimenting with new social inventions for distributing pay among employees, and this book sifts through the various pay innovations and separates the fads from the ones that will be around for a while. For instance, companies are increasingly basing compensation decisions on the performance of groups of people, focusing on the "team's" efforts rather than the individual's. This trend will most likely continue to spread. Thus, you should know something about how these plans work. Similarly, skill-based pay has been around, off and on, for many years. These are pay plans that reward employees for developing their abilities and acquiring new skills. You should be aware of the advantages and disadvantages of these plans as well. There are also a host of social/family issues related to pay that will be mentioned throughout the book, including working part-time, working through a temporary agency, and two-wage-earner families.

Finally, we'll examine the potential psychic rewards and pleasures that may be derived from your work, and you are asked to measure these against your current pay to determine if it's all "worth it." We'll discuss very simple, tangible things you can do to increase your satisfaction with your job and how to deal effectively with barriers to that satisfaction, such as a nightmare boss, lack of career opportunities, and too much work and too little time. If you can increase your satisfaction with your job, you'll increase your satisfaction with your pay.

Traditionally in America there have been a few ways to amass wealth: A person could create a bestselling product or start a successful business, win in the financial marketplace, or receive a hefty inheritance. Each of these things involves risk or circumstances often beyond anyone's control. But there is another way to accumulate wealth in America: working for a company. Profitable companies are monster income-distribution factories and *Are You Paid What You're Worth?* intends to make you a benefactor.

Chapter 1

Underpaid, Overpaid, or Paid Just Right?

Advice from the Pros

Most people think that the surest way to increase their compensation is to complain about it. And, sure enough, every company has a high-profile complainer who seems to get what he or she wants by irritating others. Since you don't think of yourself as a complainer and would never stoop to whining in public, higher pay seems outside your reach. Here's your syllogistic argument, then:

> People who complain receive higher pay. I am not a complainer. Therefore, I won't receive higher pay.

There is a myth or misconception embedded in these assumptions. First, complainers usually don't get ahead—at least not by the mere fact of complaining. There are salient examples of those who squeaked and sulked their way to greater rewards but these are exceptions, not the rule.

Second, many people are under the mistaken belief that complaining is their only recourse to increasing their compensation. In actuality, demand-

ing, threatening, serving ultimatums, and in general, making unsubstanti-
ated claims for more money do not elicit much from others, other than
anger. There are more tactful and appropriate ways of making a point and
increasing your compensation that are explored throughout this book.

The pros—those who work behind the scenes at a variety of typical
companies—have several suggestions for you on how you can increase your
pay. I asked a number of practicing compensation experts what advice they
have for employees who want to maximize their compensation. The fifteen
most cited recommendations appear in Chart 1A.

On reviewing the list, you will notice that certain themes emerge. Of
course, being responsible, maintaining high performance, continuously
growing and taking decisive action, are all predictable responses and things
we already know we have to do. But the two pieces of advice employees often overlook are *understanding the mechanics of compensation in the workplace* and *being your own best advocate.* You've got to know how the
system works, then work to get the best from it.

Suppose you want to buy a used car. If you walk into a dealership without any preconception of the worth of used cars or how the sales process
works between you and the salesman, I can guarantee who will come out
on top.

In order to reach a favorable settlement on any issue that is open for negotiation, as is compensation, there are certain things you should know.
Let's pursue the used-car analogy. The first thing you have to understand is
what the car is worth. And not only do you have to know the suggested retail price for a particular year, make, and model, you have to know what can
potentially affect that price, up or down, such as special add-ons like power
windows and the general condition and expected longevity of the car as assessed by mileage repair records, etc. Similarly, in compensation, you have
to know your worth in the marketplace and the attributes for which companies may be willing to pay extra. They *do* pay extra. Companies have been
known to pay more for people from certain educational institutions or companies, for people with in-demand functional/technical expertise, depending on the company and industry, or for people with specific previous
experience (e.g., working in an international office).

Second, armed with the knowledge of what you want for yourself and
how much you are worth, you have to ask the difficult questions. If you
know a used car was serviced by the dealer, ask to see the records. Don't
just take his word for it. In compensation, there are some things that are secret, because under no circumstances are you, or others, to know. A com-

Chart 1A. Experts' Suggestions for Increasing Your Pay

1. Have a mind-set that is accepting of change—change creates new opportunities and employees who are open to change will more readily locate the opportunities.

2. Correctly assess your own contributions and deal with the conclusions: Have the humility to handle weakness and have the self-confidence to communicate your value and achievements.

3. Be willing to work outside the boundaries/scope of the job (on the fringes) and to make sacrifices.

4. Use the company as a resource for heightening your skills and abilities— take responsibility for taking developmental action.

5. Make life at work a continuous learning experience.

6. Be willing to take calculated career and business risks.

7. Understand what the company needs and values, and find ways of adding value in those areas; if you are in an incentive plan, get to know the plan so you know what to do.

8. Maintain a positive attitude—enjoy what you do and contribute to a positive work environment.

9. Take on as much responsibility as possible without compromising quality of work or becoming too "scattered."

10. Be action oriented—follow through on ideas and suggestions.

11. Trade fixed pay for variable pay—that is, sacrifice a part of your base salary for bonuses. It usually pays off.

12. Work hard and long.

13. Ask for advice from others when you need it—there are people who are always willing and able to help.

14. Understand that different industries and different disciplines (e.g., engineering, accounting, etc.) pay differently—some more than others.

15. Document your achievements, let others know what you've done, and know when and how to ask for a raise.

pany won't tell you what someone else earns, for example. But many things remain secrets simply because no one has asked. The answers aren't forbidden, but they won't be volunteered either. "What is the salary range [i.e., the minimum and maximum] for this position?" almost always elicits a candid response. So does, "What are the main distinctions between a position within this level of the organization, and one at the next highest level?" "Which companies (or types of companies) do you compare yourself to when determining salary for these positions?" These are fair questions that give you a wealth of information. They give you a good picture of what a company will pay for a given job, without ever having to explicitly ask about "price."

Third, you have to have the conviction to be a resolute negotiator and the courage to walk away from arrangements that are not in your interest. Chapter 7 is dedicated to methods of negotiating salaries. Your *attitude* is what I want to emphasize here. A dealer knows from your demeanor, the way you say things and the decisiveness of your expression, just how flexible (i.e., easy) you really are. When discussing your pay with a company, if you are unsure of your value, the company will be unsure of your value. Conversely, if you have an accurate and firm sense of your worth and tactfully communicate that to your employer (I'll tell you how later in the book), you will have a better chance of getting what you want.

Fourth, you have to read the fine print. Once an agreement is finally sealed, there is not much left to discuss. Have you ever asked a dealer to fix something on a car for which you just signed and paid? There isn't much motivation there, not without a cost to you. There is quite a bit that can be agreed to and acted upon on the basis of trust without formal contract. But not promises of money. If an employer says it will do something financially for you in the future, you should test that commitment by requesting a written document.

There are two main reasons employees don't ask for compensation commitments in writing. First, there is a fundamental confusion about which party is the seller and which party is the buyer. People are often so wrapped up in the excitement of a new job or new promotion that they often don't question what's being offered. But know this: You are the seller, and the company is the buyer. Through salaries, signing bonuses, various incentives, relocation reimbursements, separation packages, etc., a company is making an offer to purchase your talents. It is reasonable to ask them to spell it out on a piece of paper. A second factor is that employees have a tendency to think that formal agreements are somehow disruptive to relationships; that it is too much to ask among "friends." It's not true. I can assure you that broken promises have broken more hearts than broken contracts have.

Finally, if you ever want to resell that old car you bought, you will have to keep it in good working order. Similarly, you are responsible for your personal development. However, you have a definite advantage over a car. You can appreciate in value if you keep yourself intellectually and technically fit. You can get more and more expensive, which is good news to you and your employer since you both benefit.

What Is Your "Blue Book" Value?

When I ask employees what they want to know about compensation, they routinely answer that they want to know what is fair and reasonable pay for them and how to go about getting it. They want the compensation equivalent to the "blue book" value for cars.

The questions, "Am I paid fairly?" or, "Am I paid enough?" or, "Am I paid what I am worth?" can be answered by you in one or both of two ways: (1) by comparing yourself to some external standard and seeing where you lie in relationship to that standard; (2) by setting a goal for yourself and striving to meet it—the gap between where you are and your aspirations being a measure of your success. For ease of communication, I'll refer to the first type of standard as "comparative" and to the second type as "noncomparative."

Comparative Standards:
How You Measure Up to Everybody Else

There are two types of comparative standards that involve comparisons between what you get paid and what others get paid. In one instance, you compare yourself to others around you within the company: to those persons' efforts, abilities, contributions, responsibilities, etc., and to their likely salaries. It is wholly natural to make these social comparisons to see how you measure up against others. You make a judgment of fairness based on what you do and offer the company and receive in compensation, and what others do and offer and receive in compensation. If these comparisons do not match up, if there is a disconnect between what you do and what you get, versus what others do and get, you will perceive the system as unfair. And you, for one, may feel undercompensated because you believe you offer as much or more to the company than others but get paid less. You will often hear companies refer to this as an issue of *internal equity.*

The other comparative standard involves comparing yourself to others who perform similar work outside of your company. Companies refer to this as *external equity*. Having a pay system that is externally equitable means that no matter which company you approach in your geographic area (often within the same industry), that company would pay about what you currently get paid for the performance of similar job duties and responsibilities. Inequity exists to the extent to which your company pays less, or more, than similar companies. I assume you won't complain if you are earning "too much." Let's take a closer look at internal and external equity before we move on.

Internal Equity:
How You Stack Up with Your Colleagues at Work

This is the most obvious, straightforward way of recognizing fairness: by comparing yourself to others who work near you. When you look at the sum total of what those around you bring to the table and see what they earn, compared to what you bring to the table and what you earn, does it make sense?

Now you know why companies don't like people talking about what they earn. In some companies, such discussions are "dismissable offenses." Polite conversation about what everyone earns is often forbidden because it leads to questions of fairness and, potentially, to employee dissatisfaction. In trying to make life fair, most attempts fall short. And it isn't because your human resources department doesn't try. Achieving internal equity is a basic tenet of any self-respecting human resources department.

There are many complicating factors that create internal inequities. First, you can't earn more than your boss. Even companies that have "flattened" the organizational hierarchy and claim workforce parity have extreme difficulty in violating this axiom of corporate life. The problem, of course, is that your boss may not have kept up with the times, particularly in areas that are rapidly changing. Your boss may not have a clue, but he or she pulls in a higher salary. I have met heads of information technology departments (of big companies!), for example, who wouldn't know a PC if it fell on them. Now I can appreciate managerial acumen but shouldn't a person in a supervisory position know something about the area in which he or she supervises? Nevertheless, these people are paid more than their underlings.

There aren't a lot of great options about how to avoid this, but let me alert you to what is futile. Don't curse and denounce hierarchy. Every complex social system has a "pecking order." Some ordering of authority will always be found and is quite "natural." Indeed, I believe organizations would be better off if they acknowledged this fact rather than touting concepts that are often meaningless like "flattening the organization" and "empowerment" (and simultaneously acknowledge that the way power is distributed within a company has very little to do with the way work is done).

Also, don't discuss your boss's incompetence with your boss's boss or seek to have him or her removed. Incompetent people have an uncanny staying power. And if you thought your life was unbearable before you complained about your boss. . . .

Fundamentally, the problem with bad bosses is that they never get anywhere. And whereas they may never have been told they are mediocre performers, their pay is likely to reflect that fact. Insofar as your boss's pay acts as a ceiling to your own, that's a problem! Conventional wisdom may suggest that having a boss with inferior skills who may someday be replaced (by you, perhaps) is desirable, but the contrary is true. Find a boss whose talents you respect and who appears to be psychologically balanced. He or she is more likely:

(1) to get better pay raises
(2) to get promoted
(3) to help you refine your own skills
(4) to help you get promoted

All of this is good news for your earnings. It is like a bicycle race; a good boss who is on the move can pull you along in his or her draft.

A second complicating factor to maintaining internal equity is inequities created by new hires. Have you ever noticed that whenever new people are hired, they earn more than you for the same work? It happens. What also frequently happens over time is that as new people are hired in, the pay between organizational levels begins to blur. With people coming and going, the nice distinction in pay between levels is often tough to maintain. Companies refer to this as "pay compression." This is when the compensation paid at one level in the organization abuts the compensation of another level—two different sets of jobs are paid similarly, which threatens to violate the rule that employees higher in the organizational hierarchy should be paid more. It is hard to control internal equity with people coming and going all of the time.

Of course, you can play the same game and hop to a new job. That is, you can be the new hire. Indeed, workers are more mobile than ever before and quite readily exercise the "move" option. It is estimated that the average employee will make seven to nine job or company changes and will have three different career tracks during his or her work life.

But let's assume that you like where you are. Having people come in at greater pay can work to your advantage if:

(1) The pay differential is noticeable.
(2) It seems to be a recurring problem; the position appears to be impossible to fill except at greater pay than your own.

Under these conditions, there is likely to be a reassessment of your job and pay that may lead to a pay adjustment. That is, if the problem of paying new employees more than the old occurs frequently enough, your pay will likely be bumped up as well. Again, such situations are a source of angst for most human resources departments who strive for fairness. But they have to notice the problem first and not all of them do.

I know what you're thinking. How can you bring it to their attention if you don't know for sure what others earn? You don't have to know in order to raise a "concern" with your boss about your salary compared to the "newcomers." One top-performing employee I met raised the subject of undercompensation vis-à-vis newly hired employees with his superior by suggesting he be the highest paid employee within his particular work group. He'll never know for sure if he is, but he received a handsome increase. His boss obviously realized that his contributions relative to others warranted higher pay.

A third complication arises because of the way pay is set by the company. Much more will be said about how this is done in the following chapters. For now, the important point to note is that pay is determined *by the job* and not *by the person*. To some extent, your "excess" skills and abilities are not recognized by your pay. If they are not required for the performance of your job duties, they are not relevant.

That, however, creates perceived inequities. Your potential, given your abilities, may be far greater than another's but your pay is comparable. The trick, then, is to find a way of using your full potential so that the compensation system can recognize it. One strategy is to think of using the skills you have in unusual ways in your current position. The best employees play to their strengths. Sally T. relied upon her strong team-building skills to become a cult heroine within a telecommunications company by going to the company's various call centers and improving their performance on the strength of her leadership abilities. There are three directions that optimizing your skills can lead and they are all positive:

(1) It can lead to a stellar performance review and increased earnings.
(2) It can lead to a redesign of your job and a salary that is adjusted upward. There are many instances where jobs are created by the jobholder who has special skills and abilities.
(3) It can lead to a promotion with the attendant pay increase.

Another strategy is to look for another job within the company that is a better "fit" with your abilities. Many companies have programs that internally advertise job openings along with the skills required to competently perform the job (i.e., job postings). Look for companies that promote internal movement.

My personal theory of the best way of dealing with internal inequities is to remove the secrecy surrounding pay and appeal to public opinion. Everyone should be required to wear their total compensation value on a name badge and allow the spectacle of public discourse to rule. Those who are clearly not "worth it" are run out of town, and those who are, are retained and rewarded. This will never happen, of course. To maintain a certain degree of civility in the workplace, employees' pay will never be widely advertised or openly discussed.

External Equity:
How You Stack Up Industry-wide

External equity is another form of fairness that companies closely watch over. Here, fairness is determined by comparison between your earnings in your position and the earnings of others in similar positions in *other* companies that may vie for your services. External equity is discussed at length in the following chapter so I'll reserve some commentary for later. Suffice it to say that setting compensation so that it is externally equitable is difficult. It could be done better, as discussed below, but it would still lead to imperfect results. If you look for social injustice, you will be sure to find it.

Just as there will always be someone who is stronger, bigger, faster, smarter, etc., there will always be someone who earns more than you. People who are unhappy with the work they are doing have a knack of finding the one person who earns more than they do.

Companies routinely participate in, and subscribe to, compensation surveys that match jobs across companies and typically set compensation at an average level. So, in reality, if you have been in your current job for an average length of time, there is a good chance that at least half of the population who occupies positions similar to yours, earn more than you do.

Does this make it unfair? Not necessarily—and here is what makes external equity hard to establish. To say that pay is truly externally equitable, your pay would have to be matched against that of others (1) in similar jobs, (2) with similar tenures in the position, and who (3) have similar talents and similar performance. Further, these comparisons would have to be *relevant*. That is, they would have to be made with other positions to which you (and others) are likely to move to or from.

There is always discussion among company insiders and consultants about what constitutes the relevant labor market: about which companies people go to and come from. This information, however, is never verified through records although ostensibly that information would be available from recruitment files and exit interviews. Companies try to collect as much compensation survey information on other companies as they can and then make educated guesses about its relevance to various jobs within their own companies. There is plenty of room for survey gamesmanship, however, particularly at the executive level. For instance, in twenty years of consulting I have never seen a company's survey information show that the company's top executives are overpaid. Never. Doesn't that sound a little suspicious?

Neither are personal attributes such as skill level and performance ever matched. Salary surveys show what a particular job is paid but don't say anything about the kinds of people in those jobs. The major consideration in compensation surveys is the job and even here there are imprecisions. No two jobs are identical and yet, for the most part, they are treated as such in surveys. Subjective judgments and leaps of faith are required when peering at jobs across organizations.

I have provided you with a number of calculations related to external equity in Chapters 2–4. In these chapters, you will be able to look at external equity from many perspectives and arrive at a pay value that is closely aligned with your own position, abilities, and circumstances.

Noncomparative Standards:
How Well Do *You* Think You Should Be Doing?

The other major way to decide upon the fairness/unfairness or adequacy/inadequacy of your pay is to reflect upon your standard of living. Is it in line with your expectations?

Admittedly, the easiest route to personal fulfillment may be to have low material expectations. That may be difficult, however, in a culture that thrives on commercialism and encourages consumption. People generally expect more, not less, and hope to gain in economic stature over time. So before you decide to lower your expectations, let's see where you are and what you could be doing differently.

If you are like most Americans, you probably do not feel that you earn enough to live comfortably. A recent poll (see the *Wall Street Journal,* September 20, 1996, p. R4) suggests that fewer than one in five Americans believes he earns enough to live comfortably and more than one in four says he lives from paycheck to paycheck. That same poll indicates that things are getting worse and not better. More Americans feel worse off today than they did just six years ago.

There is good reason why people feel financially beleaguered. There is strong evidence that income stagnation is alive and well, and will continue for some time. Recent statistics provided by the Bureau of Labor Statistics (described in *BusinessWeek,* November 19, 1996, p. 116) illustrate that, on average, wages against inflation are falling. People have been struggling to increase their incomes by working longer hours, holding two jobs, and having multiple family wage earners.

But exactly how much will you need to make to live well? The old adage that "if you do good, you'll do well" no longer holds. It is no longer sufficient to put in a hard day's work and expect miraculous outcomes. To beat the odds of slow wage growth, you will have to have a plan, and take action.

There are some rules of thumb that will help you to set an earnings target. Remember, these are just rough guidelines that are intended to give you an idea of what you should be earning in order to keep pace with changing standards of living and to help you to get moving in the right economic direction. At a minimum, you should be able to pull your per capita weight. In 1996, U.S. per capita income was $24,200. Thus, if you are a single wage earner, you should make *at least* that. If you are a part of a larger household, you will want to earn at least the median household income of $35,300. The median is the value that separates the population in half: half of the nation's households earn more and half earn less. You'll want to be in the top half!

Household incomes naturally vary with age, as shown in Chart 1B. The older you are (up to the early retirement age of 55), the greater your earning power. That fact gave rise to a longstanding rule of thumb that says, "To sustain a high quality standard of living throughout your life cycle, your salary needs to keep pace with your age, times $1,000." So, a thirty-year-old should be earning $30,000, a forty-year-old, $40,000, and so on. *Fortune* (June 26, 1995, pp. 66–76), however, recently argued that the formula needs serious updating. A lifestyle today equivalent to one twenty years ago now requires four times your age, times $1,000. Taxes, housing, medical

CHART 1B. MEDIAN HOUSEHOLD INCOMES

Age Group	Median Income
15–24	$21,400
25–34	$35,900
35–44	$44,400
45–54	$50,500
55–64	$39,800
65 and over	$19,400
Overall (2-year average, 1995–1996)	$35,300

Source: U.S. Bureau of the Census, 1996.

expenses, college tuitions, and interest from record consumer debts have taken a toll on disposable income. That thirty-year old, mentioned above, now needs $120,000 and the forty-year-old, $160,000.

These incomes are out of range for most Americans, singly or as families. Ninety-five percent of individual taxpayers earn less than $91,000. Few jobs pay these sums. A more modest and realistic proposal is this: Each member of the household should earn his or her age times $1,000, and the cumulative total is the amount of money you should be earning as a household. This acknowledges that people generally want more as they get older, can earn more as they get older, and have greater financial necessities that come with children. It also recognizes that more spouses work today than twenty to thirty years ago (about 60% of women today are employed versus about 40% in 1965).

If there is a non-income-producing member of the family, another member has to pick up the slack. Remember, children can work and it is often advantageous to employ them in family businesses—you get basic duties performed and get money out of the business while keeping it in the family at a lower tax bracket. It is "cheaper" money to apply to college tuitions, for example. Unless your children have good lawyers, you can usually "recommend" how the money is spent.

The worksheet in Chart 1C leads you through the calculations for determining the individual and family income required for comfortable living, using the revised rule of thumb that I have introduced above. Perform the calculations and then evaluate where you are in relation to the total needed. How are you doing?

Now that we've gone through several ways of evaluating your current pay in this chapter, you can start to evaluate where you stand overall. I have developed a short quiz for you to take in Chart 1D with questions based on concepts we've just discussed. Take the time now to complete it.

If you scored 36 or above, you are either doing really well, living an isolated, spartan existence, or stretching the truth a bit. Don't be discouraged

CHART 1C. HOW MUCH MONEY DO YOU NEED TO LIVE COMFORTABLY?

A Rule of Thumb

Your Age:	_____	×	$1,000	= _____
Your Spouse's Age:	_____	×	$1,000	= _____
The Total of Your Children's Ages:	_____	×	$1,000	= _____

(1) Total (what you should earn as a rule of thumb) = _____

(2) Your Current Household Income = _____

(3) Differences: (1) minus (2) = _____

CHART 1D. TEST YOUR PAY

Instructions

Check the box that applies by giving your honest answer. Add up your total points and look to the key below to see how you are doing.

	Not at all true (1 point)	Somewhat true (2 points)	Moderately true (3 points)	Mostly true (4 points)	Completely true (5 points)
1. Compared to others, I am paid just about right.	❑	❑	❑	❑	❑
2. Given my skills and contributions to the company, I think I am fairly paid.	❑	❑	❑	❑	❑
3. If I moved to another company for the same job, I would be paid about the same or less.	❑	❑	❑	❑	❑
4. Most people I know with my education, training, and experience earn about what I earn, or less.	❑	❑	❑	❑	❑
5. I make enough income to live comfortably.	❑	❑	❑	❑	❑
6. I am satisfied with the amount of money I earn.	❑	❑	❑	❑	❑
7. In terms of compensation, I am doing better than most people.	❑	❑	❑	❑	❑
8. Given my age and salary progress to date, I am definitely on the compensation fast track.	❑	❑	❑	❑	❑

Key:

36–40 points	Excellent
32–35 points	Good
28–31 points	Fair
< 28 points	Not Excellent, Good, or Fair

if you did not do well on the quiz. There are remedies. This book will help you to improve your score by helping you to successfully navigate through the corporate compensation maze. If you are only a few points away from the "excellent" range on the quiz, it won't take much to elevate your score to where it should be. You will find a suggestion or two in this book that will make a difference. The further away you are from a score of "excellent," the more work you'll have to do, including making a hard and critical self-examination of your current strengths and weaknesses; finding your way to any destination requires knowing your starting place.

Chapter 2

How Your Pay Is Set

It's the "Job" That Counts

The official "job" remains the focal point of most compensation systems. That is good news for you since jobs are "man-made." They can be chiseled and formed by your imagination.

"So, what do you do for a living?" is one of the most important questions for which you need a good answer in life. A good, prepared answer will make you look smart at parties. Your answer will also determine how much money you will make within your company.

Thus, the description of your job is a critical element of corporate life. And the remarkable aspect in all of this is that despite the significance of the description, most companies let you write the description yourself. Writing job descriptions is viewed as a time-consuming nuisance that companies prefer you handle—subject to review. Further, this is one of those grand enterprises in which all are equally motivated to exaggerate what they should be doing in favorable ways. It is a rare moment when supervisor and supervisee see eye to eye. A flash of unspoken camaraderie to embellish the truth. It helps everyone: the grander the job, the higher the pay.

Generally, the determination of your job description follows this process:

1) You prepare your job description, which then undergoes cursory review by your supervisor.

2) The description is sent to Human Resources for review; typically, Human Resources *evaluates* the content of the job. When Human Resources evaluates your job, they are making a judgment about its magnitude relative to other jobs in the company; the bigger your job compared to other jobs, the more money you will make. Some companies forego this step and move directly to Step 3, below.

In your corporate life, you will catch wind of many ways of determining the "size" of your job: whole job ranking, factor comparison, point factor, market pricing, blah, blah, blah. All you need to know for now is that all of these methods are classification systems.

Classification entails putting objects (i.e., jobs) into exhaustive and mutually exclusive groups (i.e., grades or bands) according to some attribute or set of attributes (such as level of experience and training required to perform the job), so that each job belongs to one and only one group. Our concern is not the particular method used to classify jobs, but the attributes used to distinguish among jobs.

Chapter 3 will take you through a detailed exercise on classifying your job using highly specific criteria. But there are shorthand "attributes" that we will presently discuss.

Every company has some form of "grade" structure in which jobs are ranked from high to low. The grade represents a class of jobs that have been judged to be similar. The number of grades depends upon the size of the organization. You'll see throughout this book that the size of the organization, as measured in revenue, is relevant to how and how much employees are paid. In rare instances, companies treat each job as unique. There, in essence, each job is its own class; the presumption is that there are no meaningful, common characteristics among jobs. Companies that pursue this course are taking on a lot of work for nothing.

There is generally an internal human resources staff (or internal cross-functional committee) who is responsible for classifying jobs. In touchy, highly political situations (such as human resources positions where the reviewer is being reviewed or jobs for which no clear consensus of opinion emerges), they are assisted by an outside consultant. In any case, the evaluation process determines the relative value of your job within your company.

3) Your job (or a numerical index of your job, as evaluated) is compared to other jobs like it in the labor market. Information on compensation for various jobs is readily available through surveys, mostly conducted by major consulting firms.

4) Based on all of the above information (the job description and its compensation value), your job is usually grouped with others like it into a salary grade. Some "purist" companies classify jobs into grades solely based on the description and associated job evaluation, and handle jobs that pay significantly more or less than others within a grade as special cases. This sometimes occurs with "hot" jobs and labor shortages. Currently, many companies are looking for information-systems people and, in order to attract and retain these type of employees, companies offer them a bit more salary and bonus. The market demands higher pay for positions that appear to be no different in size (i.e., in job content) than other jobs that are paid less within the same grade. Other companies look at the comparative salary data, and even though the job doesn't seem to warrant a higher grade on its own grounds, the company plops the job into a different grade based on the salary information.

5) A salary range for the grade is created that defines the minimum and maximum to be paid within the grade. The salary ranges for all of the grades are referred to as the *salary structure*.

The higher the grade that you are in, the greater your compensation potential, with a higher grade meaning about 5% to 15% greater compensation to you. With this size of pay increase possible, the onerous task of composing job descriptions is one of the most valuable and self-serving exercises that you can perform. It is the perfect occasion to influence your job by a grade. And the beauty of the process is that you will probably never end up having to do all of the work you describe. But if you did, that's okay; writing your job description gives you the chance to craft a better job for yourself that's more challenging and more fun.

What Is Your Job Description?

Most amateur writers of descriptions assume that by loading a description up with a plethora of job duties, their job will be bigger. But more is not better. It is the level of work that matters, and not so much the amount. It is a common misconception that the more worn out you get, the more pay you deserve. That's false. What good would more money do you anyway if you were really that tired?

There are many job description formats but all are designed to capture the *minimum* basic requirements needed to perform a job competently. If you ask yourself, "What is a job?" you will quickly ascertain these requirements: the knowledge you need to perform the job (education, training, and experience often serve as proxies for knowledge; the higher the standard you set, the better off you are; note, you don't actually have to have the educational background you view to be minimal—if you lack the required minimum studies, your argument is that you have more than made up for these deficits in experience); the complexity of problems that you normally confront and the difficulty of their resolution; and the amount of responsibility that you have.

Obviously, the more you have to know, the more difficult and challenging problems you routinely face, and the greater your accountability, the more you will be paid. Further, all of these elements should be consistent with one another. A seasoned reviewer in human resources or a consulting firm can spot inconsistencies; so make sure you don't write, for instance, a description for a job that requires a lot of education in order to deal with simple problems or that has very little decision-making discretion.

Again, I will discuss the finer points of the various job requirements in Chapter 3. But there are easy ways to gauge what makes some jobs "bigger" than others. Let's take a look at your own job to see how it's perceived by "the guys upstairs." Complete and score yourself on the quiz in Chart 2A. Hold on to your score; we'll be using it later.

It should be apparent from the quiz that three aspects of your job can increase its perceived market value and there are three major dimensions that companies use to distinguish among jobs. Companies may not consciously recognize these but they certainly will correlate highly with your pay.

First, the more "strategic" a job, the more highly compensated you will be. Most work performed in companies can be broken down into four major chunks: There is work that is strategic, work that is tactical, work that is operational, and work that is executional.

Strategic people sit in corner offices and think lofty thoughts about markets, products, the competition, and the like. They determine the general direction of the company and set the short- and long-term financial and nonfinancial objectives of the company.

CHART 2A. CRITICAL JOB ATTRIBUTES

Instructions: Please circle the answer to each of the items below
that best describes your job.

How would you describe what you do in general terms?

1	2	3	4	5	6	7	8
Performs specific tasks in accord with prescribed design, rules, etc., and/or close supervision.	Performs general activities according to general procedures and/or occasional supervision.	Follows a process or methodology and performs a series of interrelated activities to effect a particular purpose or result.	Develops systems, methods, and approaches to various issues and work activities.	Determines operating procedures, standards, resource requirements, etc., for a significant part of the company or significant corporate projects.	Determines how to meet/secure objectives designed by the corporate strategy.	Key adviser to the most senior management on strategic issues; determines objectives for a significant part of the company—provides direction for a significant part of the company.	Sets longer-term corporate goals; determines the corporate strategy.

How long does it take you to complete your *most important* assignments for
which there are tangible end results?

1	2	3	4	5	6	7	8
1 day–1 week	1 week–1 month	1 month–3 months	3 months–6 months	6 months–1 year	1 year	1 year–3 years	3 years or longer

How big of a direct impact would you say you have on your company's
financial results? ("Direct" means that there is a clear link between what you
do and various financial indicators of corporate success such as lower costs
or higher revenues.)

1	2	3	4	5	6	7	8
No Effect	Negligible Effect	Small but Detectable Effect	Small to Moderate Effect	Moderate Effect	Moderate to Large Effect	Large Effect	Very Large Effect

Total your points and put the sum here _____

The *tactical* people are the ones who try to figure out what the strategic
people are talking about. They decide what a strategy implies for corporate
action and what the company should do. They assess the options open to it,
the resources available, and the general capabilities of the company to move

in different directions. If there are insufficient resources, they may recommend certain capital purchases, changes in personnel, the addition of new departments, and so on.

Once a plan of action is devised, the *operational* folks take over. These are the people who make sure that things happen in the right way, at the right time, with the right people, at the highest quality, etc. They muster resources and lead (or, more typically, send) the frontline troops into battle.

The people they send into battle—the *executional* people—form the heart and soul of the organization. These are the people who *execute* tasks; they actually do the work. Well, somebody has to do it! When all of the orders and mandates trickle down, this is where they land. The first scale in the chart measures the degree to which your job is strategic versus executional.

The second scale measures how long it takes you to accomplish your most significant tasks that have tangible outcomes. (The author Elliot Jacques, in *Requisite Organization: The CEO's Guide to Creative Structure and Leadership,* Cusson-Hall, 1989, calls this your "time span of discretion.") People who perform tasks that take longer to complete get paid more. That is because tasks with longer time frames typically:

- are more strategic
- require more training and experience
- are more difficult
- have higher corporate payoffs

Thus, this scale really measures many different things and serves as a good index to the size of a job and where it will eventually be placed in the corporate hierarchy.

The third, and final, scale measures the extent to which a person, while performing his or her job, affects the company. Larger effects are:

- visible to others
- usually financial in nature
- direct (i.e., there is a clear causal relation between your actions and the results of your actions)

Sales positions are good examples of jobs that satisfy these conditions. Small effects have the opposite properties. They are harder to see and nearly impossible to trace back to their source. The effects are not very pronounced and only indirectly linked to the financial results of the company. The more distant and elusive this linkage, the lower in the hierarchy the job. Many support and backroom office positions have these attributes.

You can have some effect on others' perceptions of how much "strategy," "time discretion," and "effect" your job contains through the job description, which is, after all, a form of literature (fiction). Performance evaluations and résumés also fall into this category. In reading this material, I often wonder how an American company has ever lost a cent with such grand aspirations and magnificent achievements on record. Every résumé I have ever seen shows the millions of dollars a person has made or saved through his miraculous actions. And no one ever fails.

At any rate, I have shown in Chart 2B how modest descriptive changes to a job description can influence others' outlook on jobs without changing their essential nature or basic purposes. I showed experts in the field the three sets of descriptions in the chart and asked them to rate the size of the job on a ten-point scale, from "very small" to "very large." The enhanced description was rated higher in every instance.

To clarify this point, I've emphasized the potential to exaggerate job de-

CHART 2B. "BEFORE" AND "AFTER" JOB SUMMARIES

Before Embellishment	After Embellishment
Production Coordinator	**Production Coordinator**
Reviews contract specifications, orders materials, and schedules work.	Develops methods and procedures for the efficient handling of contract work to ensure that the work is performed to order, on time, and at the lowest cost.
Marketing Manager	**Marketing Manager**
Analyzes market trends and develops product/market plans accordingly.	Develops 1-to-3-year market projections consistent with the company's strategy in order to locate new product/market opportunities that will increase revenues.
Controller	**Controller**
Plans, organizes, directs, and controls the accounting/control functions of the company.	Formulates short- and long-range plans to ensure sound operational controls in order to reduce fiscal waste, increase cost savings, and improve corporate effectiveness.

scriptions. Writing a description is, indeed, an exercise in imagination. But that is what it takes to get organizations to work well. Managers who see the world as a series of singular, mundane tasks to be accomplished in a hard day's work are not likely to think of all of the tasks that could be done. But the whole company can benefit from people, like you, who can think of the possibilities.

The Salary Survey

The next step, following the composition of job descriptions, involves assigning a monetary value to your job. The company determines your earnings by comparing your job to others like it in the marketplace. They make these comparisons through salary surveys that they conduct, have commissioned, or purchase from consulting firms and other third parties (such as associations).

Salary surveys have all of the sights and sounds of science, with the attendant sharpening of pencils and the echoes of poignant conversation, but surveys are imperfect. Your job, as it is described in summary form, is compared to other jobs like it. Most organizations collect a number of surveys; some are general, all-industry surveys while others are more specific and feature a particular industry, size of company, functional area, or type of job.

The two most noteworthy features about surveys are: (1) they are not random, and (2) it is harder to match jobs (your job to others) than most people think. The nonrandom feature means that the survey results will be biased in some way, either because only certain types of companies that pay a certain way are selected for inclusion and/or certain types of companies routinely either agree or refuse to participate in surveys. Some companies, for example, think information on their compensation practices is strategic knowledge and do not provide that information to others.

The other problematic feature of surveys is the job matching process itself. Jobs are compared in summary form only—using incomplete, thumbnail sketches of job responsibilities, and the organizational context and importance of a job to a given company is missing from the comparative descriptions. Also, job titles vary from company to company and may yield an erroneous judgment of the status of a job; some companies are quite liberal in the allocation of titles, while others limit their use. Overall, there is substantial bias and error in the survey process that suggest *about* what positions pay but by no means describe exactly what they pay. Companies take the accuracy of this information far too seriously but they do take it seriously. It forms the basis for your company's salary structure.

There are many salary surveys available, and you may get your hands on one at some time. Don't wave one in front of your human resources department in order to make a case for yourself. For every one survey you whip out, Human Resources will pull out ten. This trick of "survey wars" doesn't work—the best it can do, and it happens often enough to suggest it be used as a tactic, is to offer a survey to Human Resources as a way to open an investigation. This works best when the request for a Human Resources audit and review comes from management and when there appears to be genuine concern about the ability to attract and retain talent. It is very difficult to offer up a survey on one's own without appearing self-serving; you generally have to wait until your manager sees a problem and argues for more money in everyone's behalf.

Compensation Philosophy and Salary Structure

Now to the real interesting part: how this salary information is used. The company uses various statistical techniques to bundle and summarize the compensation data in order to develop a salary structure either on a job-by-job basis or, more typically, for groups of jobs within the same job class (or grade).

A salary grade has certain components that you should know about. That is, each grade (or job) is defined in a particular way, as illustrated in Chart 2C.

Every grade has a *midpoint* that represents the competitive wage for jobs in that grade. In most instances, it represents a central value or average of the survey results—usually the *median* salary in the labor market for which the company competes for talent. (Technically, an "average" can be a mean, median, or mode.) The median represents the point that divides a sample of cases in half, with 50% of the people above the point, and 50% below. Most companies strive to be average payers as defined by the median.

An emerging trend is for companies to set their midpoints *below* the median by a certain percentage, such as 5% to 10%—usually no more than that. Why would any company do that? Because they try to make up for the shortfall through "variable" pay programs. The different "variable" programs will be described in Chapter 8 and include cash bonuses and profit

Chart 2C. The Elements of a Typical Salary Range (sample)

150% From Minimum to Maximum

$32,000 Minimum:	$40,000 Midpoint:	$48,000 Maximum:
Usually 80% of the Midpoint	Usually the median market value as determined by salary surveys	Usually 120% of the Midpoint

sharing. The philosophy of these companies is to pay everyone below average if there are no profits and everyone above average if there are. In exchange for taking a lower salary, you have the opportunity to make more than most everyone else in other companies, *if the company performs well.* Presently, emerging companies and high-growth companies such as technology companies are most likely to engage in this practice.

A few companies believe that they can better attract and retain talent if they set their compensation sights higher, to above-average levels. Some companies, then, set their midpoints (their "competitive" salaries) above the median, generally at the 75th percentile (only 25% of employees in similar jobs earn more, and 75% earn less). The companies that do this are usually the large consumer products and investment banking institutions.

This strategy does work. Companies develop reputations as being "high payers." That, in turn, attracts unusual numbers of résumés. What employees get in exchange for high pay is: (1) the smug feeling of superiority, (2) a lot of money, and (3) long work weeks and hours. When a company "overpays" someone, the employee can never quite even the score. You are forever in the company's debt.

Before you join such a company, consider the following parable: Once there was a father whose daughter had two suitors who were equally desirable to the daughter. Her father's advice would be instrumental to the daughter's decision as to which man to marry. The father met with and talked to each suitor as they strolled along a high and narrow path. The father slipped and fell from the path as he walked with the first suitor. As the father precariously clung to life, suitor number one lifted him to safety.

When the father was walking with the second suitor, it was the suitor who slipped and who was aided by the father. Who did the father suggest his daughter marry? The one that would be eternally indebted to him (suitor number two) and not the one to whom he'd be forever indebted. Companies that pay high, as fathers, like their children-in-law to be obligated. They exact a price in long hours and hard work that can never be repaid in full.

There are a couple of corollaries to this story. The first is that there are obviously many awkward and clumsy people in this world. The second is a piece of advice: Watch out for making others feel obligated whether or not it is related to salary decisions. People like to believe that they have free will. Block that presumed "will" and you're in trouble. People just don't want to be around those they're indebted to. For example, I recall the executive who was asked to hire his superior following a merger of two companies; he would remain the head of the human resources function within one of the companies and his new boss would oversee the function for both companies. I cautioned him about the counterintuitive nature of this. His future superior will not feel grateful but obligated, and that will be problematic for him. Sure enough, he selected and hired his superior and within three months was asked to leave the company.

But back to compensation. It is perfectly legitimate to ask companies about their compensation philosophies. If they know, they'll probably tell you something about how they position their grade midpoints against the market (below, at, or above) and how much variable (bonus) compensation is available to you.

As a rule of thumb, compensation professionals place ranges around salary midpoints that serve as salary minimums and salary maximums. These ranges are normally ±20% of the midpoint. Thus, Chart 2C illustrates a minimum of $32,000, which is 20% below the midpoint; the maximum of $48,000 is 20% above the midpoint. Some companies use tighter ranges for jobs lower in the company hierarchy. When used, these ranges are typically ±15% of midpoint. Tighter ranges are sometimes used because the learning curve for these positions is shorter and people move through these grades more quickly. Thus, not as much room to pay people is needed within the grade since people will soon advance to the next grade anyway.

Whether jobs are clustered into grades or "priced" separately, they are all wrapped within a range. One new development in compensation is to disguise this fact through the use of "Broad Bands." Broad Bands, on the surface, are salary ranges that are much wider than the ± 20% rule of which

I just spoke. The ranges may stretch as wide as ±50% of midpoint. This gives employees the illusion that the sky is the limit when in truth there are internal caps. We'll talk more about Broad Bands when I consider them and other trendy policies in Chapter 4. Companies have fooled themselves into believing that by calling a square a circle, they have a ball instead of a box. Calling a salary grade "broad" doesn't make it so.

Midpoints are often thought of as "control points." Companies do not like to pay beyond this level, on average, across all employees. So when they add up all of the salaries and all of the associated midpoints for each employee and form a ratio between the two (salaries are the numerator, midpoints are the denominator), they want the ratio to be under 100%. The ratio of your salary to your midpoint is called a *compa-ratio*.

Suppose your salary is $45,000 and the midpoint of your salary grade is $50,000. Your compa-ratio is $45,000 ÷ $50,000 times 100 or 90%. When the company performs this calculation for all of its employees, the usual corporate ratio is between 90% and 95%. Companies tend to pay employees slightly below average.

If you knew the midpoint and salary range of your grade, you would have real power. In essence, the salary range represents a company's bargaining range. If you are changing jobs, asking for a raise, or moving into a new grade, and you are a valuable member of the company, you may want to deal a little. For new entrants into a grade—whether an internal promotion or external hire—most companies will pay as high as 105% of midpoint (that is, up to 5% over midpoint). Any higher than that would require special permission or a rethinking of the job and its placement within the overall grade structure.

If you take what you're given when you are given it, your pay will be about 90% of midpoint. That's about 10% to 15% less than you could be earning just within the same grade. You might be thinking, if only you had some idea about your company's salary structure—about not only the salary range of your current grade, but of all the grades piled up. The good news is that from my years of working in compensation, I've learned what your salary structure probably looks like. They are surprisingly similar from company to company. You might want to do some innocent snooping on your own as well; these salary structures have a way of getting around. There is someone there at your company, someone you know, who has it. A few companies will tell you the range of pay for your position, but conceal the ranges for other positions/grade levels.

Sample Salary Structures

Chart 2D shows illustrative grade structures for companies of various revenue sizes. The greater the revenues, the greater the number of grades. That is because bigger companies have more people and require more "layers" to integrate work. With a stack of blocks, to keep the stack from tumbling over you have to build in supports. In organizations, the supports are people who, at each level, serve to integrate or fuse the work performed below them. As in a stack of blocks, the top layer is usually unaffected—the supports are needed toward the foundation. Thus, the top layer does not change much with the revenue size of the company.

For every major increase in the revenue size of a company, about an extra three salary grades are needed and inserted. You will also notice that each salary structure is broken up into four major segments. These correspond to the extent to which your job is strategic, tactical, operational, or executional. We captured these concepts with the quiz you took earlier. Now look back to Chart 2A and retrieve your score. As a starting working hypothesis, categorize yourself as follows:

YOUR SCORE	YOUR CATEGORY	TEXT REFERENCE
21–24	Strategic (top salary structure box)	Band 1
15–20	Tactical (next highest box)	Band 2
9–14	Operational (next highest box)	Band 3
3–8	Executional (next highest box)	Band 4

Next, locate the revenue size of your company. If you work for a bank that measures corporate size by assets, the revenues-to-bank comparison, in descending size, is roughly as follows: large money-center banks (corresponding to "greater than $5 billion in revenue"); superregionals (multiple states); regionals (statewide or other significant area of coverage); midsize (one or more counties); small (generally a local community bank).

Most people in companies are concentrated in Bands 3 and 4. Generally, the further up the organization you go, the fewer the available positions and the smaller the number of people. Thus, again, there is a pyramid-like structure.

However, there are frequently grade anomalies where an inordinate number of people are found within a particular grade. I call this the "grape effect" because employees tend to bunch up within particular grade levels. The levels at which they tend to bunch are precisely the ones at which eligibility for certain extra cash benefits, such as bonuses, begin. Employees tend to congregate just below and/or right at the bonus-paying grade. It's like a club membership: Some people are asked to wait outside while others are permitted inside.

Let's get back to you and the two main questions that remain to be answered. What are the salary ranges for each of the grades, and what grade are *you* in?

The salary ranges also are given in Chart 2D. Developing a salary structure in which salary ranges are applied to a series of grades is not at all like building with blocks; it's more like constructing a puzzle. There is a logical way of doing it and, when it is completed, the pieces should all fit nicely together.

It is easy to know what the CEO/president earns, the very top grade, because in a public company that information is readily available from the company's several government filings and securities disclosures. The proxy statement is the customary source of this information found in just about every university and large public library. It isn't as easy to find out what the top person earns in privately held companies. Only the IRS knows for sure. The largest privately held companies in the United States participate in salary surveys, but they generally don't reveal what the top executives make.

The average salaries of CEOs are given in bold print in 2D. The bolding indicates that the CEOs' salaries are treated separately from the rest of the structure. They have a life and rules of their own that we will discuss in Chapter 9. The ranges, too, do not conform to the ±20% of midpoint rule I offered earlier. Instead, the ranges represent average pay ranges for CEOs in companies of various sizes.

Note that salary grades between companies of different sizes have overlapping structures. For example, it is possible to earn the same wage as a big fish in a small pond or a smallish fish in a large pond. Of course, there is nothing quite like being a big fish in a big pond with lots of space and fine food.

Now let's go to the bottom of the grade structure with a midpoint, or competitive wage, of $16,500. This lowest grade is never called grade "1" in any organization, ostensibly because it would demoralize people to know that they are in the lowest grade. This grade is usually called grade "3" or

CHART 2D. PROTOTYPICAL SALARY GRADES BY COMPANY SIZE

	Company size: $100–$500 million
	275,000–450,000
Company size:	152,900–191,100–229,300
$50–$100 million	132,400–165,500–198,600
175,000–275,000	<u>114,600–143,300–172,000</u>
99,300–124,100–148,900	99,300–124,100–148,900
85,900–107,400–128,900	85,900–107,400–128,900
<u>74,400– 93,000–111,600</u>	74,400– 93,000–111,600
64,400– 80,500– 96,600	64,600– 80,500– 96,600
55,800– 69,700– 83,600	<u>55,800– 69,700– 83,600</u>
48,300– 60,400– 82,500	48,300– 60,400– 72,500
<u>41,800– 52,300– 62,800</u>	41,800– 52,300– 62,800
36,200– 45,200– 54,200	36,200– 45,200– 54,200
31,400– 39,200– 47,000	31,400– 39,200– 47,000
27,100– 33,900– 40,700	<u>27,100– 33,900– 40,700</u>
<u>23,500– 29,400– 35,300</u>	23,500– 29,400– 35,300
20,300– 25,400– 30,500	20,300– 25,400– 30,500
17,600– 22,000– 26,400	17,600– 22,000– 26,400
15,300– 19,100– 22,900	15,300– 19,100– 22,900
13,200– 16,500– 19,800	13,200– 16,500– 19,800

"4"—it is hoped that these employees won't look over the edge and see nothing below.

Returning to our 20% rule in building salary ranges, we develop minimum and maximum salaries by adding and subtracting 20% to and from the salary midpoint. Twenty percent above $16,500 is $19,800, the maximum of the salary range. Eighty percent of $16,500 is $13,200, which is equivalent to a wage of $6.35 an hour ($13,200 divided by the number of hours

Company Size: $500 million–$1 billion	Company Size: $1–$5 billion	Company Size: Greater than $5 billion
		$800,000–$1,000,000
		559,400–699,200–839,100
		484,300–605,400–726,500
	650,000–800,000	419,300–524,100–628,900
	363,000–453,800–544,600	363,000–453,800–544,600
	314,300–392,900–471,500	314,300–392,900–471,500
450,000–650,000	272,700–340,200–408,200	272,700–340,200–408,200
235,600–294,500–353,400	235,600–294,500–353,400	235,600–294,500–353,400
204,000–255,000–306,000	204,000–255,000–306,000	204,000–255,000–306,000
176,600–220,800–265,000	176,600–220,800–265,000	176,600–220,800–265,000
152,900–191,100–229,300	152,900–191,100–229,300	152,900–191,100–229,300
132,400–165,500–198,600	132,400–165,500–198,600	132,400–165,500–198,600
114,600–143,300–172,000	114,600–143,300–172,000	114,600–143,300–172,000
99,300–124,100–148,900	99,300–124,100–148,900	99,300–124,100–148,900
85,900–107,400–128,900	85,900–107,400–128,900	85,900–107,400–128,900
74,400– 93,000–111,600	74,400–93,000–111,600	74,400– 94,000–111,600
64,600–80,500–96,600	64,600–80,500–96,600	64,600–80,500–96,600
55,800–69,700–83,600	55,800–69,700– 83,600	55,800–69,700–83,600
48,300–60,400–72,500	48,300–60,400–72,500	48,300–60,400–72,500
41,800–52,300–62,800	41,800–52,300–62,800	41,800–52,300–62,800
36,200–45,200–54,200	36,200–45,200–54,200	36,200–45,200–54,200
31,400–39,200–47,000	31,400–39,200–47,000	31,400–39,200–47,000
27,100–33,900–40,700	27,100–33,900–40,700	27,100–33,900–40,700
23,500–29,400–35,300	23,500–29,400–35,300	23,500–29,400–35,300
20,300–25,400–30,500	20,300–25,400–30,500	20,300–25,400–30,500
17,600–22,000–26,400	17,600–22,000–26,400	17,600–22,000–26,400
15,300–19,100–22,900	15,300–19,100–22,900	15,300–19,100–22,900
13,200–16,500–19,800	13,200–16,500–19,800	13,200–16,500–19,800

worked in a year, 2080). Most jobs in the United States pay at least this amount within the for-profit sector. Now all we have to do is work our way up the grade structure in 15%–20% intervals, the usual distance between salary midpoints. Notice what happens to the midpoints. They get further and further apart in dollars the higher in the organization we go, even though the percentage change remains constant. The reason that the midpoints get further apart and the ranges get wider, again in dollars (aside from the math involved), is that people spend longer periods of time within grades the higher in the organization they go. There just aren't enough positions to go around. The greater room allows an employee to spend more time at a given grade without adverse salary consequences (discussed in the next chapter). Nevertheless, remaining at a particular grade for too long a time will not be good for your wallet.

I used 15.5% increments to produce the grade structure in the chart. These increments are used up to the level just beneath the CEO. The midpoint for the level just below the CEO is between 50% and 75% of the average salary for the CEO (the midpoint of the range provided). This is the usual salary relationship between the CEO and next highest grade and a piece of the puzzle that should fit snugly in place when the puzzle is complete.

Are you ready for the dramatic finish? There are two things that you know with regard to the grade structure in Chart 2D. First, you know your company's size (if you work for a wholly-owned subsidiary, use the subsidiary's revenue dimensions). Second, you should now know to which Band you most likely belong.

If you belong to the top Strategic Band, the easiest way to determine which grade you are in is to count how many "touches" you are away from the CEO. That is, how many layers are there between you and the CEO? For example, if you report directly to the CEO, you belong to the top grade just below the CEO. If you report to someone who reports to the CEO, you are in the next highest grade; and so on.

From here, the best normative expectation of how much money you should be earning, i.e., which grade you are in, is your years of experience *within your current Band*. Chart 2E shows how many grades to count up from the bottom of the Band based on years of experience. Simply add up the years you have had of directly relevant experience within a given Band, either within your current organization or elsewhere, and look to see where you fall.

To a large extent, education level is incorporated into the grade structure by the Band into which you were hired. However, if you were hired into the Executional Band, and are currently within that Band, give yourself an additional 6 experience years for an associate degree or two years of vocational training; add 15 experience years for a four-year college degree, 20 for a top-twenty-five school or a master's degree. If you were hired into either the Operational or the Tactical Band, and are currently in

CHART 2E. YEARS OF EXPERIENCE AND GRADES

Company Size	0–1	1–3	3–6	6–10	10–15	15–20	20–30	>30
				Years of Experience				
Greater than $5 billion	1	2	3	4	5	6	7	8
$1 billion to $5 billion	1	2	3	4	5	6	7	7
$500 million to $1 billion	1	2	3	4	5	6	6	6
$100 million to $500 million	1	2	3	4	5	5	5	5
$50 million to $100 million	1	2	3	4	4	4	4	4

Note: The numbers in the chart represent the number of grades from the bottom of a Band one must count to arrive at his or her expected grade level, based on years of experience.

that Band, give yourself +5 years of experience for an MBA or advanced degree from a nationally recognized program (+2 for a regionally recognized program).

Now it's just a matter of addition. Let's say you're a director of product development working for a 500-million- to 1-billion-dollar company. You have worked your way up the organization and now consider yourself to be in the Tactical Band, a hunch confirmed by the quiz you took earlier in this chapter. You have been within the Tactical Band for 5 years. Chart 2E indicates that you should count up three grades into the Band shown in Chart 2D ($99,300 to $148,900).

Now suppose you work for a company with revenues in excess of $5 billion. You have a high school education and have worked within an applicable field of your current occupation for 16 years. Chart 2E leads you to grade level 6 within the Executional Band, or to a salary range of $27,100 to $40,700 within the grade and salary structure of Chart 2D.

Let's look at two other examples. You are an MBA from a prestigious program (e.g., Harvard), recently hired to conduct high-level financial analyses for a 1-to-5-billion-dollar company. You are hired into what we have been calling the Operational Band. Prior to earning your MBA, you had 6 years of relevant experience performing operational work. The 6 years of previous experience plus the 5 years of credit for an MBA places you at the 5th grade level with a salary range of $64,400 to $96,600.

A final example: You are fresh out of college. Your first job is with a company with $100 to $500 million in revenues. You start within the Operational Band as an environmental engineer, designing and performing basic tests for water quality. You would start at the first grade level, with a midpoint of $33,900 and a range of $27,100 to $40,700.

This grading exercise is not exact but it should give you a good idea of what your company's salary structure looks like and about where you fall within it. Keep in mind that what I have presented is descriptive. The grade structure illustrates the way things generally look and where people are generally located based upon their job Band as well as their education and experience. In your particular case, you may find that you have advanced in grade and pay far beyond expectations. Good for you. You are obviously doing many of the right things. Some of you may be below expectations. But a healthy start to higher pay is to have higher expectations.

Many people work for companies that are smaller in size than those illustrated in Chart 2D. The chart, however, is applicable to your circumstance; let me show you how.

I have provided, below, the approximate earnings of CEOs in companies that range in size from $1 million to $50 million.

Company Size (Revenues)	CEO Salary
$20–50 million	$150,000–$200,000
$10–20 million	$125,000–$175,000
$1–10 million	$100,000–$150,000

As a company gets smaller and smaller, the strategic level of the organization gets smaller and smaller, until the limiting case, when the CEO is the strategic level (at $10 million in revenues, or less).

Thus, look at Chart 2D. Go to the structure for companies of the smallest revenue size. The salaries for the CEOs of smaller size companies replace certain strategic layers and, in effect, create a new ceiling to the structure. For example, the salary of the CEO for a 20–50-million-dollar company replaces the top strategic grade (leaving two strategic levels below); the salary of the CEO for a 10–20-million-dollar company replaces the second strategic grade (leaving one strategic level below); and the salary of the CEO for a 1–10-million-dollar company replaces the lowest strategic grade—there are no strategic players other than the CEO.

You now know some of the jargon and have ample background to proceed to our next step. The language and fundamentals of compensation should no longer be a barrier to your understanding of your worth. You're ready to look at your worth from a variety of angles. The next three chapters are devoted to this cause.

Chapter 3

What You Are Worth—
Part I

How to Determine What Your Job Is Worth

To help you arm yourself with the hard information needed to negotiate your best possible pay, we will now begin a three-chapter journey in which you will make various pay calculations and adjustments. Don't worry. They are easy to do and, more important, you'll have fun seeing the results.

In this chapter, we will discuss what your *job* is worth. That is, we will calculate what people earn, based on a national average, in a job like yours. We will then make certain adjustments based on

- geography
- industry and your functional area (e.g., finance)
- your proximity to power
- the scarcity of your skills

In the next chapter, we will take a look at what *you* are worth in your job. You are worth more or less than the "job" based upon such things as your skill sets and your past and potential contributions and performance. We'll see how these can affect your market value.

Then, in Chapter 5, we will cover a few compensation-related topics not covered in previous chapters, such as sales compensation. We will also see how working for a small, private company or a nonprofit organization may force you to revise your thinking on your estimated worth in the workplace.

Of the many thousands of jobs, each is distinct on the surface and also has common characteristics that give it value. We are now prepared to translate these job characteristics more directly into money. In essence, a job derives its value from a set of minimum requirements needed to perform the job competently. Defining "minimum requirements" can be tricky because people who hold a given job have different backgrounds, experiences, and skills, and it is tempting for each job incumbent to think that the qualities he or she possesses are precisely the requirements needed for the job. They aren't. You have to take a step back and look at your job as objectively as possible. What are the minimum requirements you need to fulfill the essential duties of the job? We're not looking for superstars here. We're looking for the qualifications and requirements needed to get the job done—nothing more and nothing less.

The "Value Drivers" of Your Job: What Determines Its Worth?

A job has three basic underlying components:

- things you have to know
- things you have to do
- things you have to produce (including ideas)

All of these are related. The more knowledge required for a job, the higher the general expectations about the work that can be performed and the results that can be achieved. Again, the basic elements of a job should be consistent. For example, you wouldn't design a customer service representative position that requires a person to respond to the most complex and potentially costly customer problems, but at the same time suggest that a newly minted high school graduate could do the work. It's a good check for what is to follow: knowing, doing, and producing should be at about the same relative conceptual levels.

The questionnaire in Chart 3A asks you to answer a few questions. Following the instructions in the chart, go ahead and complete the questionnaire and score yourself. Then read on for a brief discussion of the questionnaire and what your score means in terms of money.

Things You Have to Know

There are lots of things you need to know to satisfy the minimum requirements of a job. First, you have to have the technical skills to perform it. This just means that you have to know what you're doing (although we've all worked with people who clearly don't see this as a precondition!). If you are in the legal department, you have to know the laws and procedures germane to your area of focus. If you are in the accounting department, you have to know generally accepted accounting procedures. You may also have to know certain things about the company, the business, and the industry: operations, trends, competitors, cost structures, etc. The longer it takes you to acquire this knowledge through formal education and previous experience, and the longer it takes you to become proficient in the application of this knowledge in the performance of your job duties, the more things you obviously need to know. Thus, education, previous experience, and on-the-job training and experience are all indices of the knowledge and skills you need to perform a job to par.

Things You Have to Do

The way you use your knowledge defines the role you play in an organization. When someone asks you, "What do you do?" he or she is asking you about the activities you perform. He may also be putting a move on you, so stay alert. You reply by talking about your primary activity:

"I write code for our managed care information system."
"I manage a customer call center."
"I am the ruler of the free world."

The levels in the questionnaire under "Things You Have to Do" correspond to the Executional, Operational, Tactical, and Strategic levels we dis-

CHART 3A: DEFINING YOUR JOB

REQUIREMENTS: Things You Have to Know

Instructions: You are provided with five criteria with which to view your job: education, previous experience, on-the-job training/experience, activity, and planning horizon. Within each criteria set, mark the description that best represents the *minimum* standard required to perform your job and then use the key to determine your score.

Education: Indicate the education you need to perform the job — not necessarily the education you have.

High school . . . . ❑

Associates/2-year post–high school apprenticeship . . . . ❑

4-year college . . . . ❑

Master's degree . . . . ❑

Other advanced degrees (e.g., Ph.D., J.D.):

4 years or more of post-collegiate education . . . . ❑

Previous Experience: How much experience working in previous jobs do you need before you are qualified to do what you now do?

0–2 years . . . . ❑

3–5 years . . . . ❑

6–8 years . . . . ❑

9–12 years . . . . ❑

More than 12 years . . . . ❑

On-the-Job Training/Experience (80% proficiency): How long does it take to become reasonably proficient at your job once you are in it?

0–1 month . . . . ❑

1–3 months . . . . ❑

3–6 months . . . . ❑

6–12 months . . . . ❑

More than 12 months . . . . ❑

cussed in Chapter 2. You should consult that discussion to round out your understanding of these levels. If you are on the cusp between two levels, round downward: It has been my experience that employees tend to overstate their level. There are more people who "execute" than "operate," more

ROLE: Things You Have to Do

Activity: Check the one box in this "role" section that best describes your work.

Executional: Performs, carries out, or puts into effect what is required in accordance with set directions or prescribed design usually by . . .

comparing:	judging or verifying completeness or accuracy
compiling:	gathering, collating, classifying, etc.
copying:	typing, transcribing, entering, posting, etc.
computing:	making basic arithmetic calculations
conveying:	carrying, informing, loading, etc.
other:	stamping, pressing, applying, punching, etc.

. . . in order to complete a given task or set of tasks . . . . ❑

Operational: Follows a general process or methodology (which may be theoretical and nonspecific) and/or performs a series of actions usually by . . .

processing:	following a system of operation in the production of something; goes through a process in order to produce, prepare, treat, or convert something
constructing:	building something by systematically assembling or arranging parts or ideas

. . . in order to achieve a particular end result . . . . ❑

Tactical: Determines the best way to fulfill objectives and accomplish work usually by . . .

analyzing:	examining something methodically and presenting alternative courses of action
coordinating:	harmonizing into a common action or effort by determining the time, place, and/or sequence of actions or operations
synthesizing:	integrating or combining separate pieces of information

. . . in order to develop new systems, products, methods or approaches and/or new operating procedures and practices . . . . ❑

Strategic: Establishes plans, objectives, policies, or initiatives usually by . . .

creating:	giving rise to ideas and action through imaginative effort
fostering change:	reconciling, adjusting or changing internal organizational structures or modes of operation

. . . in order to best position the company against the competition and to broadly direct the work activities of others . . . . ❑

RESPONSIBILITY: Things You Have to Produce

Planning Horizon: How far out do you regularly need to plan to achieve your most important concrete results for which you are accountable?

Daily to weekly . . . . ❑

Weekly to monthly . . . . ❑

Monthly to quarterly. . . . . ❑

Quarterly to annually . . . . ❑

Longer than one year . . . . ❑

Scoring Instructions: The first box in each criteria set is worth one point, the second box is worth two points, and so on. First, tally your points. Total scores can range from 5 to 24. Then change your point total as follows:

If Your Total Score Is:	Use As Your Score for Subsequent Calculations:
5 or 6	3
7	3.5
8–24	4–20 (i.e., 4 less than your total score from the questionnaire)

that "operate" than "tactize" (I've wanted to use that word for so long), and more that "tactize" than "strategize."

Most people conduct activities with various levels of authority. You may supply information or materials to someone else, you may serve as an adviser, or you may be the one who is primarily responsible for given activities or decisions. When you complete the section on "Things You Have to Do" within the questionnaire of Chart 3A, you should be describing your *primary* responsibilities for which you have the authority to act *without* approvals from others.

For example, if you are a data entry clerk, you may have the authority to change the way data is entered and the design and format of the data entry screen, but not the fields themselves. You, essentially, would be *executing* commands according to a set of instructions.

If you are an office manager, you may decide on your own how to optimize the efficiency of the office by changing work flow and internal procedures but not have the authority independently to determine the best ways of increasing volume (revenues) into the office. You would be carrying out *operations* that satisfy a set of general conditions (e.g., maximize efficiency).

If you are brand manager (of a product) you are likely to be handed a profit objective along with a number of "constraints" (you work for a particular type of company, that does business in a particular sort of way, that targets certain types of customers). Your job—the one for which you are directly accountable—is to figure out how to market, distribute, and sell your product profitably while adhering to the broad objectives and intentions of your company. You are a *tactician.*

Finally, if you are a member of senior management, say the chief operating officer, you will help to fashion the company's broad objectives and the plans, policies, products, etc. You are *strategically* positioning the company to better the competition and to grow and thrive in the years ahead.

Also keep in mind that you really don't have to do the things described in the questionnaire. For now, we're just saying that you are *supposed* to do those things; that's what your job description says, anyway.

Things You Have to Produce

You engage in activities for some purpose. There is a by-product of your efforts. In general, the longer it takes you to perform your most important responsibilities, for which you are primarily accountable and for which there is a tangible end result, the greater your impact on the organization. That is, things that take longer to perform typically yield results of greater magnitude, good or bad. Thinking lofty thoughts that others take to heart pays off. So, if after considerable thought and due diligence, an automobile executive decides to change the design on one of the lines of cars, that decision is worth a lot of money: Designers are set in motion; the manufacturing process has to change (the plant must retool); new materials will be ordered and purchased; etc. This is a big decision that will take a long time to enact. Right or wrong, there is a lot at stake.

This is why "Planning Horizon" (see Chart 3A) is a good proxy for your overall qualitative and quantitative influence on the organization. The longer your planning cycle for your most important responsibilities for which there are outcomes to which you can point, the larger your corporate responsibilities.

Computing Your Worth

Based on the little discussion we just had, go back and check your answers to the items in Chart 3A and recalculate your score accordingly. Then let's move on to Chart 3B, where you will compute the worth of your job. Using Chart 3B, you will be applying an equation that will determine your worth. For the curious, the equation is the result of a multiple regression analysis that includes interaction effects. Impressive-sounding, isn't it? The data underlying the analysis comes from my twenty-plus years of consulting experience and knowledge of thousands of jobs and their market worth.

CHART 3B. CALCULATING THE WORTH OF YOUR JOB

Step		Your Base Salary	Your Total Cash Compensation
1.	Multiply your job points from Chart 3A by . . .	$7.75 =$ _____	or by $9.50 =$ _____
2.	Multiply your job score by your company's revenues or assets (for now, leave off the last three digits of the revenues/assets) and then multiply this product by . . .	$.001 =$ _____	or by $.0015 =$ _____
3.	Add steps 1 and 2 together . . .	here $=$ _____	or here $=$ _____
4.	Multiply your company's revenues/assets (leave off the last three digits again) by	$.0065 =$ _____	or by $.011 =$ _____
5.	Subtract step 4 from step 3 . . .	here $=$ _____	or here $=$ _____
6.	Subtract from step 5 either . . .	$6.80 =$ _____	or $17.30 =$ _____
7.	Multiply step 6 by 1050 . .	here $=$ _____	or here $=$ _____

Note: Step 7 gives you your job worth. Be sure to read about the few caveats to this formula in the text.

Also "company" revenues or assets refers to the size of business with which you are primarily affiliated; if you work within a division of a company or a wholly-owned subsidiary, use the division or subsidiary revenues.

I took a sample of 100 jobs that represent all corporate functions and various job levels. I completed Chart 3A on these jobs and developed a formula that predicts the worth of these jobs in the labor market from information about the size of the job and the size of the company. We discuss the results of this analysis, below.

Notice that there are *two* separate calculations you are asked to make: one for your base salary and one for your total cash compensation (your base salary plus annual cash bonuses). I can save you a few frustrating moments if you keep three things in mind as you proceed:

(1) The computation of total cash compensation applies only if you scored "8" or higher; otherwise, your total cash compensation will be equal to your base salary only. (The smaller the size of the job, the less likely it is a bonus-paying position.)

(2) If you scored a 2.5 or a 3, use $1 billion in revenues or assets as the *maximum* size of your company; alternatively use the new minimum wage, $5.15 per hour, and multiply that by total hours worked (2,080 hours is the standard: $5.15 \times 2,080 = \$10,712$).

(3) For scores greater than 3 and less than 16, use $5 million as the *maximum* size of your company even if your company is larger; for scores of 16 or greater, use $10 million as *maximum* revenues regardless of the size of your company.

Let's look at a sample for both the salary and the total compensation calculations. Suppose you have determined that your job is worth 10 job points and that you work for a company with $1 million in revenues. Your calculations for determining salary would be as follows:

(1) $10 \times 7.75 = 77.50$
(2) $10 (1,000) \times .001 = 10.00$
(3) $77.50 + 10.00 = 87.50$
(4) $1,000 \times .0065 = 6.50$
(5) $87.50 - 6.50 = 81.00$
(6) $81.00 - 6.80 = 74.20$
(7) $74.20 \times 1050 = \$77,910$

In order to get a better idea of the dollar range of the job, the person in our hypothetical example should perform the same calculations using 9 points and 11 points. That is, to be sure you have it right, recalculate the worth of your job by using job points one greater and one less than the points you initially used. You'll have three calculations in all: one based on the score you think is correct, bracketed by scores that might be correct had you answered just one question differently. Thus, the person in our example would find the worth of his or her job to be between $68,723 and $87,098.

The total cash compensation is calculated using the exact same steps but using different numbers as shown in Chart 3B. Taking a hypothetical job of 10 points again as an example (in a company of $1 million in revenues), the steps in determining the worth of the job in terms of total cash compensation are:

(1) $10 \times 9.50 = 95.00$
(2) $10 \ (1,000) \times .0015 = 15.00$
(3) $95.00 + 15.00 = 110.00$
(4) $1,000 \times .011 = 11.00$
(5) $110.00 - 11.00 = 99.00$
(6) $99.00 - 17.30 = 81.70$
(7) $81.70 \times 1050 = \$85,785$

Bracketing the score of 10 by a point on each side and performing the calculations yields a total cash compensation range of $74,235 to $97,335.

That's all there is to it! Answer the questions and compute the worth of your job. You can use the information in Charts 3A and 3B to experiment. Compute what you could earn if you were in a job with requirements different from those of the job you now occupy. Keep in mind that you don't really need to have all of the requirements specified by a job to fill it. If you can convince your company that you are prepared for a position and can do the work, more power to you. You'll get paid for the job even though on paper you don't meet all of the specs.

There is one annoying exception that I have seen repeatedly. It makes no sense to me and it holds back many intelligent and talented employees. Some companies put their metaphorical foot down when it comes to educational requirements. Even though an employee can obviously perform a particular job (or, indeed, would be perfect for it) some companies won't give him the job unless he satisfies the educational requirement first. Companies sometimes forget why they have job requirements: they are essential for the competent performance of the job. But if an employee can do the job, or has successfully done it on an interim basis, we can and should dispense with the formalities.

Geography

Just as the cost of living varies from place to place, some areas of the country pay more and some pay less. Chart 3C gives you summary information on how pay varies by geography. The data supporting the chart come from Department of Labor statistics, which were then manipulated using statistical techniques.

I hold to the "pebble in the pond" theory when it comes to the effects of geography on pay. Big cities are the pebbles. From Chart 3C you can see that the bigger the city in which you work, the higher the pay. These cities create ripple effects in regions: The more big cities concentrated in an

CHART 3C. CALCULATING GEOGRAPHIC DIFFERENTIALS

Start with . . .	0.00%
Then, factor in size of city	
if over 5,000,000, people add	8.00%
if between 2,500,000 and 5,000,000, add	4.00%
if between 1,000,000 and 2,500,000, add	2.00%
if under 1,000,000, add	0.00%
Then factor in region of country	
if you live in the Southeast, add	0.00%
if you live in the Great Plains (including the North Central U.S.), add	2.00%
if you live in the Southwest (Texas to California), add	3.25%
if you live in the Northwest, add	3.50%
if you live in the Mid-Atlantic (Delaware to North Carolina), add	3.50%
if you live in the Midwest (Michigan, Ohio, Indiana, Illinois), add	6.00%
if you live in the Northeast, add	10.00%
Subtotal	_____
Subtract	5.00%
Total	± 2.5%

area—and the bigger the cities—the higher the ripples and the greater their range. Thus, some areas, such as the Northeast, regionally benefit from the effects of the big cities on compensation. On the other hand, there aren't enough pebbles in the Southeast to raise compensation levels there overall.

In order to calculate your "geographic differential," start with the salary or total compensation figure you've determined from Chart 3B, then add or subtract a percentage of that number based on the information in Chart 3C (±2.5%). This will give you the likely range at which your salary compares to the national average. For example, let's say your job is worth 6 job points (in a company with $1 million in revenues) and that based upon that, you've calculated the worth of the job to be $41,600. You work in the Midwest within an area with a population of fewer than 1 million people. Using Chart 3C, you see that your geographic differential is 1% ± 2.5%. That is, your pay will range anywhere from −1.5% to 3% of the average paid for your job nationally, or between $40,976 and $42,848.

Geographic differentials aren't much of a problem until you move and cross noticeable compensation boundaries one way or another. Even then, there is only good news and good news for you. If you make an intracompany transfer from an expensive, high-paying region of the country to a more affordable place, companies will generally preserve your salary. You'll live like a king or queen. And if you move to a new company in a less expensive region, they generally won't expect you to accept less money than you are currently making.

Some companies will try to build up the affordability and quality-of-life aspects of an area, which may all be true, but you don't have to accept their arguments and less pay. For instance, Jack M., a manager in human resources and resident of New York City, said it best when considering a job offer from a company in Florida. When asked to take a little less money in exchange for all of the sunshine and outdoor exercise he'd get, his response was that his current salary was not a function of geography. He politely acknowledged the differences between Florida and New York but maintained that his current compensation was the result of many years of hard work and specific accomplishments, which he would be happy to discuss. The company increased its offer. The moral is this: You don't have to lower your salary expectations just because you are moving to a lower-cost-of-living area.

When moving in the opposite direction—to a more expensive, higher-paying area—do your homework. There are surveys of cost-of-living and pay differentials printed by the Department of Labor, available in most libraries. It is reasonable for you to want to preserve your lifestyle and to ask for an adjustment to your current earnings. When negotiating salary, try to keep discussion of the geographic differential separate. In this way, you'll be able to discuss your worth apart from your location. Some companies build geographic differences into their offer. Smaller companies may not know what the differential is and begin bargaining without awareness of it.

Here is how one employee responded to a company who offered an amount of compensation, for a higher-level job, equal to the geographic differential: "I'm currently making $55,000 where I am now. The equivalent earnings for the *same* position in your location is $60,000, which is what you are offering me in compensation to make this move. You apparently believe that the job you are offering me is worth about 10% more than I am now earning. Taking geography into account, that would be $66,000, not $60,000." The company conceded her position and she accepted the company's offer of *$68,000*—even more than she requested!

Functional Area

Some types of companies pay certain types of jobs more money simply because those jobs are more crucial to the companies' success. Engineering companies pay more for engineers, software companies pay more for programmers, pharmaceutical companies pay more for researchers, consumer products companies pay more for marketers, investment firms pay more for financial professionals, and so on. You get the picture. You'll earn more in a company that needs you more.

A large part of competing successfully in the marketplace is competing successfully for talent. It is important, therefore, that a company attract, hire, and retain the kinds of people it absolutely has to have. One way of doing this is through the compensation system. The general reputation of the company and the challenge of the work help as well.

I have provided below a list of industries and the functions that are usually most highly prized within those industries. This is not an exhaustive list and things may be a bit different in your particular company. But you can generally tell which functions mean the most to your company. These will be the areas that people talk (or grumble) the most about, the areas in which the company is most obviously concerned, the areas most highly esteemed, and the area to which the company most greatly owes its success. If you fol-

CHART 3D. MATCHING INDUSTRIES TO THE FUNCTIONS THEY LOVE BEST

Instructions: I have indicated, below, certain industries and functions that tend to go together. But there are many possibilities other than those indicated. So draw lines from your type of company to the functions your company values the most. If your industry or function is missing, go ahead and add it. Is there a match between the "functional values" of your company and your work?

Industry	Function	Industry Match
a. Advertising/Public Relations	Accounting and Finance	f, p, t, z
b. Aerospace	Administration/Facilities	
c. Agriculture	Management	j, u, cc, ee
d. Automotive	Art/Design	a, k, n, o, y
e. Aviation	Communications	a, g, o, s, y, dd
f. Banking	Engineering/Technical	b, d, e, f, l, bb
g. Broadcasting	Human Resources	s, aa
h. Chemicals	Information Technology	f, i, p, t, bb
i. Computers	Legal	b, d, h, j, m, o, p, t, u
j. Conglomerates		
k. Consumer Products	Marketing	k, n, aa
l. Electronics	Operations Production	d, u
m. Energy	Public Relations/	
n. Fashion	Government Affairs	a, f, m, w, bb, cc, ee
o. Film and Entertainment	Real Estate	j, m, v, w, z
p. Financial Services	Research and	
q. Food and Beverage	Development/	
r. Health Care	Scientists	b, i, l, x
s. Hospitality	Sales	a, k, p, t, x, aa
t. Insurance	Service	e, i, r, s, dd
u. Manufacturing	Other Specialty Areas:	
v. Metals and Mining	_____	
w. Paper and Forest Products	_____	
x. Pharmaceuticals	_____	
y. Publishing		
z. Real Estate and Construction		
aa. Retailing		
bb. Telecommunications		
cc. Transportation		
dd. Travel		
ee. Utilities		

low the money trail (corporate revenues) back to the people the company relies upon most for its revenues, you'll find your way to the key areas of the company.

If you're lucky enough to be in a job in the type of company that highly prizes your area of specialization or function, then you win. This is worth another 5% to 10% in compensation, and sometimes more. A 10% adjustment to the worth of your job would not be unreasonable. Take the worth of your job as you have previously calculated in 3B, as modified by geography, and add another 10% to it if you are in a coveted function within your company.

Companies are sometimes shocked by the difference between jobs from one industry to another, particularly when they are in the midst of change and are looking for new blood in areas that are gaining in importance. For example, companies within industries that are deregulating, such as utilities and telecommunications, have a tendency to become more marketing focused in their thinking and start to look outside their industry for marketing talent. Lo and behold, they have to pay a premium over their former wage to lure people away from industries such as consumer products in which marketing is traditionally more important (i.e., where these people are paid more).

This is a long-winded way of saying, "If you like sea life, you need to live by the sea"—go to an industry that will value your skills the most.

Scarcity

A job becomes more precious if there are not enough people to fill it—if the specific set of skills is in short supply and hard to find. To see how scarcity may affect the worth of a job, let's start by looking at an extreme example: the compensation of physicians.

The average total compensation for physicians is about $175,000, but there is wide variation in how much physicians are paid. Chart 3E shows how different types of physicians are paid relative to one another. The scale shown represents how similar or different certain physicians are with respect to total compensation.

In general, the higher the scale score, the more scarce the skill set (i.e., demand exceeds supply) and the more procedurally oriented (versus cognitively oriented) the physician; i.e., there is higher pay for interventions (surgeries) that relate directly to revenues. Thus, having scarce skills is one way to improve upon your compensation. Physicians achieve this through many years of advanced training and specialization, in the hope that patient need and ability to pay will persist at the conclusion of their training. You can do the same. Research departments, for example, need scientists with special skills for which companies are prepared to pay top dollar.

In the corporate world, scarcity is typically brought about by changes in technology or the emergence of new products, services, processes, or ways

CHART 3E. PHYSICIANS' SALARIES—AN EXAMPLE OF SCARCE SKILL SETS
(Among Other Things)

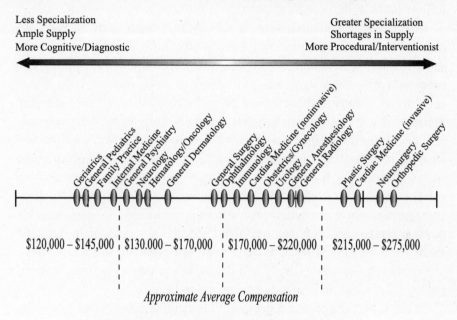

Less Specialization
Ample Supply
More Cognitive/Diagnostic

Greater Specialization
Shortages in Supply
More Procedural/Interventionist

Geriatrics
General Pediatrics
Family Practice
Internal Medicine
General Psychiatry
Neurology
Hematology/Oncology
General Dermatology
General Surgery
Ophthalmology
Immunology
Cardiac Medicine (noninvasive)
Obstetrics/Gynecology
Urology
General Anesthesiology
General Radiology
Plastic Surgery
Cardiac Medicine (invasive)
Neurosurgery
Orthopedic Surgery

$120,000 – $145,000 ¦ $130.000 – $170,000 ¦ $170,000 – $220,000 ¦ $215,000 – $275,000

Approximate Average Compensation

Note: This conceptualization was provided by Don Samples, M.D., formerly of the
Ochsner Clinic. Data are based on my experience in working with physician groups
as well as the following sources: the *Wall Street Journal,* September 3, 1996, p. B6,
and October 22, 1996. p. B1: *U.S. News and World Report,* October 22, 1997. p. 104.

of thinking. The scarcity is clearly temporary, lasting until enough people acquire the skills. Recently, marketers with systems and database backgrounds (e.g., in database marketing) have been hot as the need to store and meaningfully retrieve customer information has gained importance. Companies that introduce new information systems (e.g., SAP) need people who understand the system—and, frequently, there aren't enough people to go around.

Even outdated skills can become scarce. COBOL programmers are being sought to help resolve the "year 2000 problem" with computer systems, and it is often hard to find facilities managers who understand older mechanical systems in older buildings.

Scarcity creates the need to pay a compensation premium of 5% to 25%. The premium will vary with the perceived duration of the shortage. You'll get 20% to 25% for skills in which there will always be shortages or for which there will be shortages with no end in sight—as for neurosurgeons or orthopedic surgeons. You'll get closer to 5% for skills that will have their brief day in the sun, then be gone. There is about a 10% to 15% premium for skills for which there are known shortages that will last a finite period of time (such as two or three years).

Companies struggle to deal with scarcity, particularly when it is known to be temporary. They know they have to pay more and they also have a good idea about how much more they will have to pay, but they are just never sure *how* to pay it.

Most companies end up putting people with "hot" skills into a higher grade level—in essence, arguing that the job is worth more. Some companies ratchet up the salary structure for functional areas where a preponderance of scarce skills is found. For example, if most scarce skills are found within information technology, information technology is given its own salary structure that is higher than the structure used for the rest of the company. So a position at grade level 5 within the company, for example, that pays on average $50,000 may pay about $55,000 for someone in the same grade but who is in information technology. The problem with both of these approaches is that when supply and demand even out, a company ends up paying more for skills it is not as desperate to have.

In the short run, getting a pay premium is great news. In the long run, however, unless you have further refined your skills—creating a new niche for yourself for which there is again a sparse supply—you are precisely the person the company gripes about behind his back. You become the overpaid employee. A company won't cut your pay but pay increases may become increasingly stingy; and the company will start looking at you funny if you expect sizable raises after the perception that you're so valuable is gone.

Instead of permanently hardwiring pay increases into an employee's base salary, I have sometimes recommended that companies' offer "salary supplements." This is a practice used in academic institutions for the assumption of temporary responsibilities, as when someone chairs a department or runs a clinic. The added responsibilities warrant added compensation. But because the responsibilities are temporary, pay is delivered as a supplement or addition to base salary. These supplements are factored into benefits calculations but they will disappear when a person steps down or when the term of one's duties is up. Companies may offer employees something akin to supplements as a way to address the relative rarity of their skills: annual, special lump-sum bonuses and incentives for as long as the scarcity persists.

If you have a skill that is in short supply, it is far better for you to receive a healthy premium in pay that goes right into your paycheck as a part of your base salary rather than a one-time bonus. It will be an amount that will never go away and that you can use to your advantage during salary negotiations for a lifetime. And if you can get more put into your salary plus a bonus, all the better for you.

Back to physicians for a moment. Use of medical technology in procedural interventions (use of a scalpel but not a hand) also adds to a physician's compensation—procedures bring in more money. Generally, people are more willing to pay for things that are actually done to them. Doing things that bring in money from others is generally looked on favorably by employers. Just thinking about things and diagnosing don't attract the same zealous giving from patients. The lesson here is that the bigger your direct impact on revenues, and the larger the effect, the more you will earn. (In corporations, two groups are believed to fulfill this role: upper management, who are seen to execute the corporate "vision," and sales.) Procedurally intensive areas can add about another 25% to physicians' salaries.

Your contribution to revenues in a company is handled in one of two ways. The extent of your contribution to and impact upon the corporation is built into your job description and you are paid accordingly. Or, if you are a part of the sales force, your contribution to revenues will be an entirely separate matter from the rest of the company: You will have your own compensation program, which we'll discuss in Chapter 5.

Power

There is one other factor that I have seen influence the perceived worth of a job—proximity to power. We are all well aware of the relationship between power and money within the executive ranks, but many types of positions brush up against power and the money rubs off. There are corporate pilots, chefs, facilities managers, drivers, boat captains, security specialists, speechwriters, executive secretaries, gardeners, etc., all of whom are in regular contact with the rich and powerful and all of whom benefit from the contact. Employees in these positions provide personal services to executives.

The types of positions that benefit from power are ones (1) that often relate informally to the executive, and (2) for which there are status or level differentials, i.e., they are far apart in the organizational hierarchy as reflected by the distance between grades in the company's grade structure. In many respects, these jobs involve hazard pay. Providing services directly to executives has its risks. In dealing with people who've come to expect perfection in many aspects of their lives, you generally have to be very good at what you do in order to survive in the job. Furthermore, it takes considerable interpersonal skill to be effective in these jobs (e.g., to change an executive's mind, to read an executive's mind, to get a point across, etc.).

Because of the proximity to power and all that entails, jobs that have regular, ongoing contact with senior executives pay about a 10% to 20% premium beyond what the job may be worth in terms of what has to be known and so on. If you are in one of these jobs, go ahead and add another 15% to the calculations and adjustments you have already made.

It's Not Just the Job That Counts

As you know, a job has a certain worth in the labor marketplace based on a set of job attributes such as education, training, and experience. The appraised value of the job may vary with geography, and we figured how to account for geographic differentials using size of city and region of the country as our guide.

Next we considered how a job within a given function may be of greater value in certain companies than in others. And then we discussed how certain jobs may be worth more than others because the knowledge and skills defined by the job are hard to find. In this instance, higher compensation acts like a corporate magnet, attracting and pulling scarce talent toward it. Finally, we discussed the special role of power as it contributes to pay.

All of these aspects are instrumental in determining the worth of a job. At this stage, we still haven't talked about *your* worth in the job. We have only considered the going rate for *anybody* who might be qualified to fill it. We now have to discuss the important reason you bought this book—finding out what a company might be willing to pay *you*. That is the objective of our next chapter.

Chapter 4

What You Are Worth— Part II

How to Determine Your Personal Worth

It doesn't matter how much individual talent you have if you don't believe in yourself and have the confidence to assert your worth. You can't be timid about your abilities or play them down.

But, as a start, let's find out how good you really are. So far, we have primarily considered your worth based upon the job you are in: the average paid to people who are suitably trained. That is, we have calculated the average worth of a given job for an *average* person. You don't want to be one of the ordinary ones, though. You want to be one of the best, with compensation to match. You want to be the Michael Jordan of the workplace.

By now, you have calculated the worth of your job and made certain adjustments based on factors such as geography and scarcity of talent within an industry. We now want to make another adjustment based upon who you are in the role you fill. In essence, we now want to determine your worth to your company in the context of your job. The worth of the job establishes a starting place for discussion, but your capabilities determine how much more or less you are uniquely worth to your company.

Evaluating your "worth" to your company raises two fundamental questions. First, is it possible to distinguish yourself on the job and prove your value? Second, exactly how much can you earn if you do—how high can you go?

Competencies Count

The first question is generally discussed within the general framework of "competencies." Competencies are technical and behavioral attributes that are associated with superior performance on the job.

How can you recognize these attributes? Think about two performers who work in a job similar to or exactly like your own. One performer is average and one is clearly excellent. What is the difference between these two individuals? Write them down. This will give you a good clue on what superior performers do that average performers do not, and what average performers do that superior performers should not.

When you review your list, there are certain types of attributes that are sure to stand out in the superior performer:

- technical abilities: greater depth and breadth of knowledge and abilities
- interpersonal effectiveness: more adeptness at handling conflicts, better listening, more ability to influence, etc.
- personal effectiveness: more self-confidence and more willingness to take initiative and risks
- cognitive abilities: better problem-solving and decision-making abilities
- results orientation: more attentiveness to things that make a difference, including service, quality, and productivity

You can see from this list that it is possible to distinguish yourself, no matter what the job. Do not accept the assumption that you are an interchangeable part within a corporate machine. You are not.

In any job, regardless of how good the employees are collectively, talent and performance are normally distributed. It's the way of the world—whether it's the height of corn stalks, the amount of time lightbulbs burn, or the weight of baskets of berries—there are always individual deviations among people or objects such that most are around average and there are fewer at the extremes (really bad or really good). Performance isn't any different. There are a few individuals who are outstanding—one way or another—and most who are about the same.

If you are one of the superior ones, your worth isn't simply what the average person in the job gets paid—it's more. Can you imagine a top entertainer or athlete accepting the "going rate"? If you have more to offer than others do and can show that you do, you are worth more.

Broad Banding

One of the hottest topics in compensation over the last few years has been the concept of "Broad Banding," mentioned in Chapter 2. With a Broad Band structure, a company's many salary grades are collapsed into a few new grades with tremendously large salary ranges. You read the company literature on these compensation structures and you think the sky is the limit. For example, a "band" may stretch from $20,000 to $60,000, or more.

Conceivably, these structures give you, the employee, elbow room to grow financially without having to be promoted. That is, as long as you grow "horizontally" in your job (acquire more skills and depth of knowledge), you will get your just desserts. "Vertical," upward career progressions, so the Broad Band proponents say, aren't necessary in order to be recognized with money. No longer need you accept a job for which you are ill-equipped just for the sake of a promotion and a salary increase.

Let's get one thing straight. Broad Bands are a lot like going to Las Vegas. Everyone who goes *can* become a millionaire, but very few ever do. It's one thing for a company to say, "You can earn as much as you can," and another thing to be able to earn it. There are limits to what you can earn in a given job because there are limits to what most jobs are worth, no matter how good you are. Studies by consulting firms, corroborated by my experience, suggest that employees within Broad Band structures actually earn 3% to 5% less than employees with more graduated, "thinner" salary grades. That is because there is more upward movement (i.e., traditional promotions) within the latter systems and with each upward promotion there is a little extra put into employees' paychecks. That element is frequently missing with Broad Bands.

When Broad Bands were first introduced, they had some genuine appeal despite being a relatively vacuous concept. They seemed to have something for everyone. In an era of downsizing, "flattened" organizations, the devastation of middle management and fewer career opportunities, they held out to employees the promise of recognition in the form of money in exchange for skill development.

For Human Resources, it meant some relief from their role as compensation guards (telling managers, "You can't pay that because the structure says you can't"). For the company, it was their answer to a flatter, more flexible, and more nimble structure capable of reacting faster to market needs.

It should be clear that such a superficial change as reducing the observable number of grade levels on paper does none of these things. It's like rubbing aspirin on your forehead: It has great show appeal but no effect. At their best, and in conjunction with other genuine organizational changes, Broad Bands are theoretically useful in a number of ways:

- They are organizationally healthy in the sense that attention shifts from rules and structures to management and people; that is, they force more decisions about individuals to be made rather than allowing "the system" to dictate what can and cannot be done.
- They de-emphasize organizational layers and promotions as ways of getting ahead; growth and development in one's discipline (depth of development) as well as cross-departmental/functional experiences (breadth of development) are valued.
- They are more accommodating to the deployment of people (putting the right person in the right role job); people are moved based on organizational needs and the skills/competencies a person possesses—in contrast, fine gradations in organizational levels frequently are barriers to the movement of employees within the organization from one job to another since employees will only want to accept a move to a grade that is at least on par with their current grade.
- Broad Bands require that tough choices be made about people, particularly with regard to compensation. The Bands may signify qualitative distinctions in the nature of work being performed, but they do not specify what to pay a person within a Band.

The problem is that companies really haven't figured out how to use the Broad Bands in these ways. By and large, they don't make tough decisions about people or deploy people more efficiently. In fact, most companies end up camouflaging the "old" grade system by a Band structure; they overlay Broad Bands on the old grade structure (e.g., zones within Bands, reference levels within Bands, etc.), and nothing has really changed. It's the old wine in a new bottle. On the surface, it looks like anything is possible but in reality pay is regulated in the same old ways. Take a look at Chart 4A and tell me if you see any difference.

Determining Your Worth in Your Job

Before we do a few calculations, I want to emphasize that your worth is related to your effort only insofar as that effort yields tangible results. Otherwise, trying doesn't count. As Yoda says, "There's no try. Do or do not"— or something like that. Many employees believe they deserve more because of how hard they work but that is incorrect.

You also can't excel by just doing your job. Performing your normal job responsibilities well does not qualify as "superior performance" and generally doesn't entitle you to anything more than the going job rate.

There are four things that can demonstrate your value to your employer.

(1) You have valued skills and knowledge that few others possess, i.e., you are hard to replace.
(2) You have consistently produced superior results and have outstanding achievements on record—achievements that far exceed the usual requirements of the job.
(3) On balance, you are one of the best performers among a class of employees, past and present, who have held, or hold, similar positions.
(4) You execute tasks and activities in a manner that doesn't destroy or diminish others' ability to do work or otherwise denigrate the health of the organization, i.e., you are not a complete and total jerk.

I am constantly amazed at companies' tolerance for high performers who have a poisonous effect on the organization: people who are just plain unpleasant. I have never seen this form of devilish exchange pay off for a company. What *may* be gained in individual productivity is offset by

Chart 4A. Sample Band Versus "Old" Salary Structure

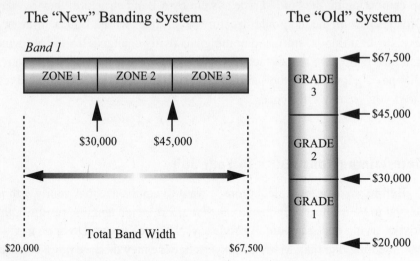

Note: This is the way it really works. You can see that "bands"
are about as useful as a chocolate teapot.

the ethically permissive culture it tends to create. It also tends to demoralize other workers and to lower everyone's sense of what "excellence" means.

At any rate, take a look at Chart 4B and take a moment to answer the questions in the chart. Be sure to give your honest and frank opinion. Ask a coworker how he or she feels you measure up on each of the questions and combine his or her answers with your own.

Your total score is an index of your personal worth to your organization. In essence, it's a measure of your "present value." The higher your present value, the more the company believes you will contribute to the company's future success based on who you are, the skills you have, and the results you have achieved in the past.

Once you have answered the questions and obtained your scores, use the key to determine how much you are worth. Here's how it works. If you score in the middle (i.e., between 2.25 and 3.74), you'll make no further adjustments to your worth: Your worth is on par with the value of the job in the open market. If you score higher than 3.74, use your score to pro-rate a percentage adjustment to your job worth. For example, let's say your average score is 4.00. You can prorate your score by:

(1) finding out how far your score penetrates a given range by applying the formula below:

$$\frac{\text{Your score} - \text{Minimum Score in the Range}}{\text{Maximum Score} - \text{Minimum Score in the Range}} = \frac{4.00 - 3.75}{4.49 - 3.75} = .34$$

(2) and multiplying the result from (1) above, by the total percent that can be earned (or lost) within a given range; using the example, this would be done as follows:
.15 (or 15%) times .34 = .051 (or 5.1%—the amount your job worth should be modified)

Next, let's say you have calculated the worth of your job from the exercises in the previous chapter to be $45,000. So the average person is worth $45,000 in a job like yours. But you've just determined that you in particular are worth more. In fact, you are worth a 5.1% premium, or $47,295 ($45,000 × 1.051), or $45,000 + 5.1% of $45,000 which is equal to $45,000 + $2,295.

You would do any calculation in a similar way. But note:

(1) It is possible to be worth less than the job, i.e., to value yourself downward.
(2) It takes extraordinary ability (or inability) to separate yourself from the pack.
(3) It is possible for your worth to a company to change over time.

Now we've reached a point where companies get it all wrong. If companies want to pay people and not just the job, why do companies use the same midpoint for everyone in the same job or same grade level? The midpoint, you recall, represents what a company thinks is a competitive wage. But should the same competitive wage be the same for everyone in a given job or grade? I don't see how it can be if the performers are different.

Nevertheless, companies use the same midpoint as a reference point for everyone in a given job. If your pay is higher than the midpoint, and you are a good performer, the general perception is that you are adequately paid and need no special recompense other than the money that is ordinarily deliv-

CHART 4B. DO YOU KNOW YOUR PERSONAL WORTH?

Instructions: Please respond to the following statements honestly and frankly by circling the answer that best represents your opinion. After you have made your responses, compute your final score as shown and look to the key for your score's meaning to your compensation.

1. There are very few people in jobs similar to my own who have the skills I have.	strongly disagree	1	2	3	4	5	strongly agree
2. I have done things that others thought were impossible.	strongly disagree	1	2	3	4	5	strongly agree
3. Compared to others doing similar work, I'd have to say I'm one of the best.	strongly disagree	1	2	3	4	5	strongly agree
4. My company has specially recognized my achievements.	strongly disagree	1	2	3	4	5	strongly agree
5. If I left my company today, most people would be sorry to see me go.	strongly disagree	1	2	3	4	5	strongly agree
6. I routinely accomplish much more than required by my job description.	strongly disagree	1	2	3	4	5	strongly agree
7. I am always pushing myself to learn something new and each year I can do something significantly better.	strongly disagree	1	2	3	4	5	strongly agree
8. I can honestly say that I have helped to raise the level of performance in the area in which I work.	strongly disagree	1	2	3	4	5	strongly agree
9. Given what I know and can do, it would be hard to replace me with someone of equivalent ability.	strongly disagree	1	2	3	4	5	strongly agree
10. I am considered by others to be a leader in my field (discipline, craft, vocation, etc.).	strongly disagree	1	2	3	4	5	strongly agree

Scoring Key (use your average score)
1.00–1.49: subtract 30%
1.50–2.24: subtract 15%
2.25–3.74: add 0%
3.75–4.49: add 15%
4.50–5.00: add 30%

Total Score =_____

Average Score (Total Score÷10) =_____

ered through the merit system—which isn't much. In fact, your raises get smaller as your salary gets higher relative to the midpoint because the company believes it is already adequately compensating you by paying you above the average. The demotivating aspects of this system (consistently better performers get less in annual increases) are obvious.

Modified Midpoints

I want you to think of yourself as having your own private midpoint that reflects both the value of the job you perform and your unique contributions to it. Think of it as a job midpoint that is modified to fit your talents. Every employee has a unique midpoint because every employee has unique worth. Just because a company doesn't assign you a unique value, doesn't mean you don't have one. It's up to you to: (1) recognize what that value is, and (2) convince your employer of that value.

Your job worth serves as an anchor or a point of departure. Companies generally won't pay more than about ±30% the worth of the job. Plus or minus 30% is approximately equivalent to ±1 standard deviation in most jobs such that about 85% of employees within a given job are paid within that range. (This is why, in Chart 4B, 30% is as high or as low as you can go relative to the average compensation of a particular job.) If anyone could demonstrate value beyond this range, chances are he or she is performing a different job; at that level of value, it may be reasonable to say that the employee has carved out a unique job for him- or herself. This is the best of all worlds when you create your own job in your own image.

Robert M. was an inspector at a midsize manufacturer. Gradually he acquired statistical skills and became schooled in quality processes. He began to introduce the company to new ways of thinking about quality standards and to new approaches to quality measurements and controls. Robert M.'s value to the company grew as he progressively enlarged his job. He eventually became the head of a newly created position: quality assurance and organization improvement. Robert kept increasing his value until, presto, a new job!

Let's look at the logic of "modified midpoints." Suppose you have calculated the worth of your job to be $30,000. Further, assume that there are three employees who have the same job title, including yourself. Now look at other conditions and states of affairs shown in Chart 4C.

The chart shows that the salaries of these employees are different, their perceived values to the company are different, and their performances for the current year are different. Which of the employees is underpaid? To whom would you give the biggest annual increase to base salary? Person A is underpaid because Person A makes less than he or she is worth. Person A should get the best increase because (1) Person A performed the best and (2) Person A is paid below the modified midpoint—the midpoint, as modi-

CHART 4C. MODIFIED MIDPOINTS—
MODIFYING YOUR JOB MIDPOINT TO REFLECT YOUR WORTH

Employee	Current Salary	Present Value (from Chart 4B)	Performance (on a scale of 1-5)	Salary Midpoint	Modified Midpoint
	—	—	—	—	—
	—			—	—
Person A	$32,000	4.49	4.5	$30,000	$34,500
Person B	$30,000	3.30	3	$30,000	$30,000
Person C	$28,000	1.74	3	$30,000	$26,960

Note: The "present value" column refers to your score in Chart 4B—it numerically represents your current worth to your company. These values are prorated as discussed previously and used to adjust the salary midpoint, up or down, into a "modified midpoint" based on the capabilities of the job incumbent.

fied, reflects the personal worth of this employee. In real life, unless Person A says something to someone, he or she would not get much greater an increase than B or C. Does that seem right to you?

The job is a relevant point of discussion when negotiating a higher compensation, but don't limit your discussion to the job. And by no means should you limit your true value to the company to the value of some market average, unless that's all you think you are worth.

Years of Experience

Before concluding this chapter, I want to acquaint you with a common compensation pattern that relates compensation to years of experience, using lawyers as an example. Other sections of this book are applicable to attorneys within corporations and firms as well as to solo practitioners. A corporate attorney, for example, would be able to calculate his or her worth using the various methods provided in this book as guides. I have singled out lawyers for closer examination because they often like to look at compensation as a function of years out of law school. You should be aware of the relationship between compensation and years of experience that pertains to any type of work.

Relating years in the workforce to compensation results in what is called a *maturity curve*. Every craft or profession has one. For illustration, I have plotted what the curve looks like for attorneys (excluding sole practitioners) in Chart 4D. The data comes from my ad nauseam analyses of legal departments and from intimate knowledge of what lawyers get paid—and then, through statistical means, converting this knowledge into a formula that everyone can use.

To arrive at the plot displayed, you begin with the approximate starting total compensation of attorneys, $52,500, then

- Add $4,000 × number of years post graduation; then
- Subtract $35 × the product of the number of years post graduation, squared [$35 × (years)^2].

For instance, if a lawyer has been out of law school for 5 years, you would calculate the total compensation as follows: $52,500 + ($4,000 × 5) − ($35 [5 × 5]) = $71,625. (If you are beginning your career in law with one of the large major law firms, your starting salary will be between $75,000 and $95,000. So use a number in that range rather than $52,500 as your starting place.)

You will notice from the chart that compensation begins to flatten out the longer one is in the workforce. (Again, for the curious, the graph depicts a "quadratic trend" which is what you normally get when compensation is plotted against years of experience.) Compensation normally follows an arc

CHART 4D. MATURITY CURVE FOR LAWYERS

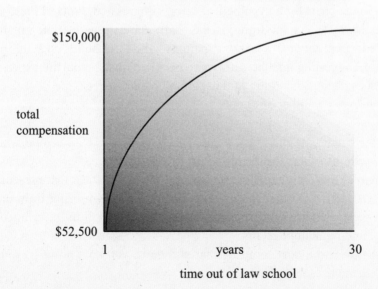

like a shell being fired from a cannon. There is an initial flash and acceleration, followed by fizzle, and free fall to the ground. It doesn't have to be that way. To maintain a steady climb in your compensation, you have to renew and reinvent yourself before your compensation begins to *plateau*. You have to energize and enliven your pay trajectory by acquiring new skills and honing your knowledge and abilities. This may be the juncture in which you try out something new to you. A physician who reached his earnings peak stepped into . . . administration. He was respected less but he earned a lot more. A highly seasoned programmer started a for-profit consulting business to other companies with his own company's blessing—with moderate success and better compensation.

The form the maturity curve takes is the same from job to job, but compensation begins to flatten out sooner or later for different trades and professions. Different trades and professions have their unique curves because they have different time lines in which people become proficient in their jobs and different progressions with differing numbers of career "steps." You can estimate the point at which your career and compensation may start to lose some of their energy by performing what I refer to as a "scree" test. Scree is the boulders and rocks that stack up at the base of a mountain—this image hints at the appearance of the results of this test (shown in Chart 4E).

Look at how many career steps you have for your given career track (and the number of employees at each step). Estimate the *minimum* number of years of experience required for each of these steps. These numbers are provided in the chart for a hypothetical career progression. Plots of these pairs of numbers produce the figure in the chart. You can see that the graph begins to level at about 10 years of experience; the scree builds up at this point onward, suggesting that there are more people with the requisite experience than the system can sustain in this particular career track.

You have a number of options:

(1) Do nothing and wait it out: You may be the chosen one who climbs (claws) to the top.
(2) Make an internal lateral or upward move to a track that presents greater opportunities to you: Gene B. did it by moving from the corporate legal department to a higher-level job in government and regulatory affairs.
(3) Move to a new company that will move you up a notch in your career.

CHART 4E. WHEN THE GOING GETS TOUGH IN YOUR CAREER

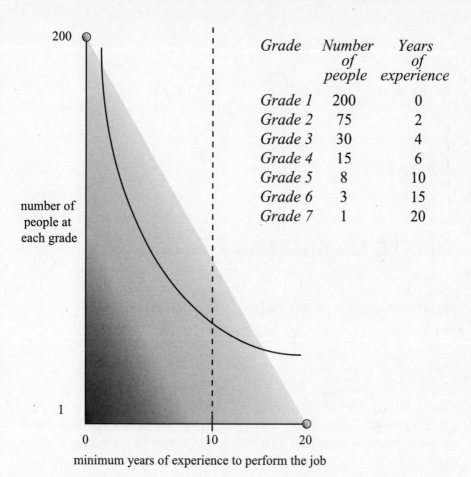

Grade	Number of people	Years of experience
Grade 1	200	0
Grade 2	75	2
Grade 3	30	4
Grade 4	15	6
Grade 5	8	10
Grade 6	3	15
Grade 7	1	20

number of people at each grade

minimum years of experience to perform the job

In all cases, you have to keep moving to prevent career inertia. Today's cutthroat job marketplace requires that you keep one eye on the present—getting the job done—and one eye on the future—looking out for the future role that you will grow into.

Chapter 5

Special Compensation Issues:

Self-Employment, Small Companies, NonProfits, and Sales Positions

This chapter addresses several situations that are not fully covered in the previous two chapters. If you're working for yourself, for a smaller company, for a nonprofit, or in sales in any size company, your compensation will have some unique features that make it difficult to neatly fit them into "standard" discussions about pay.

Working for Oneself

Working for big business historically meant job security for life. You might hate your job, hate your boss, hate your coworkers, and hate your life, but you were guaranteed a paycheck, good benefits, and retirement income. In exchange for your obedient acceptance of the way things are, you were taken care of. We now marvel at the people who had the fortitude to work a lifetime at the same place.

These days, corporate life can be nasty, brutish, and short. Any employer, big or small, can abruptly and arbitrarily end your employment. Whether forced by circumstance or of their own volition, more and more people are "going it alone." Some 1 to 15 million people in fact have started full-time home businesses (*Money,* May 1997, p. 142) and several millions of others work part-time out of their homes.

These estimates mean that about 1 in every 11 workers is now self-employed full-time. Further, most self-employed work for their own account and never hire other employees. Most self-employed are between the ages of 35 and 44 and work within the diverse services industry. As a percent of people within different age groups, most self-employed are retirees starting second careers (see *Monthly Labor Review,* October 1994, p. 29).

There are many businesses that you can start and run profitably from your home. Chart 5A lists the ten home businesses with the greatest earnings and growth potential.

Despite the inherent risks associated with self-employment, the owner-employees I have spoken with over the years have the pleasure of feeling that their destiny lies in their own hands: They are not completely secure but they have a sense of control. The insecurity they do feel has a healthy focus. It is more focused on how to succeed—on how to do and sell more rather than on failing, of being let go, of becoming obsolete, or of learning how to avoid the most recent corporate purge.

Indeed, the glamour of a home business is alluring. There are many ex-

Chart 5A. High-Income Home Businesses

Job	Potential Annual Income
Export agent	$300,000
Employee trainer	$300,000
Management consultant	$300,000
Commercial debt negotiator	$150,000
Business plan writer	$150,000
Desktop video publisher	$150,000
Computer tutor and trainer	$120,000
Mailing list service provider	$100,000
Home inspector	$100,000
Temporary help provider	$100,000

Source: *Money,* March 1996, p.76.

amples of home businesses that grew into multi-million-dollar enterprises. Earl Bakken (Medtronic), Scott Cook (Intuit), Michael Dell (Dell Computer), Gun Denhart (Hanna Anderson), Bill Gates (Microsoft), Phillip Knight (Nike), Mo Siegel (Celestial Seasonings), Lillian Vernon (Lillian Vernon), and others all started with little from a garage, basement, or dining room table.

It is rare for ideas to grow into such mammoth businesses. And even if you are lucky and skilled enough for your home business to flourish, there is a decision you'll have to make: "Is this what I want?" One employee I know, Donna B., started a successful language center from her home (later moved to an office building). Demand for her business's services were such that she could have grown the business to many times its size. But her reason for leaving corporate life was to leave the corporate rat race and spend more time with her children. She purposely contained the growth of the company to a size that produced, on balance, optimal pleasures and profits.

I have heard a lot of dreams from employees over the years—of mail order gourmet foods, craft shops, photo galleries, and so on. Most employees, however, remain employees. There are both financial as well as psychological reasons for this. Financially, the longer you wait, the more dangerous it becomes, since after years on the job as an employee your paycheck is higher. Also, the longer you wait, the more financial obligations you'll have, like a family. It raises the ante: The longer you wait, the more difficult it will be to earn the same amount of money outside your current employment on your own. You're financially hooked. The business adage of start-ups is that the best defense against going broke is to be broke.

It is difficult to get a good fix on what people working in home businesses earn. Some people have been at it a long time, some are just starting out. Some people work out of their homes full-time and some just try to pick up extra cash on a part-time basis. Some home businesses are operated with the sole purpose of making money and some make money by coincidence (i.e., they are really hobbies).

Nevertheless, Chart 5B should give you an idea of what to expect in terms of compensation when you work for yourself based on numbers I've seen over the years. If you earn over $100,000 from home, you are doing exceptionally well. You are in the upper 2% of home-based wage earners. Indeed, only about 15% of people working out of their homes earn more than $50,000 per year. And these are gross figures. Since you are on your own, you'll have to pay your own benefits and expenses.

CHART 5B. COMPENSATION IN HOME BUSINESSES

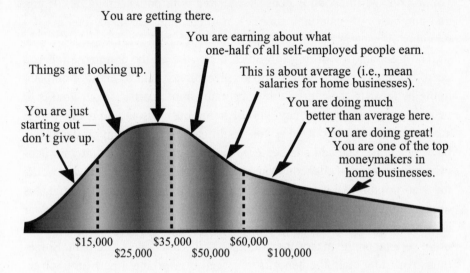

You are getting there.

You are earning about what
one-half of all self-employed people earn.

Things are looking up.

This is about average (i.e., mean
salaries for home businesses).

You are just
starting out —
don't give up.

You are doing much
better than average here.

You are doing great!
You are one of the top
moneymakers in
home businesses.

$15,000 $35,000 $60,000
    $25,000 $50,000 $100,000

As a self-employed worker, you have to subtract out certain benefits that you either must pay or would be foolish not to pay:

- Social Security and Medicare
- retirement
- health care
- long-term disability
- life insurance

Recent tax laws have tried to level the playing field between the employed and self-employed. For example, there are now higher deductions for health care premiums: 45% deduction in 1998 and climbing to 100% by 2007. Recently, tax-favored Medical Savings Accounts were introduced to help pay the deductibles associated with medical expenses. In addition, there are a myriad of retirement plan options including Simplified Employee Pensions, Simple IRAs, Simple 401(k), and Profit Sharing and/or Money Purchase Plans. In a nutshell, it's easier to put more of your money away on a tax-deductible and tax-deferred basis for retirement than ever before. Check with an accountant on all of the tax provisions that apply to the self-employed.

Despite the legislature's growing concern for the self-employed, the items previously listed can do big damage to your cash flow. In addition, you'll have the time and expense associated with bookkeeping, tax filing, and purchases of materials, supplies, postage, and so on. Various tax deductions offer no immediate consolation for the cash outflow.

The freedom of working for yourself may be all the compensation you need. But many people who work for themselves want to know if they are doing better than their miserable corporate counterparts. If your goal is to make at least as much money in your home business as you could within a corporation, figure out what you could earn in a corporation using this book as a guide and add another 20% to that to take into account your benefits and other miscellaneous expenses. If you have a spouse who works for a corporation, and you can obtain benefits inexpensively through his or her employer, then just add another 10%—you can pick up your health care coverage through your spouse's employer and your spouse can make sure he or she makes maximum contributions into retirement. Sometimes you can obtain the benefits you need by working a part-time job on the side.

Small Companies—Private Companies

"Small" is a relative term that varies by government agency and from law to law. The Age Discrimination in Employment Act is enforceable in companies with twenty employees or more. The Occupational Safety and Health Administration exempts companies with ten or fewer employees from record keeping and health and safety inspections. The Family and Medical Leave Act applies to companies with more than fifty employees—this act allows employees to take time off to attend to personal or family emergencies without risk of losing their jobs (a company does not have to pay for FMLA excused absences—up to twelve weeks—but some big companies do pay). Advance notice of plant closings applies to companies with at least 100 employees. And so on. For our purposes, "small" means a company with fewer than 100 employees.

Small business accounts for a disproportionate share of the job growth. It is estimated that such companies will add two out of every three new jobs in the near future, whereas mega-companies with over 10,000 employees are projected to create just three out of every one hundred new jobs (*American Demographics,* October 1996, pp. 17–18).

Most small companies are privately held, family-owned concerns that raise special compensation issues. Some of the complications at the management level are illustrated in Chart 5C.

You can see from the diagram that you can play a number of overlapping roles in a family-owned business. You can play the part of whining family member who wants to become "more involved in the business." Or you can play the part of family owner who, if only you raised someone who is competent, wouldn't have to go to work every day. Or you can be neither family nor owner but in management and think of yourself as a son or daughter—except without ever being invited over to the owner's house or being given stock in the company.

The arrows in Chart 5C indicate the typical desires of the occupants of

CHART 5C. ROLES IN FAMILY-OWNED BUSINESSES

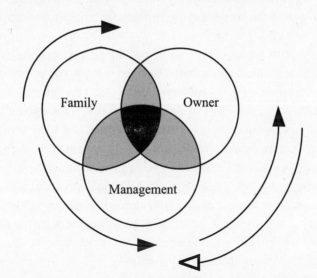

Note: This conceptualization was personally communicated to me many years ago by a former Yale professor, Ivan Lansberg.

the various circles. The arrows point to what the occupants often want to be. Key managers who contribute to the success of a company often want to become owners. If you are in this position, the easiest way to become an owner is to marry the owner's son or daughter. Or you can wait until the company "goes public" through an initial public offering. At that juncture, many owners are willing to reserve a small share of stock (but a handsome sum) for you in the form of stock options (discussed in Chapter 9).

To retain the talents of management, the owners of small companies hold out the prospect of fat bonuses to you. These bonuses won't be as juicy as the bonuses that go to family members, but they won't be shabby either. It will be like getting the ten-ounce versus the twelve-ounce filet. In smaller, privately held companies, these bonuses are often discretionary in nature. The owner looks at how much money was made during the year, thinks about how much he or she enjoys having lunch with you, and makes a decision on how much to give you.

The informality of small companies is what makes them vibrant and enjoyable places to work. But that same informality around compensation can be quite irksome. One thing you shouldn't do, for example, is compare your compensation to that of a family member with comparable duties. Although there is a ready business rationale for what family members get paid, this logic often shrouds other reasons behind compensation ranging from tax considerations to family needs (e.g., money for a new home, additional support for a new child).

As for equity (stock) ownership, owners of privately held companies don't like to give their stock away. Besides, giving you a tiny interest in a company whose stock is not publicly traded won't do you much good. You'd end up putting it in your dresser drawer. Even if you were given stock, don't count on it having much value. Owners often try real hard to minimize the value of the company and the stock for tax-related purposes. You want it to be high, they want it to be low—it's not a good situation.

A good compromise position in privately held stock companies for non-owner managers is the use of phantom stock. Phantom stock is discussed at greater length in Chapter 9. Essentially, phantom stock mirrors stock ownership without providing actual equity—but it delivers the same monetary value as the real thing through appreciation.

We have looked at the effects of company size on compensation in an earlier chapter, but small companies often are private companies, and private companies are more frugal than public ones with compensation "expenses," all else being equal. The relationship between what comes out of an owner's pocket and what goes in is very evident to owners. As a consequence, compensation is carefully watched and prudently given in small, privately held concerns.

The top management of the privately held companies, primarily the owners, do quite well. In fact, I have received many frantic phone calls over the years from the delegates of owners seeking justification for enormous pay packages in the face of IRS audits. When the IRS reclassifies compensation as a stock dividend (i.e., it judges executive compensation to be excessive), it has major implications on company taxation and profits. I don't touch these babies anymore, having learned that you really can't make a silk purse out of a sow's ear. I don't want to be overly discouraging, however: Individuals sometimes win these "compensation" cases in tax court when all of the facts and circumstances are considered.

As for the rank and file, it is very hard to say precisely what private versus public means in terms of compensation. My experience suggests "not much" when the private employer is larger (over 100 employees) but about minus 5% to minus 10% with smaller employers. That is, smaller, privately held companies pay roughly 5–10% less for a given job than would be paid in a larger, publicly traded institution for a similar position.

I have yet to see the definitive study that proves this. It would be a hard study to conduct because there are other things that change with a company's size (in addition to public versus private) that may affect wages—larger companies are more likely to be subject to collective bargaining agreements, smaller companies are more highly concentrated in service industries, etc. Equating jobs across companies of different sizes can be tough as well.

Even without a complete base of research in comparing public company versus private company pay, one thing we all know is this: It really is easier spending someone else's money (public company) than one's own (private company). I have seen many comparable jobs over the years in similar industries of differing sizes and the compensation data I see keeps leading me down the same path: Small, privately held employers don't pay as much.

Nonprofits

This "compensation deficit" is more severe when it comes to nonprofit organizations. Nonprofits have to be frugal for two reasons. First, they depend for their sustenance upon grants and gifts, neither of which are perfectly dependable. Second, they have to make sure they have the money they need to provide their essential services. There is tremendous public scrutiny of nonprofits to make sure they use the funds they take in for the good of those they serve.

If you work for a nonprofit, subtract 10% from your calculated job worth from Chapter 3, regardless of the size of the nonprofit. If you work for a nonprofit with fewer than 100 employees, take another 10% off. Clearly, if you work for a nonprofit, your lifetime refrain will be, "I did something useful" versus "I made a lot of money."

But you must know that except for being poorer, nonprofits look and act like every other organization. They have organizational levels and career progressions, performance appraisals, petty politics, offices of various sizes, reserved parking places, executive dining rooms, etc. They have it all. Human behavior doesn't change as a function of an organization's tax status.

You can work your way up the career ladder within a nonprofit just as in any other organization. And just as in every other organization, you have to point to yourself so others can see your good works. For example, Susan Y. worked for a large multi-site nonprofit organization in one of its satellite offices in the Northeast as publicity director. She frequently appeared on local television as a discussant on issues dear to the nonprofit she represented. She would forward her tapes of her public appearances to the home office and, over time, became a kind of cult hero. When the job of head of public relations became available at the headquarters office, she was the logical and emotional choice.

The other piece of related advice I have for you with respect to nonprofits is this: Don't be seduced into a career stupor. It's easy to dismiss personal ambitions when one is working for grander purposes. There is nothing wrong or inconsistent with wanting to improve one's abilities and to advance, *and* simultaneously supporting the mission of the nonprofit. You can care about your career and the organization for which you work at the same time.

Benefits Within Small Business

We will explore the value of your benefits plan in greater depth in Chapter 11. For now, suffice it to say that smaller businesses are not known for their benefits largesse. Benefits cost money and once a company starts a benefits program, it's hard to take it away even if the company could.

It is possible for two companies to have two identical benefits programs that would be perceived by employees much differently, depending upon the evolution of the program. If one program is a product of cutbacks, it will be viewed more unfavorably than a company that never offered certain benefits in the first place.

Most small businesses tread cautiously around benefits. Chart 5D shows how the benefits programs of small versus big business stack up. In every category, smaller businesses provide fewer of the traditional benefits. This gap was larger, however, not that long ago. Low unemployment has forced smaller businesses to enhance their total packages while big businesses have tried to shed some of their benefits costs, mainly in health care and defined benefit (pension) plans.

Even if small businesses offer the same type of benefits as large businesses, however, they are unlikely to offer them to the same degree. They do not contribute as much to health care premiums, for example, nor are they as likely to include family members in health coverage unless you pay for it. They are also less likely to make matching contributions into retirement funds. This all adds up and one way or another, sooner or later, it will cost you money.

Smaller businesses, nevertheless, excel at offering glitzy benefits and perquisites that are valued by employees but don't cost the company that much. These include items like cars, cellular phones, and club memberships. They also excel at nontraditional benefits like sabbaticals, telecommuting, and group activities and clubs ranging from yoga classes to going to the movies. In addition, they are more likely to provide a host of conveniences such as casual dress and dry cleaning drop-off/pickup services.

As appealing as certain benefits are to your lifestyle and their psychic value to you, take a hard look at what they mean financially. By all means,

CHART 5D. BENEFITS IN SMALLER VERSUS LARGER ORGANIZATIONS

Benefit	Small	Medium and Large
Vacations	86%	97%
Holidays	80%	91%
Health insurance	62%	82%
Short-term disability	56%	87%
Prescription drugs	56%	80%
Life insurance	54%	91%
Jury duty with pay	51%	90%
Sick leave	44%	65%
Funeral leave	42%	83%
401(k)	29%	49%
Sickness and accident leave	24%	44%
Dental insurance	23%	62%
Long-term disability	14%	41%
Personal leave	11%	21%
Vision care	9%	26%
Pension plans	9%	56%

Note: The table represents the prevalence of benefits in companies with fewer than 500 employees versus companies with more than 500 employees.

Source: *The Wall Street Journal*, May 22, 1997, p. R6.

consider the nonfinancial benefits of working for smaller companies, and there are many of them that you may decide no amount of money can replace; but consider the monetary consequences as well.

Sales

Sales personnel are almost always on compensation plans separate from everyone else within the company. The obvious difference between salespeople and others is that salespeople clearly and directly bring money into the company.

When paying salespeople, the amount of money the company pays out in itself becomes irrelevant. The more pertinent question is, "Is the amount paid consistent with the employee's contribution?" A company pays a salesperson based on the amount of money he or she brings in. Therefore, paying salespeople is never simply a matter of "how much," but "how much" in exchange "for what." This should be the question a company poses with any employee anywhere within the company—but frequently doesn't. That shouldn't stop you from raising the issue of what the company gets from you in return for its compensation outlay.

Since the sales function is the point of organizational consumption—the means by which the organization is fed—the contribution of salespeople to the organization is most evident. Everybody else serves some systemic purpose, extracting what is needed for survival and disposing of the rest, so that the company can go on feeding and reproducing (through start-ups, mergers, and acquisitions).

Because money is a measure of a salesperson's contributions to the company, and an index of his or her success, this group does something interesting with respect to their compensation. They set earnings goals for themselves: "I want to earn six figures within three years"; "I want to double my income every five years"; "I want to be the top producer and highest paid in the division."

They say these things not because they have a special love of money. They say them because money is a trophy; the amount they earn more directly signifies how proficient they are at their craft than it does for the rest of us. Their pay is quite public and other people respect the top earners because they are recognized as the best. The story isn't the same elsewhere in the company where higher paid people often *are not* perceived to be as talented as lesser paid employees.

Take a clue from your sales force. Set a compensation goal for yourself. This is the great lesson of salespeople. Their pay doesn't magically increase. Compensation for salespeople is a planned event. The day you finish reading this book and have developed a pretty good sense of your worth, write down what you want to be earning a year from now, and five years from now—and develop a plan that will help you get there.

There are three elements to sales compensation, which can be paid singly or in combination: base salary, bonus, commission. Most often sales compensation is a mixture of base salary with bonuses and/or commission, where commissions are payments (or accruals) for sales transactions, and bonuses are payments for reaching specified sales hurdles or goals. Thus, most sales forces use a combination of base salary plus incentive compensation (bonus and/or commission) as a method of reward.

The relative mix of base salary to incentive compensation varies by industry and depends on a number of factors. Generally, companies put more into base salary if the following conditions exist:

- The duration of the sale is long and complex (high-tech goods sold to corporate customers are often of this ilk).
- The sale is equivalent in importance, or secondary to, other transactional features such as ongoing advice and service; sales of technical, industrial machinery frequently require after-sale counsel and advice to nurture the client's understanding of the equipment and its proper and safe operation.
- There are many factors and many people that affect a sale, making it difficult to pinpoint a given person's specific contributions.
- The demand for the product or service comes and goes, i.e., demand is volatile, making sales nearly impossible at certain times and a sure thing at other times. The bulk of manufacturers' toy sales occurs before the Christmas holidays and sales are made to the usual suspects (the major super-retailers, who have already previewed the manufacturer's products and consented to carrying a certain amount).

Put differently, the less fluctuation in the demand for a product or service, the more accountable a particular person is for a sale, the less important follow-up services and advice, and the shorter and less complex the sale, the more your compensation will be driven by commissions and/or bonuses. The potential swing in compensation mix can be substantial from job to job and company to company. A salesperson may be paid 100% base salary or 100% commission/bonus, although a meaningful blend of base salary and incentives is most common.

The size of the organization also makes a difference in how sales professionals are paid. Smaller organizations that are more strapped for cash on hand are more likely to put more money into incentives.

Incentive payouts are influenced by a number of criteria. Revenue is the most commonly used measure of a salesperson's success, but the following are often used to gauge a salesperson's compensation as well:

- profit margin
- product mix
- revenues from new accounts
- units sold

The beauty of sales is that your pay becomes effective when you do. There is no one to blame and nowhere to hide. It's up to you. And there is nothing more gratifying than accepting a check from a customer who has placed his or her trust in you.

And speaking of earning, I have provided in Chart 5E what salespeople in different sales positions generally earn, adjusted for company size.

Compensation plans for salespeople are developed "backward." A company figures out what it wants to pay for and how much it is willing to share with the salesperson, then produces a plan that will generate the intended results. Said differently, a company thinks about what it is willing to pay for a given return. The answer is remarkably similar from company to company, so much so that I have a shorthand formula for you to use. Sales compensation is usually about 2% of sales revenues plus $32,500. This is not a perfect index of your worth, but it seems to approximate what most salespeople get in return for given revenues that the salesperson secures through his or her efforts. A more precise formula is:

$$\text{Your Sales Compensation} = (.022 \times \text{Sales Revenues}) - (.000001 \times \text{Sales Revenues, Squared}) + \$35,000.$$

The formula uses an abbreviated version of sales revenues, so when making your calculations divide your actual sales by 1,000—and use that number. For example, instead of using revenues of $4 million, use $4 million divided by 1,000, or $4,000. After you've worked through the equation,

CHART 5E. SALES COMPENSATION

Position	Company Size				
	Under $5 Million	$5–25 Million	$25–100 Million	$100–250 Million	over $250 Million
Vice president, sales	$65–$85	$80–$100	$110–$130	$125–$155	$155–$185
Regional sales manager	$60–$70	$70–$85	$75–$95	$85–$105	$115–$145
District sales manager	$50–$65	$60–$75	$70–$85	$80–$95	$95–$115
Senior sales rep.	$60–$75	$75–$85	—	—	—
Intermediate sales rep.	$45–$60	$45–$60	$45–$60	$50–$65	$55–$70
Entry sales rep.	$35–$45	$35–$45	$35–$45	$35–$45	$35–$45
Major account manager	$50–$65	$55–$70	$65–$80	$70–$85	$75–$90
National account manager	$65–$75	$70–$80	$80–$95	$85–$100	$90–$125

Note: Figures are in thousands (000).
Sources: Based on data from: *Sales and Marketing Management*, February 1995; *Sales and Marketing Management*, October 1996; *Working Woman*, February 1996.

Organizational Hierarchy in Sales

Top Sales

Regional Sales Mgr.   National Acct. Mgr.

District Sales Mgr.   National Acct. Rep.

Senior Sales Rep.   Major Acct. Mgr.

Intermediate Sales Rep.

Entry Sales

convert your answer back to thousands by multiplying your answer by 1,000.

Let's look at an example. Let's say you bring in $2 million in sales during a given year. Then your total compensation, which may be structured in a variety of ways (e.g., base salary, commission, etc.), will be:

- .022 × $2,000, minus
- .000001 × ($2,000)^2
- plus $35,000
- add three zeroes to your answer to change to thousands and add and subtract $12,000 to your answer to give you an idea of the range of pay you are likely to receive for given sales volume; more guidance on how much money to add or subtract to your answer is provided below

If you work out the calculations you'll find that a person who sells $2 million worth of product, earns about $75,000, plus or minus about $12,000. Perform these calculations for any amount. Someone who sells $4 million of product should earn somewhere between $95,000 and $119,000, or $107,000 on average, plus or minus $12,000. Someone who sells $500,000 of product would earn, on average, $45,750 or roughly between $33,750 and $57,750.

The higher your company's profit margin, the higher your salary will be within the range. Companies with higher profit margins can afford to give more away for a given level of sales' revenues. As an approximation to your worth, calculate your average total compensation based on the formula above, and apply the following:

COMPANY PROFIT MARGIN	WHAT TO SUBTRACT OR ADD TO THE AVERAGE
less than 3%	subtract $12,000
3%–5%	subtract $5,000
6%–8%	add $0
9%–11%	add $5,000
12%, or greater	add $12,000

You can find or calculate the profit margin for your company by looking in your annual report. Take your company's net income after taxes and divide it by total revenues. That's it. This ratio tells you how much out of every dollar your company brings in, it gets to keep. If profits at your company are kept secret, you can still find the average profit margin for companies like yours (i.e., of similar size and industry) by going to published sources available at most public libraries—the librarian will help you to find the right set of numbers. If you still can't find the figures you are looking for, you can always estimate them by making a visual inspection of your surroundings. If leaks go unfixed, the tears in the carpeting are taped down rather than replaced, and machinery is painted but not repaired, your company isn't doing so well. If everything seems to be tidy and well furnished, your company is doing okay and/or is fiscally prudent. If your surroundings are lavish, your company is rolling in dough and/or is a quasi-governmental agency extravagantly spending the taxpayers' money.

Most people in sales ultimately confront "the wall." It seems no matter what you do, after a point, it's hard to make more. That's because there are just so many hours in a day and only so much you can achieve personally. You have three options at this juncture: (1) be happy with your level of achievement; (2) find a way to work smarter so that you can leverage your time better (e.g., hire an assistant to help you with paperwork); (3) join management. That's right. You can join sales management where you can do less and earn more. It's a big headache and not as much fun but you'll get to "revenue share," i.e., take credit for someone else's production. And you'll get to hire and raise little salespeople who will want to be just like you some day. Really! Taken seriously, this is a great responsibility for you and a great opportunity for them.

Chapter 6

How to Increase Your Base Salary:

Merit and Promotional Increases

Aside from moving to another company, there are two ways to increase your base salary on an annual basis: through your company's merit system and through promotions. In this chapter, we discuss what you can expect from your company from each of these pay delivery mechanisms. With each, you will be fighting the forces of nature—the inflation rate and related corporate budget—which try to contain how much of an increase you can receive during a given year.

The Merit Program

Think of something that you don't like but must do regularly: dust, visit an intolerable relative, commute, pay bills. That pretty much summarizes the experience of most employees with the performance review process.

Merit pay is tied to companies' performance review programs. Employees often look at these review times with dread or disdain, but the ostensive aims of these programs are to motivate employee performance and to reward employees for their contributions to the company. Managers typically review employees' performance annually, and these reviews, and recommended salary increases, occur either on an employee's anniversary date from date of hire or at the end of the company's fiscal year (usually at the end of the calendar year). Overall, companies are split roughly 50-50 on when they conduct performance reviews. There are advantages to each method of timing: Anniversary dates make it more feasible for a given supervisor to review many people by dispersing the reviews throughout the year, whereas conducting the reviews close to the fiscal cycle corresponds to the company's business planning and goal setting processes.

Regardless of the timing, performance reviews are generally entrusted to a theoretically omniscient and omnipresent manager. Most of the time, supervisors and managers have an idea of what you are doing and how you are doing, but they frequently don't know the whole story. A supervisor, for instance, can sometimes see the results of your work but rarely sees the process you used to reach the end result: your decisions, your demeanor and poise, your problem solving and initiative, etc.

Your antidote to performance ambiguity is to help bring clarity to your reviewer's judgments. You will have to build a case for yourself. There is nothing prohibiting you from documenting your achievements throughout the year. The temptation is to try to recall everything you've done at the year's end—but, again, much is forgotten, taken for granted, or, in retrospect, deemed unimportant. There is quite a bit that you do in the course of the day that is beneficial to the company but goes unrecognized and, due to faulty memories, is forever lost—little things with big impact like teaching a peer a new statistical method, fixing a machine, applying a new quality control technique, or solving a recurring customer problem. Build a portfolio of evidence to support all of your accomplishments. It is difficult to refute the hard facts.

Think seriously about what your general behavior conveys to those around you. It is well documented in the psychological literature that people make inferences about others based on limited knowledge of them: Knowing a few things about someone implies other things. The more you like someone, the more wonderful you believe he or she is. "Liking" in a corporate setting doesn't mean "friends outside of work" or "social friends" but rather "being a good corporate citizen."

Being a good corporate citizen means being well mannered, respectful, and even-tempered; being accepting of authority and of the rules (i.e., not being difficult); and being gladly willing to do extra work when asked. Coming to work in battle fatigues, persistently challenging authority, and ranting on and on about vague injustices is typically considered rude. A good citizen is someone who always seems to be there when you need him or her. If you unfailingly disappear from work at 4 P.M. every day, your chances of being considered a superior performer are minimal regardless of your productivity during regular hours. (If you really don't want to work, take the afternoon off if you can and show up at 6 P.M. Then people will just wonder why someone who seems to work so hard never seems to get anything accomplished—you're inefficient, not lazy. I recently met an employee who has a novel approach to work—or work avoidance—she comes into the office, turns on her computer, puts a steaming cup of coffee on her desk, and leaves for a couple of hours to run errands.) Your unavailability for the little extras after normal working hours will cost you a heap of goodwill. No, you don't *have* to stay and, yes, it's a problem if the requests for additional help become too frequent and come with little forewarning; in that case, you will have to have a candid conversation with your boss.

After-work tasks have a life of their own and an annoyance factor that far outweighs the actual quantity of the work. Still, when you stay to help, you are not merely completing an assignment—you are helping another human being who, like yourself, doesn't want to be there. And even if he or she did, you'd still be helping and that goes a long way.

This may sound obvious, but it is also important to look and act intelligent. If you look professional, people will actually assume that you are. Surprise, appearances matter! Most companies have an implicit dress-code ethic; know it and follow it. This may be shallow and you can protest that "people should get to know me for who I am," but those people won't want to if you don't project the right image. Or worse, people will tend to look for evidence that confirms their hypotheses about you: If the hypothesis is that you are unprofessional, they will look for samples of your work that confirm that. The reverse is true as well: The assumption of professionalism will generate a search for evidence that confirms that assumption. People are poor amateur scientists and end up believing what they are predisposed to believe.

Looking and acting intelligent is particularly valuable in jobs in which there is little produced, making it difficult to quantify results. These are largely "talking jobs" which include many office employees, professionals, and middle management. These employees are often measured on "proxy" performance—on how well they communicate (i.e., talk about performance) versus how much they actually influence the overall corporate results. Thus, being able to articulate ideas, regardless of what becomes of those ideas, is important. Those staff and project planning meetings that you attend and think are so trivial and a waste of time are actually display cases of verbal affluence and often the primary forum in which others form their opinions of you—so, be prepared, be persuasive, and by all means participate. Take it upon yourself to understand the goals of the meeting and insist that materials be sent to you beforehand for study.

Since surviving meetings is one essential feature of corporate life, remember these tips as you're swimming in the shark-infested waters:

(1) It may be necessary occasionally to whack particularly irksome sharks on the nose "to keep them away."
(2) Don't ever start to bleed. Even sharks that you thought were of the harmless ilk like a good meal now and then.
(3) Although it is considered by some to be impolite, pointing out nearby swimmers often succeeds in diverting sharks' attention, giving you time to swim to safety.

Impressions are susceptible to what are termed "primacy" and "recency" effects. Things that happen first and last have a bigger imprint on memory than all of those things that happen in the middle—which tend to be forgotten. This makes it especially important to work particularly hard at the onset of the performance year and at its conclusion because these performances will disproportionately affect assessments of you. If you don't believe me, try this simple experiment: Generate a list of ten words that have approximately equivalent usage rates (e.g., pencil, chair, etc.), slowly read them to a friend, and ask your friend to recall as many words as possible. If your friend follows the usual pattern, he or she will recall the words at the beginning and at the end—and forget most everything in between.

Of course, you can always obtain kudos and superior ratings the old-fashioned way, by being a truly superior performer. I wasn't going to bring this up but . . . aside from the requisite technical knowledge and skills that anyone needs to perform a job well, high performers share four attributes.

(1) They establish specific, challenging goals for themselves and monitor their progress.

(2) They remain focused on those goals and are not easily diverted away from them.

(3) They manage their time effectively, concentrating the most time on what is most significant to goal achievement.

(4) They have an action orientation and feel empowered to act. They are willing to take reasonable risks and are not incapacitated by indecision.

The Merit Budget: It's a Shallow Well

Most companies budget a certain amount each year for annual merit adjustments with a fixed pool of funds created to distribute among employees. Sometimes companies approve special allocations to address specific problems or issues (e.g., to increase the starting wage to attract more people or to strengthen parts of the company apt to lose employees fleeing to competitors). Otherwise, there is no manna from heaven. A reserved storehouse of money is used in a zero-sum game—the more you get, the less someone else gets, and vice versa.

To create these budgets, companies consider what other companies plan to do and examine their own ability to pay based on corporate earnings. For you, this means that working for a growing, moneymaking company is a wiser compensation decision than working within a declining company or industry. Companies can only pay what they can afford; when they spend more than they can afford, your entire paycheck is at risk through job elimination.

According to the Bureau of Labor Statistics and the Bureau of Economic Analysis, the fastest growing sectors of the economy are business services (e.g., personnel supply services, data processing), recreational services (e.g., amusement park operators), nonbanking financial services, social services (e.g., welfare workers), and brokerage services. The emphasis is on *services*. Goods-producing sectors of the economy unfortunately continue to decline, although there are pockets of good news. Construction trades such as electrical work and masonry have grown, and the following industries continue to do well: meat products, periodicals, commercial printing, plastics products, and home and personal care products (e.g., drugs, soaps, cleaners).

But you must keep in mind that economic conditions and markets change. Also realize that certain industries are in upheaval and, while they may create opportunities for some, the job instability is not for the faint-hearted. The following industries are going through major transitions: banking, media/entertainment, retailing, telecommunications, and utilities.

It's notable that, of the jobs created in the past two years, almost half pay salaries above the national average. Furthermore, many of the jobs that are expected to show the greatest growth over the next ten years are in highly specialized fields and offer good wages and career prospects (see Chart 6A for a comprehensive list of growth fields and their attendant salaries).

To find out what everybody else is thinking of doing with regard to merit increases, companies often hire consulting firms that poll other companies. The results shouldn't mystify: The collective corporate wisdom suggests that companies should pay employees about what they paid them the year before, adjusting for inflation. Thus, it is no surprise that merit increases, for companies in reasonable health, generally mirror increases in the cost of living as measured by the consumer price index.

Salary increases that are closely tied to the cost of living have two major implications for you. First, it is extremely hard to make significant salary progress if you remain in the same job. Your income advances are too marginal and too gradual relative to inflation to have an appreciable effect on your standard of living. Companies with "flatter" organizations—with fewer layers and less upward-mobility options—are struggling to figure out what to do with their employees. They may take issue with the claim that higher positions are essential for significant salary movement. But telling employees that they can materially benefit by remaining in place is false. Why? A company will never pay $60,000 to an employee who is in a job worth $30,000—unless he or she is a friend or relative of the ruling family.

Second, this salary structure makes your first job the most important one you will ever get—that salary will be with you like a financial fingerprint your entire working life. As you move from job to job, prospective employers will not want to pay you more than about 10% to 20% of what you currently make; and your first job and salary will serve as the starting baseline for all future jobs and earnings.

The Problems of Merit Systems

For now, let's return to a discussion of the mechanics of the merit system. As you read this, you should suspend any belief that these systems are truly effective in motivating and retaining employees given the way that

CHART 6A. SALARY DATA FOR THE FASTEST-GROWING FIELDS*

Occupation	Average Pay
Accountant	$30,000–$35,000
Auditor	$34,000–$39,000
Auto body repair	$22,000–$27,000
Baker (bread, pastry)	$16,000–$21,000
Bank loan officer/counselor	$30,000–$35,000
Bilingual teacher	$34,000–$39,000
Child care worker	$17,000–$22,000
Commercial cleaning supervisor	$45,000–$50,000
Computer scientist/engineer	$60,000–$70,000
Computer programmer	$38,000–$43,000
Computer repair	$28,000–$33,000
Computer systems analyst	$38,000–$43,000
Construction and building supervisor	$30,000–$35,000
Construction manager	$54,000–$59,000
Dental assistant	$19,000–$24,000
Dental hygienist	$36,000–$41,000
Employee/labor relations specialist	$42,000–$47,000
Food service/lodging manager	$65,000–$70,000
Hairstylist/cosmetologist	$27,000–$32,000
Heating/air/refrigeration	$23,000–$28,000
Home health aide	$25,000–$30,000
Household workers	$14,000–$19,000
Insulation worker/drywall installer	$24,000–$29,000
Insurance adjuster/examiner	$22,000–$27,000
Legal/medical secretary	$28,000–$33,000
Licensed practical nurse	$21,000–$26,000
Media records technician	$27,000–$32,000
Nuclear medicine technologist	$27,000–$32,000
Occupational therapist	$42,000–$47,000
Optician (staff)	$24,000–$29,000
Painter (construction, maintenance)	$22,000–$27,000
Paralegal	$28,000–$33,000
Paramedic/emergency medical technician	$26,000–$31,000
Pharmacist	$47,000–$52,000
Physical therapist	$49,000–$54,000
Physical therapy assistants	$21,000–$26,000
Physician assistant	$51,000–$56,000
Private investigator/detective	$34,000–$39,000
Property manager (commercial)	$58,000–$63,000
Property manager (residential)	$43,000–$48,000
Radiologic technician/technologist	$28,000–$33,000

Registered nurse	$39,000–$44,000
Restaurant cook (sous chef)	$23,000–$28,000
Respiratory therapist	$27,000–$32,000
School counselor	$38,000–$43,000
Social worker	$33,000–$38,000
Speech pathologist/audiologist	$37,000–$42,000
Sports instructor and coach	$26,000–$31,000
Teacher (pre-school, kindergarten)	$21,000–$26,000
Teacher (secondary school)	$34,000–$39,000
Teacher (special education)	$34,000–$39,000
Technical communicator	$39,000–$44,000
Vocational education teacher	$27,000–$32,000

Sources: *Money*, March 1995, pp. 114–117.
Kiplinger's Personal Finance, January 1996, pp. 51–53.
Woman's Day, April 25, 1995, pp. 60–66.
Salaries also are based on author's personal experiences with these jobs.

*Salary data reflects all-industry averages for employees who generally have 3-5 years of relevant prior experiences.

they are usually practiced. There are a host of reasons why these systems really don't work, but here are my personal favorites:

(1) Itzhak Perlman was once asked what makes a great musician; he replied that it is not just playing the notes that matters but playing in between the notes as well. Excellence, whether in the orchestra or in the corporation, has a beauty that is not easily captured by forms or the mere application of rules or theory. Yet many corporations only see, hear, and understand the notes.

(2) The system presumes that employees would like to spend the bulk of their lives making money in return for their hard labor; the intrinsic values of meaningfulness and creativity and contribution are secondary in the design of these systems. In fact, studies of employee behavior have shown that the consistent offer of money as the sole incentive actually undermines the intrinsic satisfaction derived from performing the work—that is, money makes people *less* motivated to do the work.

(3) Many employees have a certain distaste for a system that makes financial reward the dominant form of recognition in situations where other forms of recognition might be more suitable—Olympians are given medals, not checks.

(4) Merit systems often have no behavioral credence: The contingencies between behavior and reward are unclear, and the time frame is too long to imbue rewards with value. The behavioral expectations for rewards are only vaguely stated, if ever. Also, the psychological value of an incentive varies indirectly with the amount of time it takes to get it. Thus, a relatively small reward that is held out after a year's wait (i.e., the merit cycle) has little or no motivational value. Even if rewards could be tied to very specific behaviors, the behavioral effects might not be considered a virtue in a dynamic business climate in which goals and priorities are subject to change; flexibility and adaptiveness might be more important than the rigid execution of duties.

Other drawbacks of the merit pay system are that it encourages short-term versus long-term solutions, creates an environment filled with fear and anxiety, and discourages teamwork. I should mention that most criticisms of the merit system are not indictments against the system per se, but against how it is implemented and practiced.

The misgivings about the merit system have not been lost on employees. The employees I have spoken with over the years find the merit system to be woefully inadequate. Nevertheless, there may be side benefits to such a system, including the availability of a structured means of communicating mutual expectations and organizational standards. There very well may be overriding reasons for retaining the system but, in practice, dispensing money according to true performance isn't one of them.

How to Deal with Your Performance Review

Your company will measure your performance in either relative or absolute terms. With relative measures, one employee is compared to another. These, as you can imagine, are delicate assessments and are rare. A manager may be asked to "prove it," and mustering a defense when there are generally no uniform and clear criteria for the distinctions can be a breathtaking exercise. Employees usually hate these systems as well since they invite uncomfortable comparisons among colleagues (i.e., who's better than whom) and force performance distinctions to be made among employees—which, of course, is the purpose of the performance exercise in the first place.

With "absolute" assessment methods, each employee is simply measured along a series of performance yardsticks. These "yardsticks" are usually rating scales that measure (a) how much of an attribute you have, such as how much initiative, (b) how well you do something, such as communicate, and (c) the extent to which you have achieved important end results such as met performance objectives. I won't dwell on the many problems associated with these scales, but I'll mention a few:

(1) They are often not related to the job—the same criteria are used throughout the company for all jobs. Could all jobs possibly have the exact same prerequisites for success to the exact same degree? For instance, "influence" skills often appear on performance reviews. Does a machine operator need this skill as much as the foreman?

(2) Most managers are not able to specify exemplars of excellence on these generic scales. This is like using a ruler without the numbers.

(3) The scales are seldom tested for reliability and validity, suggesting that there is little certainty about what is being measured or how well it is being measured.

Some companies are experimenting with the trendy concept of having multiple raters in which your underlings, peers, and bosses evaluate your performance. This approach, referred to as the 360-degree method, because you are assessed by everyone around you, is mostly billed as a developmental exercise used to build employee character and skills, and it can provide you good feedback. But when it comes to handing out money, guess whose opinion counts the most?

Whatever your company's system, when you're sitting down for your annual performance review, you need to be conscious of how you behave, as it's easy to get caught up emotionally in a review, especially if it's not entirely positive. When getting feedback, do not become defensive or counterattack. That only hardens the other person's point of view and makes him or her less open-minded in the future. Clearly, if the feedback is abusive or separated from reality, then you have an obligation to right the wrong—but this is probably best achieved through a neutral third party. Otherwise, use this opportunity to look for the kernels of truth in the feedback that you can use to improve your performance. Listening is a business trait that is greatly admired—and rarely practiced!

At the end of the performance review process, as in school, you will usually end up with either a numeric or an alphabetic grade ranging from 1 to 4 or 5 or from A to D or E. The final grade usually consists of 4 or 5 categories. A high rating is generally labeled "excellent" or "superior" or "value added." Euphemisms are used for average and poor performances: "average" becomes "competent," "good," or "satisfactory"; "poor" becomes "below average" or "has developmental needs."

Managers have a tendency to de-emphasize differences in performance among employees, particularly at the low-to-moderate end of the scale. Don't be content with average ratings no matter how appeasingly they are labeled. When it's time for corporate heads to roll, it's the "average" performers who often are rounded up. You will always want to be in the top one or two performance categories.

Keep in mind that you can exert some influence on these ratings by considering some of the tactics mentioned earlier in this chapter and by subtly conveying your firm belief in your above-average skills and abilities. If your manager is particularly timid and reluctant to make any distinctions among employees whatsoever, there is a discretionary part to this process that you can influence. I'll get to that in a moment.

How Do They Come up with My Raise Percentage?

Managers essentially take their performance ratings and consult with the corporate oracle—the merit grid. This grid outlines permissible salary increases, and two factors play central roles: where you are currently paid within your salary range and how your performance is rated. These two items interact in interesting ways. Let's take a look at a standard merit grid in order to examine some of its nuances (see Chart 6B).

There are hundreds of variations on this theme, but the logical underpinnings are the same. This grid breaks up performance and salary ranges into four buckets each. The percentages in the grid are guidelines that managers use in recommending salary increases. Merit budgets are fixed and so the grid is devised to yield a certain overall outcome—say, a 4% increase for the entire corporate population. The company works backward: It determines the solution, then creates a plan of action that will yield that solution. As a company begins work on its annual grid, here's what it will know: what the merit budget will be for the coming year; where people are in their salary ranges; and what the distribution of performance usually looks like.

CHART 6B. STANDARD MERIT GRID WITH ANNUAL REVIEWS

	Performance			
	Below Average	Good	Very Good	Excellent
High 111%–120%	0%	0%–2%	2%–4%	4%–6%
Medium High 101%–110%	0%	1%–3%	3%–5%	5%–7%
Medium Low 91%–100%	0%	2%–4%	4%–6%	6%–8%
Low 80%–90%	0%–2%	3%–5%	5%–7%	7%–9%

Position in Range

So they will know what they have to spend and a have pretty good idea of where their compensation costs will lie, i.e., how many people will fall into the various boxes in the grid.

The darkened boxes on the grid show where most compensation costs reside for most companies. These are the cells in which most of the employee population will be found. Most employees (usually about 85%–90%) are rated as good or very good, suggesting that the parts (the employees) may be greater than the whole (the corporation). The majority of employees are paid between 90% and 95% of the midpoint, as discussed in Chapter 2. The places where these "performance" and "position-in-range" columns and rows intersect is where you will find most of the employees. So if a company wants to pay an average of 4% it will fix up those cells of the grid to generate 4% increases.

If an employee is paid below minimum in a range, he or she may receive a special equity adjustment and if a person is above maximum, there may be no recommended increase at all. The reasoning for the latter is this: The company is already paying a rate reserved for very high performers (at least 20% above the midpoint). Why pay more when the company is already paying a competitive wage? Some companies admit that this practice lacks incentive value and give lump-sum bonuses to compensate employees for their contributions. Lump-sum bonuses do not get added into base salaries, so the company doesn't increase its benefits costs by this practice nor compound what is perceived to be a compensation problem. Some companies will offer nothing but sympathy. If a person who is new to the company is a below-average performer and low in the range, a company may elect to partially excuse the performance by maintaining that the employee is still learning, and give a "developmental" increase. Most companies, however, are extremely tough on the 1% (a very small percent) of the population that falls into the lowest performance category.

Sometimes you will see merit grids that appear to be more generous than the one depicted in Chart 6B. For example, look at the grid in Chart 6C. Note that some of the figures are slightly more substantial for high performers who are highest in their salary ranges. However, the time frames for the increases have been changed as well—a bigger increase but a longer wait. It is not necessary to dwell on the relative advantages and disadvantages of the two merit-grid methodologies, since the real differences are infinitesimal. The intent and outcomes are the same: to give something to employees to keep them economically whole, given inflation, while controlling costs.

You should be aware that there are methods of increasing pay other than merit, such as step rate plans, or seniority systems, which I'll just mention here briefly. These plans are found primarily in manufacturing and/or union environments. Essentially, per-hour rates are increased on a fixed schedule and at specific times; employees receive specific increases assuming their performance is adequate. Thus, the longer an employee is on the job, the more he or she will earn. Pay increases and pay levels are calibrated to coincide with market salaries at various stages in an employee's development. This is not really different from merit systems: Without extra effort on your

CHART 6C. STANDARD MERIT GRID WITH LENGTHENED PAYOUT PERIODS

		Performance		
		Below Average	Good	Very Good	Excellent
Position in Range	High 111%–120%	0%	0%–2%	2%–4%	5%–7% beginning in 15th month
	Medium High 101%–110%	0%	1%–3%	3%–5%	6%–8% beginning in 15th month
	Medium Low 91%–100%	0%	2%–4%	4%–6%	6%–8%
	Low 80%–90%	0%–2%	3%–5%	5%–7%	7%–9%

part, you'll end up at about the same place regardless of the method used to adjust your salary.

Merit—In the Long Run

Let's reflect on the implications of merit adjustments. First, promotions are indeed important. Why? When you move into a new salary range you will be lower in that range (i.e., further away from the new midpoint) and, consequently, will have a greater salary increase opportunity for a given level of performance (employees generally end up at 85% to 90% of midpoint following a promotion). Second, influencing a manager either to give you a higher performance rating or to recommend a higher percentage increase within a grid cell can mean a couple of extra percentage points to you in your paycheck.

Remember the discretionary component of the performance review process that I mentioned earlier? A reviewer frequently has a couple of percentage points of latitude within a given cell of the merit grid. Many reviewers like this discretion because it gives them the opportunity unobtrusively to make distinctions among people. Do you see the simple elegance of this? Managers don't have to differentiate on the basis of performance at all but can still deliver more or less in salary increases. Most people, managers included, can identify the better performers within an organization. The problem is that no one wants to openly say who they are ostensibly because the less able would be offended. But it is possible within most merit systems to secretly slide the better performers envelops with a little extra cash and give them a knowing wink and a nod. Everyone can feel good and no one is the wiser. It happens all of the time at all levels in the organization.

Despite an extra percentage point or two in your paycheck, you may still believe the process is unfair, given your effort and what you were paid versus others and what they did and were paid. I'm not saying that the process is necessarily fair. In fact, its inherent flaws give everyone a fighting chance. But small differences do have major impact on your pay over the long term and it would be premature to summarily dismiss nominal adjustments as substantively insignificant. In fact, consistent above-average increases amount to a heap of money over time.

Chart 6D shows you precisely what a 1% or 2% extra in base salary each year can do for you. Here's how to use the table in the chart. Take your

CHART 6D. COMPOUND EFFECTS OF SMALL MERIT INCREASES OVER TIME

Number of Years	1%	2%
1	10	20
2	20	40
3	30	61
4	41	82
5	51	104
6	62	126
7	72	149
8	83	126
9	94	195
10	105	219
11	116	243
12	127	268
13	138	294
14	149	319
15	161	346
16	173	373
17	184	400
18	196	428
19	208	457
20	220	486
21	232	516
22	245	546
23	257	577
24	270	608
25	282	641
26	295	673
27	308	707
28	321	741
29	335	776
30	348	811
31	361	848
32	375	885
33	389	922
34	403	961
35	417	1000
36	431	1040
37	445	1081
38	460	1122
39	474	1165
40	489	1208

current base salary and divide it by 1,000 (e.g., 50,575/1000 = 50.575). Multiply that number by one of the figures in the table to see how much an extra 1% or 2% will yield. If you want to know what an extra 2% will yield over 10 years on an existing salary of $50,575, multiply 50.575 by 219. The answer: an extra 2% over 10 years would produce an added $11,075.93. An extra 2% per year over a 30-year career would generate an extra $41,016.33 in income. And the more you earn, the better it gets. As you will see later in this book, many cash and noncash benefits are tied to earnings: To him that hath, much is given.

If your merit increases outpace inflation for several successive years, great. But there are limits to the good times. As your salary grows compared to the midpoint of the salary structure, your company will stop giving you as much because, again, it will be felt that you are already being paid a handsome amount. Ultimately, to avoid "shrinkage" in your annual increases because you advance too high into your salary range, you will have to move on—it's time for a promotion.

Things could be worse. Most employees end up treading water: their salaries relative to position in the range stay about the same. Their salaries move in synchronization with movement in the pay structure—a 4% pay increase and a 4% increase in pay structure. Most people start out at around 90% of the midpoint within their salary range, and never make it to 100% of midpoint.

Promotional Increases

A promotion happens when there is a substantial increase in your job duties and responsibilities. This can occur in a number of ways and for a number of reasons. Job responsibilities can be added to your existing job and, upon scrutiny, the job is deemed "bigger" than before. This type of change requires a reevaluation of your job. That doesn't usually occur unless the change is dramatic or until there is a critical mass of jobs that has to be re-examined. If a job changes significantly in content, moves up a notch in title or to a higher grade level, you have a promotion. Moving up two grade levels is a big promotion. Moving up three grade levels is practically unheard of.

There are many reasons for promotions, and not the least is well-deserved recognition and a chance to excel on a new proving ground. But there are also corporate events that lead to a reshuffling of job responsibilities throughout the company, including reorganizations, mergers, acquisitions, and workforce reductions. For example, I have often seen people heaped with new responsibilities following mergers and acquisitions where the scope of duties is enlarged by the newly combined company: Treasury has more money to watch over, human resources more people, marketing more customer segments, etc.

Promotions bring booty: about a 5% to 10% increase in salary for a one-level promotion and 10% to 20% for two levels. This raises the question, "How do I get a promotion?" There are a few obvious ways. You can truly be a superior performer who has made a real contribution to the company through your services. It happens.

Since everyone gets a promotion sooner or later, another strategy is to "stay on the bus." As other employees climb off, you will become the rider with the longest tenure. It becomes increasingly difficult to ignore someone who has been sitting there forever. It is the age-old principle of turn taking: If you are first in line, you're next. And no cutting! It would be extremely rude—although we've all seen it happen!—for a company to give a promotion to someone who has less "experience" regardless of whether the suitor comes from inside or from outside the company. Eventually, you will reach a place in your career where it will be extremely difficult for someone to nudge past you—there will be too few candidates with the same tenures.

Linking promotions to longevity treats promotions as rewards for corporate loyalty. This is largely what they are. This means that companies often fail to consider what you should reflect upon: whether the promotion is right for you. Can you do it? Do you want it? The Peter Principle, being promoted past one's competence, is alive and well in corporate America because the anticipated competence of an employee in a new position is only a remote consideration for everyone involved.

The ideal way for promotion, open to a few, is to become a part of a company's "fast track" program. In these programs, employees are exposed to challenging assignments throughout the company and often have classroom work that they must complete as well. Promotions for employees in these programs are accelerated but not automatic. These employees are believed to be critical to the company's future prosperity and are, therefore, closely monitored. Reviews of their performance are much more rigorous and honest than the reviews of the rank and file.

These programs are mainly reserved for MBAs from prominent business schools (*U.S. News & World Report* has an annual ranking of such schools) and those with degrees in companies' core areas. For example, technology

CHART 6E. COMPANIES THAT DEVELOP TALENT

Company/Headquarters	Industry Rank	Quality Training For . . .	Industry Buzz
Allstate Corp. Northbrook, IL	Largest publicly owned property casualty insurer in U.S.	Insurance adjusters	Spends $30 million a year on training (plus $13 million in 17 regional offices). Allstate usually settles claims faster and more efficiently than other insurers—to the tune of $15 billion in '95.
American Express Financial Services New York City	The biggest U.S. financial planning firm	Financial and investment advisers	Even with huge assets of $132 billion under management, AmEx encourages nimble entrepreneurial skills. Recently, to protest reported planner poaching, AmEx temporarily stopped doing business with Merrill Lynch.
U.S. Department of Defense Alexandria, VA	The nation's largest employer	Labor and employee	With 1,700 union affiliates and hundreds of regulation handbooks, the Defense Department is a trial-by-fire bureaucracy that only the sharpest survive.
Arthur D. Little Cambridge, MA	The oldest management consulting firm in the world	Management and technical consultants	Boasting an 80% repeat business rate from about 2,500 project accounts annually, Little hires pros who have engineering and science degrees as well as M.B.A.s. "They turn out problem solvers who aren't clones," says a competitor.
Marriott International Bethesda, MD	The largest U.S. retail food provider	Food service staff especially managers	Marriott offers broad opportunity and the world's best-run hospitality operation in more than 1,000 hotels and about 3,000 restaurants under management.
Merck Whitehouse Station, NJ	The largest pharmaceutical firm	Pharmaceutical sales staff and managers	As HMOs and managed-care companies turn up the cost-cutting heat, Merck's sales staff has in-depth product knowledge and consistently top-ranked performance.
Microsoft Redmond, WA	The largest independent maker of PC software	Software designers and programmers	Sign on for the 100-hour workweeks and the hotly competitive culture, and you're anointed throughout Tech Land. Plus, stock bonuses could make you a "Microsoft millionaire."
Morgan Stanley New York City	Fifth-largest global investment bank	Systems analysts and designers	With $100 billion in assets under management, Morgan Stanley provides analysts with state-of-the-art equipment and topnotch training.
Motorola Schaumburg, IL	The leading cellular phone producer	Software and hardware engineers	Technical specialists must spend an average of one month each year at "Motorola University," the in-house employee-training program. Annual company cost: $81 million.
Procter & Gamble Cincinnati, OH	The leading U.S. soap and detergent manufacturer	Marketing and advertising professionals	The 159-year-old industry leader teaches classic marketing skills. Example: LensCrafters co-founder Dean Butler used his P&G experience to revolutionize the eyewear biz.

Source: Consensus view of experts as reported in *Money*, May 1996, p. 117.

companies may have special programs for engineers and computer scientists. Anyone with the requisite qualifications can usually get into these programs; you don't have to be a new college graduate.

Also, some companies are noted for developing their people in special areas. I have provided a list of the best companies to put on a résumé (see Chart 6E) because of the thorough training they provide and the high standards to which they aspire. These are great companies to work for or to be from. Alumni from these companies often get choice jobs elsewhere.

Ten Ways to Boost Your Career

Apart from performance, longevity, and special fast track programs, here are ten specific things that employers recognize as good ways to improve your career prospects:

(1) *Seek out experiences that are essential for promotions.* It is critical to investigate and develop skills that are needed for the next logical career step. Many companies post or make job descriptions available to all employees (make sure that they are current). Research the descriptions of interest, and fashion your training and work experiences accordingly. These experiences need not be direct linkages to the next job; they can be special projects that demonstrate general competencies required for the next job. You have to be inventive. If you have your eye on a job that requires excellent organizational skills, project management, and basic accounting/fiscal responsibility, then successfully overseeing a major conference or convention, for instance, can be a great argument for having the requisite skill set to be promoted to that level.

Also, certain assignments are considered essential for promotions, particularly at high levels within the organization. Experiences in "line" areas and overseas assignments are critical. At some time in most careers, it helps to be affiliated with the section of the company that actually produces the goods or delivers the services. You are sure to make important contacts there and to learn about the core operations of the company. For international companies, it is important to become acquainted, firsthand, with foreign markets and operations. Be sure to raise your hand for these juicy assignments lest you be overlooked.

(2) *Get yourself recognized.* People who get ahead are masters at self-promotion. As a modest beginning, it is important to be able to accept a

compliment without bowing your head, pawing at the dirt with your foot, and saying, "Shucks, it was nothing." It is equally important to point at an accomplishment and say, "I did that," in order to take credit for credit due. Be sure to thank others for their interest in your achievement, and if they were instrumental in securing the opportunity for you, be sure to thank them for that as well.

(3) *Work for a growing company.* Companies that grow create new jobs and not just any jobs—good ones. Job duties tend to expand proportionately to the expansion of the company. If you are fortunate, you will join a successful, emerging company at its inception and grow right along with it.

Each year, *Inc.* magazine reports the fastest-growing companies. These surveys indicate growth in a number of areas: companies involved in arcane technologies such as highly specialized software producers; refurbishing and recycling businesses (of everything imaginable); temporary-employment services; importing/exporting; computers, particularly systems integration and networks; companies that specialize in government compliance/regulations (e.g., how to dispose of wastes); social services such as mental health clinics and correctional facilities (public goods formally supplied, in total, by government); and a host of businesses that "mass customize" (tailor goods and services to specific people or needs).

(4) *Enhance your functional skill set.* Depth of skills remains coveted over breadth for most jobs, all else being equal. There is always something new to learn with respect to your specialty and something new for you to undertake in order to perfect your craft—new analyses, new equipment and technologies, new methods, new content, etc. Don't just keep up, go deeper. "On-the-job retirement" is a surefire way to emphasize how expendable you are.

What does developing your functional/professional skill set mean to you financially? By most estimates, about 10%–15% in increased wages through participation in formal training programs. You are worth more when you can do more and companies must protect their investment from walking out the door by offering more money. There is little reason *not* to participate in these programs. Most companies with more than 250 employees offer some kind of formal training. (Companies with fewer employees tend to provide training as well but it is less formal, on-the-job training). There are skill-enhancement programs such as apprenticeship training, basic skills training, and a variety of job-skills training related to such topics as computers, sales, management, clerical and administrative support, etc.

Additionally, roughly 90% of midsize to large companies offer educational reimbursement to employees for job-related study. On average, companies will pay $1,000–$5,000 per year toward your educational expenses (but no more than a tax-free limit of $5,250). Some companies will pay for everything and some, like United Technologies, will give you stock after the successful completion of coursework. Only about 10% of all eligible employees take advantage of these lucrative corporate offers that can enhance your most valuable financial asset, your earning power.

(5) *Find a mentor.* For every job within every company there is a seasoned veteran who knows things that you don't and who can help you to gain access to the people and resources that you can't. Find someone who seems interested in teaching and with whom you are psychologically and professionally compatible. It does not necessarily have to be your boss but it should be someone whose corporate authority and influence exceeds your own. Further, you need not restrict yourself to one mentor. You might consider having two mentors: one to provide technical guidance and expertise within your discipline and another to provide managerial or operational direction.

Some companies, like Citibank and NYNEX (*Supervisory Management,* January 1996, pp. 5–6), have formal mentoring programs; take advantage of those programs if you have the chance. However, most mentoring occurs informally, and there are no prohibitions against finding an experienced coach who can guard you against adverse political fallout and who can provide you with occupational guidance. These days, there is also a growing cadre of professional counselors who can work through job-related issues with you and advise you on your career.

Have you ever wondered how people, with no greater talents than your own, started at the bottom and worked their way to the top? There are numerous examples: There is the CEO of a major insurer who started in the mailroom, the head of human resources of a *Fortune 500* company who was once a secretary, and countless manufacturing executives who operated lathes and grinding machines. I can assure you that they didn't do it alone. No one succeeds alone. Someone in the company believed in them, served as their advocate, and helped them along.

(6) *Be accountable for results.* It is one thing to have an idea or to make a suggestion, it is quite another to follow ideas or suggestions through to their conclusions. Everyone does the former, hardly anyone does the latter. That is, when everything is said and done, usually much more is said than done. If you make a suggestion, also make a quality argument for its im-

plementation and try to muster internal support for and allegiance to the idea. If the company intends to adopt a suggestion that you made, ask to be a part of the implementation team, or better, the leader. If you believe something is amiss with equipment or the production line or the customer—find out why and offer to be a part of the solution.

(7) *Have the right attitude.* It is important to have a positive orientation to work and the workplace. Some traits are more important in today's work environment than in the workplace of the past. An employee today needs to be open to change and willing to learn and take risks. In addition, employees must be able to work collaboratively with others, for instance on teams, as well as independently, i.e., without much supervisory oversight. You should understand the corporate meaning of these traits in the specific context of your corporation. It is easy to self-destruct through a misinterpretation. For example, your company may condone free thinking but not free action without first informing interested parties and obtaining the necessary approvals. Traits like independence and risk are on a continuum and a part of corporate life is recognizing the specific tolerances a company has on the traits it values.

It is sometimes difficult to figure out just what behaviors a company values. Some companies have split personalities: They say one thing and act according to a different set of principles. They may, for example, espouse the virtues of quality and service, but reward and promote on the basis of production and sales. Follow the money.

I was recently reminded how assumptions about corporate values can be wrong. A company was in the process of hiring a senior-level manager when I inquired how their search was progressing. They laughed and said, "Not very well" and here's why. The company values consensus and joint decision making, not independence. All of the candidates assumed that independence was a virtue and in the course of the selection interview would go on and on about how they virtually spit on authority. Wrong answer.

(8) *Create an internal network.* Get to know people outside of your department or area. This can expedite your work: Contacts within informal networks can be instrumental in supplying information, services, or materials and in circumventing tedious internal rules and procedures. Also, you will be more likely to stand out when, for example, a special interdisciplinary project or task force is being formed. You are not just another name but a person whom others have seen and heard.

There are different avenues for getting yourself known internally. Concentrate on activities that will attract people from all levels and functions of the company such as clubs devoted to public speaking. If there are company newspapers, bulletins, or newsletters, tactfully submit an article on what you have achieved or what your department has to offer the rest of the company. Finally, remain alert for opportunities and volunteer if the assignment seems right—i.e., if it enhances your skills and/or puts you in touch with others who can positively affect your career. By the way, if you volunteer for chores outside of your department, you may have to fulfill your obligations on your own time. However, no one will hold doing extra work against you, except perhaps your family.

(9) *Develop cross-functional skills.* The importance of developing interdisciplinary skills is a wee bit overstated. You can always be wary of advice that has pictures and cute sayings attached. Breadth of skills in jobs has been symbolized many ways over the past several decades. The current portrayal of jobs is as a "T"-shape. Get it? Length (depth) and width (breadth) are both important. Conical models are also popular—you can advance or develop "in" (depth), "up" (promotion), or "around" (breadth).

Breadth of skills probably is important, but I'm not convinced that companies understand why. Being able to make connections between seemingly disparate pieces is a form of creativity that would benefit most companies, yet most companies maintain a specialization mind-set. To make "breadth" pay off for you, you will have to help your company see the relation between various skill sets or bases of knowledge and the possible relevance of one discipline to another. Learning about or acquiring new skills consistent with the company's main focus (e.g., technology, manufacturing) is usually advantageous.

Generally, however, "job breadth" means honing multiple abilities that have logical connections and professional overlaps. For example, a design engineer may learn more about manufacturing or a paralegal may seek out experiences within human resources that tend to have legalistic components. Just make sure that there is a clear rationale for your myriad experiences so that when you vie for a new job you don't appear to be wishy-washy and indecisive about your career. You will need to convince others that what was lost on intradisciplinary experiences was more than offset by rich, lateral experiences.

(10) *Communicate your interests.* Other people don't always think to ask you what you may want for yourself. You have to let people know. If it is unknown whether or not you want a particular job, it is easy to presume that you do not because it makes choosing one person over another simpler.

It affords the perfect, guiltless excuse, "Oh, I didn't know you were interested." Too late. You have to let others know about your ambitions so they know and can help.

Whenever you are considering a career or job change, make sure your move is properly motivated. It is easy to be tempted by escape from an undesirable job or circumstance. But "freedom from" is just half of the story. You have to know where you are going as well. There are plenty of self-help books that are available to help you assess your strengths and interests. Career counselors, too, can help you to think carefully through job or career transitions. Most importantly, it is critical for you to understand and communicate what you want to move toward and not just what you would like to leave behind.

Return on Your Personal Investment: What's the Value of Your Human Capital?

Your merit and promotional increases are enlightening because they represent a return on your personal investment of your energies and talents. They are gauges of how your relative worth to the company changes over time. In truth, you are an asset of conglomerate abilities deserving of a certain yield. I know that you have heard the "Our people are our most important assets" line before, but hear me out.

It is fashionable for companies to speak (or double-speak) of employees as their most valuable assets. And, unfortunately, what they often mean is that employees are the most *expensive* assets, i.e., the biggest corporate cost. Corporate assertions regarding the value of the people who produce the goods or deliver the services are too frequently hollow and made as a matter of convenience rather than as a matter of fact. Despite the rhetoric of human potential and human capital and its many contradictions, companies do in fact invest heavily in people. They sometimes don't realize the magnitude of those investments and the longer-term consequences of reductions in the size and scope of those investments. For example, high-tech companies estimate that they sink about $150,000 into each new engineer before they begin to see a return. Premature loss of an engineer is a real loss in terms of both the actual costs and the contributions foregone.

The mathematics of corporate investment in employees is fairly straightforward. Investment monies include salary, benefits, training, and the space and materials to ply one's trade. Your salary plus another 50% would not be too far off the mark of a company's annual investment in your talents. Therefore, a company that hires an employee at $50,000 has decided to make an investment of approximately $75,000 in that employee for one year alone.

Most economists would view investment in human as well as physical capital to be essential for economic growth. As a measure of human capital, educational attainment (and length of training) often serves as a proxy: Higher wages go to those who are better educated (e.g., a college education is worth an estimated 70–75% more in pay to new graduates versus recent high school graduates; said differently, each additional year of education, starting at high school, adds about 10–20% to your future income). When companies pay you for your educational prowess, as they tend to, they assume that you will provide greater benefit to the company. Maybe.

There are surely enough irregularities in the labor market that an employee's human capital cannot be exactly measured by the wage he or she receives. But your wage will incorporate the human capital that you possess. The more you know, the more you are able to do; the greater your potential contributions, the higher your wage should be. Thus, although not perfectly correlated, your earnings do serve as an index of your value to employers, and changes to those earnings reflect how your capital appreciates over time. If you think of yourself as an entity that accumulates skills and knowledge and experience—that is, that grows—you can see why your wages should grow along with you.

How large a return would you expect for your human capital? An index of no growth would be the inflation rate where the overall value of your earnings remains static over time. This is where you would end up with average performance ratings and few promotions over a prolonged period of time. At the other extreme, your earnings may grow at a rate commensurate with the stock of small public companies—very fast. The appreciation in the price of small capital stocks reflects their rising profits, wealth creation, and market value, mixed with speculation on potential. If your income is increasing at this rate, you are doing well: It signifies recognition of special qualities and capabilities that someone thinks are hugely beneficial to the corporate cause. You can achieve this rate of salary increase through consistently superior performance ratings and lots of genuine promotions.

There are other intermediate, historical investment returns that are shown in Chart 6F. Obviously, the more your income growth surpasses the inflation rate, the better off you are. Interestingly, the high returns posted by equity investments such as stock are like progressions in one's discipline: They average out favorably across time, but advancement often involves

CHART 6F. AVERAGE ANNUAL RETURNS ON A $1,000 INVESTMENT

Number of Years	Inflation (3.1%)	Long-Term Corporate Bonds (5.4%)	Large Company Stocks (10.2%)	Small Company Stocks (12.2%)
1	31	54	102	122
2	63	111	214	259
3	96	171	338	412
4	130	234	475	585
5	165	301	625	778
6	201	371	791	995
7	238	445	974	1238
8	277	523	1175	1512
9	316	605	1397	1818
10	357	692	1641	2162
11	399	783	1911	2547
12	442	880	2208	2980
13	487	981	2535	3466
14	533	1088	2895	4011
15	581	1201	3293	4622
16	630	1320	3731	5308
17	680	1445	4213	6077
18	732	1577	4745	6941
19	786	1716	5331	7910
20	842	1863	5977	8997
21	899	2018	6688	10216
22	957	2180	7472	11584
23	1018	2352	8336	13120
24	1081	2533	9289	14843
25	1145	2724	10338	16775
26	1212	2925	11495	18944
27	1280	3137	12769	21377
28	1351	3361	14174	24107
29	1424	3596	15723	27170
30	1499	3844	17427	30607
31	1576	4106	19307	34463
32	1656	4381	21378	38790
33	1739	4672	23661	43644
34	1824	4976	26176	49091
35	1911	5301	28948	55202

Your Starting Salary . . . . = _____

Your Current Salary . . . . = _____

Your Number of Years in the Workforce . .= _____

Are You an Equity?

Note: Average returns come from *Stocks, Bonds, Bills and Inflation: 1995 Yearbook*, Ibbotson Associates.

ups and downs and the assumption of risk. The road to higher wages is not necessarily straight and narrow.

Now let's put Chart 6F to use. The chart shows what happens to a $1,000 investment in various financial instruments as well as how it is affected by the average compounded annual inflation rate. Locate the row that shows the number of years that you have been in the workforce. Include years of self-employment and company-sanctioned periods away from the workplace such as sabbaticals and paid leaves of absence. Do not include *bona fide* departures from the workforce such as returning to school full-time or deciding to stay home with the kids. Unfortunately, those years only count toward your chronological age.

Next, perform the following calculations:

(1) Round the starting salary of your first real job to the nearest hundreds place (e.g., $25,575 becomes $25,600)

(2) Divide the rounded number by 1000 (e.g., 25,600 becomes 25.6)

(3) Multiply the result from step 2, above, by the appropriate value in the table. For example, to compute the income that would be equivalent to the return produced by small company stocks over a five-year period, take your result from step 2 and multiply it by 778 and add the product to your original starting salary (e.g., $25.6 \times 778 = 19,917$; $19,917 + 25,575 = \$45,492$, which would be your approximate salary if you were materially progressing like a high growth equity).

Proceed in like manner for all of the investment options. How do your current earnings compare to the values that you computed? What kind of return are you getting for the physical and intellectual capital you take into work? Are "You, Inc." like an equity investment?

Feel free to experiment with different scenarios and to set goals for yourself. What income level would you have to achieve in ten years in order to satisfy a 12.2% rate of return (small growth stocks)? Regardless of the actual accumulated returns you have garnered or the ones for which you will strive, one outstanding item that you probably noticed through this exercise is that the higher your starting salary, the higher your current salary, all else being equal. This brings us to one of the main purposes of the next chapter, namely, how to get the best deal for yourself when you are first starting out in the workforce (and afterward).

Chapter 7

Getting Your Due
Through Negotiation

By now, you should have a keen sense of your worth and a better understanding of what is fair compensation for yourself. Now all you have to do is get it. This frequently involves a process in which you and another person, usually your boss, openly communicate about mutual expectations and money. In other words, you negotiate.

Negotiation often conjures negative images of conflict, of smoke-filled rooms, and of side agreements and secrets in which one party attempts to batter another into submission. Bad negotiation pursued in bad faith may take on this character, but good negotiation conducted in good faith is a just method of problem solving. It is not unlike the processes you use to solve any problem you might encounter from time to time. With negotiation, however, the acceptance or consent of two or more people is required. That is, everyone involved has to agree to the solution.

The issue, then, becomes, "How do you gain that acceptance in a way that maintains the health and stability of the relationship and your integrity?" The goal of negotiation is to fulfill your interests in a manner that is fair and honorable through a process that leaves both parties satisfied with the results, where "fair and honorable" generally excludes the use of brute force and many other subversive tactics.

Whether you are new to the job market, changing jobs, or seeking improvements in your current pay and circumstances, the suggestions in this chapter will give you ideas about rational arguments for increasing your pay. I use the word *rational* for good reason. Everybody *wants* more money, and many people, for all kinds of reasons, believe they *deserve* more. Some reasons I've heard over the years are, to paraphrase: "I just had a new baby"; "I've been here five years"; "I am the best performer in the unit"; I'm trying to put my kids through college"; "I have just acquired a new and valuable skill"; "I make less than John, and that isn't right"; "I could get more elsewhere—everyone who leaves gets more"; "I'm embarrassed by how little I now make."

Now imagine hearing these reasons as a boss or head of human resources. Let's say you are the head of human resources in a company with five thousand employees who are at different levels, in various functions, and who have varying abilities. You subscribe to several salary surveys and have a staff dedicated to matching each job and associated pay against the market.

Then one day an employee comes to you and says he feels underpaid and would like more money. He feels that he has earned it through his many years of service and loyalty to the company. What would you say? If you could contain yourself, you would politely say, "We already pay you for your years of service as reflected in the job you perform and the duties for which you are responsible." If you can't contain yourself, you would say, "What kind of reason is that? Everybody wants more money! Do you know how many people walk into this office thinking they deserve more? I wish *I* had a dollar for every time that happened. Then I'd have the money I deserve."

That, my friend, is the end of the story. If the employee is lucky, he will engage the boss or human resources representative in a tit-for-tat debate about money—you give a little and you get a little. But nobody will feel good about it and the result will be arbitrary. You see, it is very hard for anyone to respond positively to a single claim that someone wants more money without some sound grounds for the appeal. There has to be a rational appeal or objective criteria which everyone can agree upon. If there is agreement in principle, agreement on terms is not far behind.

I am often asked to help companies reorganize departments, divisions, etc. If I told them how I thought the company should be organized, half the company would agree, half would disagree, and another half would emerge asking, "Who hired this guy?" I know that I can never get a consensus on such emotional issues without first gaining agreement on the principles or criteria on which our decision will be based. It's only when I can repeatedly point to the standards to which we have all agreed rather than having to advocate my own point of view that we're able to make progress. I learned the hard way that my point of view is but one of many.

Now imagine getting agreement on a topic that touches everyone deeply, money—that great symbol of accomplishment and worth. Unless there is a way to evaluate the fairness or rightness of a position, the discussion gets reduced down to personal interests and opinions: You want more, someone else wants to give you less.

Think about it. If you and I are just debating the price, there is not much to discuss. Furthermore, the relationship from the start is adversarial. It has all of the appearances of a zero-sum game. If I give you what you want, you win and I lose. If you give me what I want, I win and you lose. Clearly, nobody really wins. Hurt feelings and personal affronts abound. Some people feel underappreciated. Others feel misunderstood and no one has any better understanding of what anyone really wanted.

The issue, then becomes how to get someone else, who has his or her own ideas of what is correct, to modify his or her position. In the next section, I will discuss different ways of doing precisely that. But keep in mind that negotiation is a skill that requires a lot of practice to perfect.

Also keep in mind the important personality attributes of good negotiators. First, a good negotiator is able to "depersonalize" the situation and remain focused on the issues. Do not allow yourself to be caught up in the emotional aspects of money talk and lose your mental agility and quickness. Never care too much, and be prepared to walk away from situations in which there is no satisfying solution. Do not let the other party believe that you won't walk away.

Second, a good negotiator is unfazed by high-pressure tactics. Either directly question the motives of the other person ("It appears that no matter what the consequences to me, you are going to insist that I . . .") or ignore the tactics altogether. To use an analogy from Thomas Schelling's seminal work *The Strategy of Conflict,* if a crazed truck driver, who is heading straight for you on the highway, rips his or her steering wheel off, you can negate the other driver's advantage when you pretend not to see him or her driving toward you. Just whistle a happy tune.

Third, a good negotiator is both persistent and adaptive. Stay true to what you believe is right, but be prepared to change your approach or method of presentation to better represent your point of view to someone else.

Fourth, a good negotiator has an uncanny sense of posture and timing. It is important to know what to say, how to say it, and when to say it. It is equally important to know when to shut up and let the other person talk. I have seen many perfectly good and seemingly settled negotiations turn sour by innocent "add on" phrases like, "I thought that if we discussed this, you'd come around to my way of seeing things." In other words, "I won and you lost." When you have gotten what you want, stop talking!

Managing Expectations: How to Get Your Employer to Think What You're Thinking

Every manager has in mind a general amount of money he or she thinks should be spent on a given position. Generally the range a manager would like to spend for someone who can perform a given set of job duties is between the minimum and the midpoint of a salary range. Your goal is to shift the manager's "negotiating" range upward.

In essence, you have to change a manager's expectations about what he or she will have to pay to hire you or to retain you. The manager must come to believe that the low point of his or her range is too low (no way could a company offer you that without offending you) and the high point is similarly too low (the company may have to offer more than what is customary to win you over).

Before talking about what you should do, let's first talk about the one thing you should *not* do: be the first to mention a salary figure. Why? Because it won't affect a manager's expectations of what he or she will have to pay. It will only affect a company's response to you.

There are three things that can happen when, in response to the question, "So what kind of salary are you looking for?" you just blurt out a number:

(1) The number is low in the range. Result: The company accepts (if they want you) and can even appear gracious and throw in an extra $1,000.

(2) The number is higher than the upper limit of the range. Result: You are deemed too expensive and are eliminated for consideration for a new job or thought to be "unreasonable" if looking for a raise.

(3) The number is squarely within the range. Result: The number is accepted, and you live with the uncertainty of whether or not you should have asked for more.

Do not be the first to give a salary figure. It usually can only hurt you. The best it can ever do is get you engaged in "dueling salaries." This is where you name a number, someone else names a lower number, you name another number, and on and on you go until you end up about in the middle of the first two numbers mentioned.

You want a salary that is fair and that reflects your worth, not a number pulled out of thin air. Furthermore, discussing only price will never allow you or the company to explore mutual needs and other issues that matter. You may be worth more on the "open market" because of the skills you possess, for example, but the company you work for isn't taking advantage of those skills. Most companies would actually be glad to pay you more if you could help them to find ways of using your abilities to the fullest.

Most successful negotiations require discussion of multiple issues. Some of these issues, such as career advancement, your job responsibilities, your grade level, and money will matter more to one party than the other. This feature is precisely what makes negotiation work—trade-offs between what is important to you and others, and what isn't. Think, therefore, before you begin to negotiate about everything that is important to you (not just money) and raise them as discussion points. A company may not be able to give you much more in salary, but it may be able to help you with commuting expenses or child care costs or flexibility in your work schedule. These are economic benefits that can put more money into your pocket.

By the way, people do not always provide their actual salaries when pushed to provide them. Are you surprised? Many people provide estimates of their worth in the open market, or desired salary figures, which are always higher than current earnings. To put it more succinctly, they lie and it seems to pay off. The ethics of this position may be in dispute and one can always resort to the "salary negotiable" option on job application forms.

I saw something rather interesting recently at a major corporation. The recruitment office had posted average starting salaries earned by graduates of various universities. They presumably thought that by publicizing salaries they could dispense with negotiations and demonstrate their fairness. Recruits wanted to know, however, why they couldn't be paid what the kids from Harvard and MIT were being paid for similar positions. Negotiations got tougher, not easier.

One other caution before moving on. Don't be persuaded by moral arguments unless a company is willing to pay for its ethics. Companies, for example, may insinuate that asking for more money (particularly when combined with the possibility that you may take your talents elsewhere) is an act of disloyalty. In that case, ask them what "loyalty" means. Does it mean that you are guaranteed employment for life? Does it mean that you will receive regular promotions? Does it mean that you will be taken care of financially for life? You know the answers.

Companies will also suggest that by giving you more money, the entire fabric of social justice will break down and the fine balance of fairness will be forever lost ("If we pay you more, then your salary will be greater than that of these other people, who we'll have to pay more"). This isn't relevant unless the company is asking you to compare what you can do to what "these others" can do. If you know that these comparisons will be favorable for you, invite the company to explain why these "others" deserve more than you. If it comes down to differences in position/job, ask, "If I were in the same position, how would I be paid?" You have just introduced something new to the discussion. In addition to focusing attention on contributions and work results as potential differentiators in pay (versus occupancy of a job), you have raised the issue that maybe you should be in a higher-level job.

Okay, let's go on to the positive steps you can take to modify a company's expectations of what it will have to pay you. You will need to put four things into your negotiating tool kit to accomplish this: information, value, timing, and power.

Information

Information is what this book is all about. Before discussions of money ever begin, you will have to be aware of the realm of possibilities and of your worth in total compensation dollars. It's like a good game of chess. Before you sit down to play, you have to know the objective of the game and all of the legitimate moves that can be made. From there, you can begin to form your strategy.

Value

The next thing you should do is think about your strengths and play to them. What is it that you can do particularly well that helps the company to achieve what it values the most? Does the company value efficiency, quality, growth, innovation? Find out and then map your own skill sets against those values. You should be able to do this no matter what your job or your level in the organization, or whether you are a current employee or a prospective employee.

The worksheet in Chart 7A can help you to think about your strengths in the context of the company's values. List what the company values most in the left-hand column. You can easily find out what the company values through:

- *Direct observation* (or, if you are a prospective employee, through conversations with current employees): the behaviors that the company rewards, how the company spends its money, etc.; for example, I have been at companies that have sincerely proclaimed the value of their "human assets" but who have virtually no human resources department, no training budget, and few creature comforts.
- *Company literature:* A lot of this is propaganda, but there are usually recurring themes that run through a company's publications that highlight what the company values most.
- Publications: Read what analysts, consultants, journalists, and others are saying about the company.
- *Asking:* Interview the interviewer; whether talking to your current or prospective boss or an HR representative, be prepared with carefully crafted questions that get to the heart of the company's belief system. Ask for examples.

Once you've gotten a sense of the company's values, reflect on your skills and abilities. What are all of the things that you can do that are consistent with what the company most highly prizes? List them in the right-hand column. These are the items you will want to emphasize in salary discussions. They are worth more to the company. That is, the company expects to pay you more if you have them because from its point of view you are worth more.

As you discuss your salary, revisit these special strengths occasionally. At times, you will have to refocus the conversation back to your strengths. The perfect opportunity to do this is when the company makes you an offer either in the form of a starting salary or raise. You will then respond with the six most powerful words in negotiation:

"How did you arrive at that?"

CHART 7A. MAPPING YOUR SKILLS AND
ABILITIES TO CORPORATE VALUES

Instructions: List a skill or ability that you have that matches the value the company is looking for and provide an example of how you have exercised that skill or ability in the past—either on the job or off.

Corporate Values   **Your Skills and Abilities**

What the reward (compensation)
system appears to value:

_____   _____

_____   _____

_____   _____

What the company literature says
about values:

_____   _____

_____   _____

_____   _____

What the company seems to be
like based on what you have
heard and read:

_____   _____

_____   _____

_____   _____

What you have learned about the
company's values from interviews
with company employees:

_____   _____

_____   _____

_____   _____

Most often, the reason is that the company thinks you'll take it. But noooo. What you want to know is the criteria the company used to determine its salary figure. Force them to explain what went into the decision and react by describing your criteria—your strengths against the company's values.

Timing

Every child can tell you that the time to ask for something is when it is easiest for the parent to say "Yes": (1) when the parent's enthusiasm for the child is greatest and (2) when the child has been able to get the parent to make mini-commitments in preparation for the coup de grâce.

The time to ask for a raise is when you are at the peak of your game, not in the twilight. All of the wonderful things you can do are most evident when you've just done them. If this sounds excessively opportunistic or like crass capitalism, what's the alternative—to ask for more money when you are at your all-time low?

The time to negotiate a starting salary is when the company has made the decision to hire you: not before and not long after. Remember, companies don't make decisions—people do. And most people are slightly anxious about the decisions they make. To relieve themselves of this anxiety, they begin to think about a candidate's positive qualities and the wonderful decision they have really made. For some employees and employers, the marriage is all downhill once the romance is gone. So, get it while you can: when you have just been hired. Postponing earnest discussions of money until "later" will be too late.

Now imagine a child asking you to take him or her bike riding. You're watching television, the bike is in the basement, and he or she wants to go riding in the park which is a half mile away. Think of what's involved with your compliance: You have to stop sitting, turn off the television, go into the basement and carry the bike outside, walk a half mile to the park and back again. "Not right now," you reply. But your child is cunning. Your child, who has just learned to ride a two-wheeler, asks if you would mind taking off the horn on the bike during an advertisement. The horn is for "babies." "No problem," you say.

While you're in the basement, the child asks if you would mind carrying the bike outside. "No problem," you say. Do you want to watch him or her ride the two-wheeler? "Okay, sure." You see how the story unfolds: "Let's ride down the street." "Let's go around the block." "Let's go to the park." Before you know it, you're in the park.

Sometimes asking for a raise is like asking the parent to get up and go to the park. It can be remarkably inconvenient. It can be very disruptive of one's routine. It requires effort, approvals, activity, etc. So, sometimes in negotiation it is prudent to start with first things first before tackling the monster issues. Middle East negotiators don't begin negotiations with the thorniest issues like land rights because there won't be any progress on those until other issues are settled first.

Therefore, try to obtain "mini-commitments" that get you closer to your overall goal if the ultimate goal seems too far off to reach. Asking your boss to recommend you for special assignments, or special awards (e.g., service awards, employee of the month, etc.), to support you on a special project, and to publicly recognize your achievements (through a note to human resources or to his or her supervisor), brings you closer to the coveted goal of higher pay while en route you receive kudos for your hard work. Sooner rather than later, it becomes evident that a good raise is warranted. Why else would your boss have nominated you for special awards and publicly praised you if not to say you are a valued employee? These mini-commitments and expressions of appreciation are important because they prevent you from being taken for granted and help to set a rewarding course of action.

Power

You have power to the extent that you are capable of controlling or inflicting harm on others through the choices that you make. The most familiar form of power, and the one we will consider first, is the power of alternatives. To illustrate the power of alternatives, imagine asking for a raise knowing that you have a more lucrative offer in your hip pocket. Now imagine asking for a raise without that offer. Big difference, isn't there? Under the former scenario you will exude much more confidence knowing (1) that you are worth more (because someone else is willing to pay more) and (2) that you can just say "No."

Having an alternative that is preferable to the position you would be in should no agreeable solution to your compensation be reached means you can walk away. This is why, in interpersonal relationships (as in companies), the mention of "commitment" and "loyalty" is so common—it is an attempt to limit options outside the present relationship. You will *always* increase your compensation if you find an acceptable alternative either because you will accept the new job or because your current company, noting your value on the open market, will increase your compensation.

The second form of power is the power of indispensability. This means that in some sense the company finds you difficult to replace because you have acquired rare skills and knowledge. You can do things that most others cannot. You have carved out a piece of the company for yourself. It is possible to become irreplaceable by having highly specialized skills, knowing things (about systems, the industry, etc.) that others don't, or knowing where to find things that others can't.

Your value lies in there being no suitable replacement. If you go, something doesn't get done or doesn't get done well. So, a surefire way to up your compensation is to become indispensable to your company. Victor G. did it by learning a rare programming code and storing data in a way that only he understood. Kathy D. did it by having "intuitive" design (engineering) skills that couldn't be taught to others—she turned engineering into an art form.

There is one problem with indispensability that you should know about. Look at Chart 7B. It shows that there are levels of indispensability. You can be indispensable to your department, for example, but in the scheme of things your department may not be very critical company-wide, or *is* replaceable (through outsourcing, for example). Go ahead and measure yourself on the scales provided and if you are in the low or medium ranges, start thinking of ways to increase your indispensability factor. Your options range from bolstering your abilities to transferring to another business unit.

25 Frequently Asked Questions About Negotiating a Higher Salary

Raising your salary is a delicate, and often complicated, process. Over the years, many employees have asked me about their pay and the tactics they might use for increasing it. Here are the most commonly asked questions and concerns, and my replies.

1. *I am upset by my pay. I think I am worth much more. Should I threaten to leave?*

Before you threaten, remember what a threat is—you have to find an alternative that you are prepared to accept if you don't receive the compensation for which you are looking. If through honest discourse you've gotten nowhere, and *warnings* or statements like, "It would be a shame to think another company might see more value in me than the one I work for," have also not yielded results, then having viable alternatives can serve as a powerful motivator for companies. But give the company a chance to

CHART 7B. THE INDISPENSABILITY FACTOR

Instructions: Please answer the questions below. Add up your scores.

How indispensable are you?

Indispensability Level   Your Indispensability Factor

Your job	If you left the company, realistically, how easy or hard would it be for the company to replace you?	Very Easy 1 2 3 4 5 Very Hard	
	To what extent do you have abilities or possess knowledge that most others, both inside and outside the company, do not have?	Do not have specialized knowledge/ abilities 1 2 3 4 5 Have a great deal of specialized knowledge/ abilities	
Your department	If your company had to eliminate departments, what would happen to yours?	It would be the first to go 1 2 3 4 5 It would be the last to go	
	Is your department very respected by other parts of the company?	Not respected at all 1 2 3 4 5 Very respected	
Your business/ division	How much does your business/division contribute to the profitability of the company?	Contributes the least 1 2 3 4 5 Contributes the most	
	Does it look like your business will grow or shrink in the years ahead?	Will definitely shrink 1 2 3 4 5 Will definitely grow	

High indispensability factor	= 4.25–5.00
High-medium indispensability factor	= 3.50–4.24
Medium indispensability factor	= 2.75–3.49
Low-medium indispensability factor	= 2.00–2.74
Low indispensability factor	= Under 2.00

Put your average score (total points divided by six) here: _____

respond before you threaten. Threats are measures of last resort and good negotiators rarely use them. Threats have that potential of getting you what you want but damaging the relationship in the process.

2. *I know what some people get paid and, believe me, they are not worth it. Should I point this out when asking for a raise?*

That's an argument that others are overpaid, and saying something like, "Sally makes more than I do," sounds a lot like whining. Your argument is that your pay doesn't measure up given your performance and accomplishments. To generate debate, you may want to pose your dilemma as a question, "Do you think my pay is in line with my contributions to the company?" This is a good way to test a company's position; you've given the company the room it needs to reach its own conclusion without coercion.

3. *Do I always have to ask for a raise or are there ways to get a company to "volunteer" an increase?*

Companies will voluntarily correct pay that they recognize to be unusually low through so-called equity adjustments. Although most of the time you'll have to explicitly request more money, I have seen the grapevine effectively used to employees' advantage. Planting rumors of alternative, "unsolicited" offers can produce spontaneous meetings and salary reviews. The thrust of this approach is to suggest that one is being sought after but is satisfied with one's current company and if at all possible would like to remain. I have also seen increases that follow employees' discreet inquiries into departments that oversee EEOC concerns, women's issues, etc. Here, the implicit message is that an employee is wondering about the fairness of his or her pay which, in turn, can spark an investigation and pay increase.

4. *If I'm not given one right away, how many times should I ask for a raise?*

As many times as it takes. Seriously, if you believe that something is wrong, you shouldn't let it pass. An important trait of a negotiator is persistence. Indeed, one negotiating tactic is the "door in the face technique." Essentially, this is a tactic that wears the other side out: After so many rejections, a person feels compelled to yield. A person can only say "No" a certain number of times before saying "Yes." Children are masters at this technique with their parents. Just make sure you distinguish "No" from "I'm working on it." It sometimes takes a little time to make pay changes, particularly in big institutions. Give the person time and periodically ask if there is anything you can do to facilitate the process.

5. *What if a company says that it can't give me everything I want? What do I do?*

Find out what the company can do. If the discrepancy between what you are currently getting and what you should be getting is sizable, there is a good chance that the company really can't give you what you want *immediately.* But it can give you what you want in chunks. You have several options: (a) ask about the best the company can do; (b) ask if there are alternative ways of making up the difference such as lump sum bonuses; (c) create a multi-year plan that stipulates what the company will do from year to year. The latter tactic is known as the "foot in the door technique." Getting the company to make small, successive concessions serves to validate your position and commits them to future actions. If you know it's unlikely that you will get everything at once, think about the steps that will get you closer and closer: a slightly larger bonus, an upgrade on your position, a review in six months versus twelve months, etc.

6. *Do all companies negotiate starting salaries?*

Most are willing but certain companies in high-paying industries will be less likely to budge because they pay more than other companies. Investment banking, entertainment, and consumer goods companies, known for their comparative largesse, are most likely to stick to their opening offers, which they consider to be fair. Once you have the job, it will be up to you to prove your worth to increase your compensation.

7. *I was recently promoted but didn't get a raise. Does that make sense?*

It does if your company is broke. In most instances, however, increased responsibilities should bring you more money. Ask your employer what it believes to be a fair wage given your new job role and increased responsibilities. Promotional systems are more meaningful in some companies than others but all promotions imply that you will be doing "more" work or "different" type of work. If your current pay is about right for the "old job," it can't be right for the new one.

8. *Should I ever display my excitement about an offer or a raise?*

Not unless you want it to be your last. Veil your enthusiasm. You can express interest as a way to signal that things are heading in the right direction and that discussion should continue, but if you convey that it would be very hard for you to walk away from a particular job and company, then the company may assume that you are willing to accept less compensation in exchange for a job—and company—arrangement that you like. Pretending not to care too much is a great negotiating weapon because it suggests that you might leave if you don't get what you want. Once you receive a salary increase, it wouldn't be a bad idea to acknowledge others' efforts expended in your behalf. Even though you may view the entire episode as "business as usual," those who supported and endorsed you will want to be thanked.

9. *I asked for a raise and didn't get it. Now what?*

First, find out why you didn't get it. Most of the time the reasons have to do with "internal equity": if you get more, everybody will have to get more (or so the company imagines). In essence, the company is evaluating your value relative to others and generally time on the job is the deciding factor. Review your strengths and how you exercise them on the job—focus on those areas where you have clear advantages over others (a unique skill, rare knowledge, etc.) and use that as the criterion on which you will appeal for higher pay.

10. *I am a consistently good performer but don't seem to be getting ahead. Any suggestions?*

One thing companies do not do very well is pay their best performers. But they do recognize their shortfalls once they are pointed out. Ask the company about its criteria for job performance and job success and how you measure up. Discuss whether your history of raises seems consistent with its assessment of your performance. You will note, however, that discussions of this nature involve risk. You may discover that, in the company's eyes, your performance is not all that great. But then you will be in position to do something about it. It's better than not knowing or finding out too late.

11. *Our company has very strict rules on raises which limits the amount of increases employees get. Can the rules be changed?*

First of all, the rules are not rules: they are guidelines. Second, as guidelines, it is possible to work outside of them. But you will have to overcome a powerful negotiating adversary—an authority (the "rules") that says "Nothing is possible." Change is sometimes costly and inconvenient, but it is usually possible. And often obstacles provide the best opportunities. The opportunity here is to get your direct supervisor to admit that if it wasn't for those darn rules, you'd be paid more. You will next want to invite your supervisor to discuss his or her opinions with human resources (with you present). You can say something like, "Even if nothing comes of it, it couldn't hurt to let human resources know our thoughts about their rules: They may have some interesting ideas on what can be done." One of the best means of getting a raise is to enlist your supervisor as an ally who objectively argues in your behalf. Recruiters, too, can be important "neutral" third parties who serve as advocates. Indeed, their job is to place the right person into a company for the right price and, in so doing, to mediate a fair solution.

12. *When it comes to pay, does the squeaky wheel on the cart get the grease?*

If the cart is still functional, yes (i.e., if you are deemed to be "worth it");

otherwise the company will just want to throw the annoyance away. If the company can't easily get rid of you, it may squirt a little oil your way to shut you up—but it know this will only be temporary and will be looking for less costly ways to quiet you. This behavior pattern is like the child who screams for candy in the store and gets it—it's not likely to produce quality relations because it is a win-lose situation. The employee wins if the employer gives in and vice versa if the employer doesn't.

13. *I work in a factory with fixed raises given at fixed times. I don't think there is anything I can do to get more money.*

Of course there is. Your starting rate, and subsequent rate, is determined by your job. The more you can do, the more you will make. More than any other industry, manufacturing pays for skills because there is a close tie between the skills employees possess and the results to the company. By developing new skills, learning how to perform a related job, etc., you will increase your rate of pay.

14. *I don't seem to be getting anywhere with my boss regarding pay. I have talked openly with him about my pay and what I have done for the company, but nothing ever happens. He kind of snorts, says that it is too bad, and then goes on about his business. Should I go to his boss?*

Sounds like the kind of boss where nothing will ever happen. Making an idiot look like an idiot generally doesn't go over very well with idiots. They retaliate in unseemly ways, i.e., ask you to work overtime, give you lousy assignments, not talk to you. If you work for someone who is unable to recognize the unique contributions that people make, then it is better that you begin looking for a different boss.

15. *I like my work very much. I don't have to make more money to make me happy, do I?*

Yeah, but it couldn't hurt. You'll still have your job, you'll just be making more. The money, in this instance, will not make you like your job any less. There's no excuse for not asking for an amount that you believe is a fair evaluation of your market worth. And bear in mind that it isn't just a meager percentage point or two for which you are asking; it's 1% to 2% compounded over your entire work life, which is a significant amount that you should care a great deal about (how much you earn during your work life will also most likely affect how great your income will be during retirement).

16. *How much more should I ask for when I ask for a raise?*

By reading this book and doing some homework, you'll have an idea. You have to know the negotiating range. By asking for much more than can be delivered, negotiations may cease because it is believed that no middle ground will, or can, exist. That's also why it is important to introduce other issues, like greater responsibility so that you can make trade-offs: You don't get as much money as you hoped for, but you get more status through a choice assignment. This gives everybody some "wiggle room"—"I can't give you this but I can give you that."

17. *I'm thinking of going to my boss and saying, "If I don't get more money, I'm out of here."*

This will only embarrass you and your boss. There are tactful ways of threatening. People like to think they are free, sentient beings; when cornered, people fight back. Private threats of this magnitude are sure to elicit defensiveness and/or combativeness. Public threats of any magnitude have the same effect. No one wants to appear weak to others. You may feel like saying, "I'm out of here," but good negotiators maintain control of their emotions. Try to get what you want without resorting to threats.

18. *I do whatever is asked whenever it is asked. I'm the one who works overtime and weekends. I'll come in early and stay late. I take on extra projects and make sure my work is always thoroughly and accurately done. I am just not appreciated.*

The social science literature refers to people who constantly give of themselves without recompense by various names, but "suckers" pretty much sums it up. Most relationships fall into patterns, but when they become one-sided they are no longer viable. To create a true relationship of give and take, you will have to stand up for yourself.

19. *Is it possible to ask for more money without asking for more money? Do you know what I mean?*

I think so and "sure." Executives are experts at this. They never ask for more money—how vile! They ask that their "interests be properly aligned with the company" and that they "be duly motivated to work hard for the shareholder." Recently, I saw Human Resources announce a new incentive plan to its workforce. In response to the question, "What do you think?" the reply from an employee in the audience was, "It's between working harder or mowing lawns this summer." A few days later, the company increased the incentive award amounts.

20. *I don't believe that I can actually make more money. I'm fifty-six years old, and no one is going to pay me that much more.*

So, what's the question? The point at which you truly have no more options is when you believe you have no more options left. I have seen fifty-six-year-old college students, fifty-six-year-old entrepreneurs, and fifty-six-year-old employees who were as enthusiastic as anyone else on the payroll. If you are learning and growing and open to new career and job ideas, you have options available to you for which you will be duly compensated.

21. *Have you ever come across a company that is willing to pay an employee more than his or her boss?*

Sure have, and so have you—professional sports teams. The manager is not the highest paid person on the field or court. I have also seen businesses with elements of sports teams pay some employees more than the boss. This happens where it is easy to measure the value or worth of a person to the success or profitability of an organization. Salespeople fit this mold but so do employees in other professional disciplines (e.g., consulting firms, law firms), creative organizations (e.g., entertainment, publishing, advertising), and universities (e.g., professors).

22. *Do companies make counteroffers to employees when employees get job offers elsewhere?*

Sometimes they do. When they do, it is usually an equivalent offer if it is for the same job. If an employee is thinking of taking a higher-level job elsewhere, there's more than an issue of money involved. If an employee is remotely interested in remaining with his or her current employer, a candid discussion of career prospects may be in order. If you find yourself in this situation and your employer makes you certain promises so that you'll stay, make sure these promises are documented in writing. Promises are easy to make, but hard to keep—and on the basis of that promise, the employee may be forgoing an opportunity that will never come again.

23. *My company froze salaries for two years while we were doing poorly. Now that we are doing well again, shouldn't the company make up for the years we lost out on raises?*

Executives are genuinely thankful to the employees who stuck by them when times were tough. Unfortunately, those same executives will try very hard not to dig themselves into the same financial hole again. So, instead of making up for foregone raises by putting money into your base salary (which the company will have to pay for year after year), they are more apt to add to your total compensation through "variable" pay such as profit sharing, participation in stock plans, and/or various bonus programs. (Variable pay is pay that varies according to company performance and other possible measures.) In this way, if the company does well, so will you.

24. *I recently asked my boss for more money and was told that there were people without jobs who were not making any money at all. In other words, I was told to forget about it. Is there anything I can do?*

This is a ploy to control your aspirations. It's the "be thankful for what you've got" argument. It also can be interpreted as a threat: You might be asked to join the ranks of the unemployed unless you behave yourself. Politely clarify your boss's position and the criteria he or she uses to set pay, either ignoring completely his or her stupid argument or only casually referencing it to make a case: "Then do you believe that all people who do work should be paid alike?"

25. *Everything is so political. Why can't I just be recognized for my accomplishments without always having to beg?*

If you have to beg, you are not very good at politics. There is the kind of politics that is practiced in Washington, D.C., that gives politics a bad name. And then there is the kind of politics that you should play—which involves good judgment, communication, and diplomacy. There is nothing wrong or evil in that. You see, most people aren't great at doing things that they don't have to do and often don't notice things for which they are not looking. You have to help the process along and whether you call it politics or common sense, it has to be done.

A Word on Starting Salaries

Before moving on to discussion of other compensation-related issues that you can negotiate, let's briefly look at starting salaries. Having an idea of what the market will bear will help you to get a financial head start if you are just beginning your career.

Look at Chart 7C. I have provided ranges of starting salaries for various educational disciplines. As you examine the chart, you will notice two things:

(1) The physical sciences pay more than the biological and social sciences and liberal arts, and
(2) Applied fields (like engineering, marketing, and business administration) pay more than basic fields.

Keep in mind that "applied" is relative to a specific job and industry. Having a degree in literature is applicable to the publishing industry and to such occupations as journalism and communications, but not to financial underwriting, for example. Also keep in mind who is looking real hard for graduates right now: computer and business equipment manufacturers,

CHART 7C. STARTING SALARIES

Starting Salary Buckets

-1-	-2-	-3-	-4-
$25,000–$30,000	$30,000–$35,000	$35,000–$40,000	$40,000–$45,000

Answer these questions to find out what starting salary bucket you fall in:

Is the discipline of your major field of study:

   a physical/computer science (e.g., physics, computer science, chemistry)

                                 or

   biological or social science/liberal arts (e.g., biology, history, psychology, literature)?

How would you best characterize the orientation of your major field of study relative to the position/industry in which you are seeking work?

   Applied: There is a clear, evident application of your knowledge in industry.

                                 or

   Basic: Your knowledge base may be useful to industry but there is no apparent, immediate link or direct application.

Basic/biological, social sciences, or liberal arts	=	Salary Bucket **-1-**
Applied/biological, social sciences, or liberal arts	=	Salary Bucket **-2-**
Basic/physical or computer science	=	Salary Bucket **-3-**
Applied/physical or computer science	=	Salary Bucket **-4-**

computer software development employers, automotive and mechanical equipment manufacturers, bankers, consulting organizations, and merchandisers (*HRMagazine,* May 1997, p. 79).

If you have a master's degree, you can increase your starting salary by 15% to 25%. Disciplines with higher-paying starting salaries for four-year degrees are affected more. For instance, if you found from Chart 7C that you belong in bucket 4, increase your starting salary by 25% if you have a master's degree. However, if you found that you fall within bucket 1, increase your starting salary by 15%.

If you have a Ph.D., increase your starting salary by 40% to 60%. Again, increase your salary more if you are in a higher salary bucket.

An interesting new way of looking at your worth emerges from this analysis even if you have been in the workplace for some time. In fact, let's say you have been in the workplace for fifteen years. If you were just starting out anew today, which starting salary bucket would you be in? For purposes of illustration, let's say you are a chemistry major involved in basic research—bucket 3. Your starting salary today would be between $35,000 and $40,000. Over fifteen years at the current average inflation rate, your salary would be between $55,300 and $63,200. This is your inflation-adjusted value today. You will want to be higher than this because this salary assumes you haven't increased in value over the years: You are qualitatively no different from the day you were hired. Where is your current salary compared to the starting salaries of today adjusted for time? Another way of looking at this is to take your current salary and discount it by 3% (the average inflation rate) for each year you've been in the workforce. Say you are a college graduate in the liberal arts, currently earn $42,000, and have been working ten years. Dividing $42,000 by 1.03 (which is equivalent to a 3% discount) ten times would yield a current inflation adjusted starting salary of about $31,250. If you are above the current "going rate" for starting salaries you're doing all right.

There are many differences of opinion on whether or not, when pressed, you should give a potential employer a salary figure. Recruiters whom I've spoken with over the years have generally maintained that when specific salary history (or current salary) is requested, it is wise to provide it. In tight job markets company recruiters are looking for ways to eliminate people, and ability to "follow directions" is one criterion. Invariably, companies want to know what your salary ambitions are because they don't want to waste their time or yours if expectations are too far apart. Ask the company for the salary range of the position and then let the interviewer know whether or not further discussion would be worthwhile. They may not be.

Other Items That Are Negotiable

You will discover during your corporate life that there are many things that are negotiable. Most employees learn the hard way, however. They learn after the opportunity to do anything about it has passed: "Oh, I didn't know I could have asked for that!" This is your chance to find out what you can do and ask for before the chance passes you by.

Sign-on Bonuses

Sign-on bonuses have become an increasingly popular way to attract highly qualified workers and/or employees for which there are shortages. Increasingly, employees with the requisite skill sets expect these bonuses. The advantage to the company is that the extra incentive may induce you to join it versus a competitor without tampering with its internal compensation system. As the fight for key talent heats up in our "information age," sign-on bonuses may become more widespread. Right now, the fields and industries most likely to offer sign-on bonuses are:

- technology and information systems (all industries)
- sales and marketing (this includes everyone in a selling role: editors, consultants, recruiters, etc., are included in this group)
- financial services
- medicine
- mid-level to executive management (across industries)
- MBAs from top schools

The big question, of course, concerns the amount of these bonuses. Ten percent of your salary would be the typical amount offered or paid. So, if you are offered a position that pays $50,000 per year, a $5,000 sign-on bonus would be customary.

Once again, however, there are normative ranges for sign-on bonuses. Five to 10% of salary would be considered to be at the low end of the range and 20%–25% would be considered to be at the high end. Let's stop and think for a moment: Wouldn't 20% of $50,000 be better than 10% of $50,000? How do you get more as opposed to less? You *could* negotiate the sign-on bonus along with your salary but that would allow a company to make trade-offs between your salary and your sign-on bonus. This would be like negotiating price and trade-in value with the car dealer: You can get a lower price but only with a lower trade-in value. You never seem to get anywhere. Therefore, try to negotiate your salary first and when you have reached an agreement, pop the question: "What is the sign-on bonus for this position?"

Think about what has transpired to this point. The company has already decided that it wants you. Further, it has gone through negotiations with you and you have settled upon a mutually agreeable salary. Then, suddenly, when the company thought it was over, you ask a harmless question about a sign-on bonus. By this stage, the company is not inclined to let a little thing like that stand in the way of consummating the deal: Psychologically, it has already committed to you and has devoted a great deal of time and energy to capturing your talents. In addition, by phrasing the question in the proper way it is possible to subtly convey:

(1) You expect a sign-on bonus, and
(2) You would like the company to throw out the first number (no tice that you haven't asked whether or not the company gives out sign-on bonuses, which would demand a "Yes" or "No" response; you've asked how much the sign-on bonus is—this makes it much harder for the respondent to say what he or she now knows you don't want to hear: that there is no sign-on bonus).

If, however, the company seems to be taken aback by your request and stumbles out a response like, "Well, we've never done that before" or "We don't believe in sign-on bonuses," then it's time to negotiate once again. There are lots of good reasons for receiving a bonus upon entry into a new company, whether it's called a "sign-on" or not:

(1) It gives you time, with pay, to make the transition to your new position (i.e., take a couple of weeks off).
(2) It makes up for lost bonus opportunities (it may be that when you move from one company to another you will be sacrificing a bonus from your old company that the acquiring company should make up).
(3) It may cover extraneous expenses associated with the change.
(4) *Most important,* it is required to get you to move.

The last point is critical to negotiation. Whenever someone says "No," you must unapologetically and with a straight face look that person in the eyes and say "Yes."

People in general expect compromise. You must douse another's expectations early in the negotiation so when he or she says, "$5,000" and you respond with "$15,000," you don't end up at $10,000—you end up at $12,000 or more. The rule is this: Give concessions reluctantly, accept offers graciously. Thus, the less willingly and the less quickly you move on your position, the more you will get in the end—you will force the other person to adjust his or her expectations. If you hold firm, rather than $10,000 being the upper anchor, a position developed by anticipating compromise, the person across the table from you will begin to think that he or she will be lucky to settle for less than $12,000.

Severance

Now that we have discussed coming, let's turn our attention to going. Many companies do not have formal severance policies or standard severance formulas, particularly for the nonexecutive employee population and in small companies. From the company's point of view, this affords maximum flexibility. Treating everybody the same is not usually the fair solution. People have particular needs and issues. Even if your particular company has a formal policy, you can still negotiate based on your unique needs and circumstances.

Most typically, severance becomes an issue through job elimination and downsizing. It can also emerge in unexpected ways. For example, you may lose your job when you refuse reassignment or relocation, or are terminated for performance-related (or other) reasons. Each of these events may trigger severance payments—or discussion of severance payments.

For the purposes of this chapter, we'll assume that the goal of your company is not to retire you and your interest is not in retiring (thus I'm not going to discuss potential sticky legal issues that sometimes arise from severance). Further, we'll assume that severance payments are not triggered by a merger or acquisition. We'll discuss severance as it relates to change in corporate control in a later section of this book.

Companies that offer severance do so because they believe it is the right thing to do. It provides an economic bridge for employees as they make a job transition to a new place of employment. It pays off in terms of goodwill from the perspectives of both departing and remaining employees.

You might ask yourself, "Why do I need to worry about severance *now?*" With all the good feelings surrounding a new job or promotion within your company, it's easy to ignore the hard reality of having to find a new job down the road. In the typical job environment, the rule of thumb is that you will need one month to find a new job for every $10,000 you earn. So, if you currently earn $30,000, it will take you roughly three months to locate your next job. These *months* you could go without pay make it essential that you consider severance an important part of the total compensation bailiwick.

Companies that provide severance benefits make them available to the entire employee population. Many companies will exclude employees from severance only when their tenure with the company has been less than a year. Most companies will place ceilings on severance payouts and benefits. These ceilings will vary with your level within the organization. In general, employees in the lower third of the organization (in terms of grade level) receive caps of 8 to 12 weeks of pay, employees in the middle third receive caps of 12 to 20 weeks of pay, and executives receive caps of 20 to 52 weeks of pay.

The most common amount of severance pay is one week of pay for each year of service, although two weeks of pay for each year of service is not unheard of. Companies often add a few extra weeks of pay for given lengths of service. For example, if you have worked at the company for at least five years, the company will add another two weeks of pay to your total.

Payments are generally made in either of two forms: salary continuance or lump sum payouts. The method of payment is generally determined by the company but some permit choice. Be careful. The method of payout often has implications for you that you will want to consider. Companies that pay out in lump sums typically cease medical coverage in the month of the payout whereas employees who are paid over time usually have their medical coverage paid for during that same period. So, if the company pays you in a lump sum (or if you elect this option), you will want to explore the possibility of continued medical coverage: If the company doesn't want to carry and administer the coverage in your behalf, perhaps it will contribute to the cost.

There are a couple of additional noteworthy features of severance. First, if you get a new job right away, few companies will stop payment and none who paid out in a lump sum will ask for this money back. Second, your payouts will almost certainly be based on your salary only, and not other cash incentives you might be receiving. Third, severance is often offered as a part of a voluntary separation package during downsizing. The cash amounts and benefits offered depend on the demographics of the workforce and the number of employees the company would be interested in having accept the offer. These offers are a little like getting bumped from overbooked air flights in that there is some trial and error involved. The question is whether you should sit tight and hope for a better offer or take the first offer that has been placed on the table. You can't control what will or what will not transpire but you can review your financial needs and health to determine a financial cutoff that serves as your point of departure. Once the offer hits a certain level, you raise your hand. Fourth, most employees I have spoken with over the past several years who have received severance benefits have believed that their treatment was fair.

Employers are usually equitable with severance packages, especially during downsizing situations; they are loath to damage their reputations within the industry and are usually willing to pay up to acknowledge years of good service. Levi Strauss is a good case in point: It spent $25,000–$30,000 per employee (more than 6,000 workers were eliminated) on severance related benefits and took other measures designed to soften the economic blow on communities affected by the reductions in force. These benefits included up to three weeks of severance pay for every year of service. Levi Strauss offered the generous package because it believed it was the right thing to do for employees who had served it well and who needed support in making job transitions.

To help with this transition, companies often provide various outplacement services in addition to the salary replacement we have just discussed. These generally consist of the following:

- workshops on job-finding and résumé writing
- job-search skills (and search resources)
- career counseling
- sometimes, office support (use of phones, typing and mailing services), particularly for higher-level employees

The important thing for you to do is think about what will help you to get your next job. What will help you to make the necessary transition? What extenuating circumstances do you have of which your employer should be aware? These are all items that would be useful to discuss. It may be that the company can provide benefits more tailored to your needs (a little less of "this" and a little more of "that") without compromising the overall framework of a policy (or process) or its fairness—if you raise it as a point of discussion.

Relocation

Current employees as well as new hires are sometimes asked to relocate. The costs of the move can be substantial to both the company and the employee. Indeed, many employees who accept corporate relocation do not feel the move has left them financially whole, nor do companies rejoice in the financial consequences of employee moves. The average company cost to move an employee who owns a home is $35,000–$55,000 per person. The cost of moving a renter is much less: $10,000–$20,000 per person.

Additionally, the cost of moving a newly hired employee is less than the costs of moving a current employee. The cost of moving a new hire is about $10,000–$20,000 per person for the simple reason that companies usually won't offer as many goodies to new hires. The most notable difference is that new hires usually are not given the same types of housing allowances as current employees. Companies do not feel compelled to incur additional costs attributable to lifestyle decisions a person has made before he or she was an employee. But keep in mind that there are exceptions. There are always exceptions.

Overall, companies try to balance the costs of the move with the needs of the employee. After all, the company wants you to upend your life, so it has to make it worth your while. That is getting more difficult to do for reasons other than financial ones. In particular, it is getting much harder for employees with families to accept relocation.

A few decades ago, companies were dealing with just the husband-earner, whose relocation was typically associated with a promotion and a salary increase. He had a stay-at-home spouse and a couple of kids—all of whom used to defer to the dad much more readily than today's families do. Also, he didn't have elderly parents who needed some extra attention. He married younger and started his career sooner than contemporary male wage earners, so his father was, in fact, still working.

Today, the female spouse works (and in many instances earns more than her husband), the parents are old, and the children will chant: "Heck no, we won't go." In addition, relocations are often about moving the right person to the right place to do the job needed. Flattering, to be sure, but more times than not, it is a lateral move and not a promotion. So unless the job builds your "equity" in some fashion, you have to think hard about whether the move is worthwhile.

If you choose to move, the new realities suggest a few things for which you should be looking. Spousal assistance is a hot item right now and growing in popularity. If your husband or wife works, he or she will have to find a job in the new locale. To help, companies will often provide career counseling, résumé writing, and job-search strategies. Some major companies in a region form local alliances and swap résumés in search of work for relocator spouses. A few companies will offer temporary income relief to a family while the relocating spouse looks for work. Where offered, the company usually replaces up to about three months of the spouse's lost wages. Additionally, some companies will offer to reimburse the spouse for job-hunting trips.

For many families, these benefits are gratifying to employees and make a difference in whether or not relocation is accepted. For some couples, typically those in higher income brackets, the thought of relocation is more troublesome and requires much more. I have seen spouses request, and receive, interviews with company board members, as well as additional cash to temporarily maintain two households (the old and the new) and for weekend travel between the two sites. A company must really want you (or want you to move) to do these things, but if it isn't going to otherwise work out for you, there is no harm in asking.

By the way, in corporate America, more and more, "spouse" means "partner." Therefore, it is conceivable that "spousal" benefits could be extended to any person with whom you have a committed relationship regardless of the specific gender configuration.

It used to be that children were often neglected in relocations. Many relocation policies did not even cover children's visits to the new site. That is rarer now. Indeed, if you want your children to feel good about the relocation, you will want them to become acquainted with the new residence. Most companies should be willing to sponsor a visit or two. Children have fears and biases about different parts of the country. They should be assured that people who share their interests aren't confined to a particular geographic region of the United States.

With regard to elder assistance, not much is being done—yet. But if it is going to cost you peace of mind and money, it is an issue that you will have to raise and discuss with your employer. For example, if you provide some services to an elderly parent that will have to be replaced by a hired worker, that will cost somebody money. One cosmetic option for the company is to let you know about available elder services in the new community. Another option with more financial bite is to see if your company will help to move your parents. If there is a genuine need, your company may very well be willing to help out.

Your company can help you with most things but it won't know about exceptional items unless you tell it and probably won't discuss certain "contingencies" unless you bring them up. One big contingency is this: What if you don't like your new location? What if every night at the dinner table you are chastised for your stupidity in getting the whole family caught in a fine mess? What if the relocation becomes blameworthy for everything from bad grades to bad hair days? Will the company pay for your return home? It is not likely unless (a) you have arranged for this option ahead of time or (b) the company needs you back at the old location anyway.

Another area where you could lose big if you don't think ahead is in cost-of-living differentials between locations. You don't want to end up living on your same salary in a more expensive place. You will find that to be a financially draining experience. And it could happen if you are not careful. Indeed, next to family-related issues, being worse off financially in the new location is a frequent reason for relocation failures.

Cost-of-living differentials can be tricky business. There are tremendous cost-of-living differences even within a circumscribed territory. For example, it is relatively inexpensive to live in Georgia, but not in Atlanta. If you want to live in Atlanta, you will have to pay. And there are many other regions of the country with pockets of expensive areas surrounded by less expensive ones. The question you should ask yourself is, "What will it cost *me* to live in this new area, given my interests and inclinations?"

The Department of Labor publishes (available in most major public libraries and universities) cost differentials by city/metropolitan area for most essentials that you will purchase such as housing, clothing, food, etc. This provides a good estimate of how much more or less it will take to support an average person at one location versus another, but make sure the new location supports your specific lifestyle. If you or a family member have special needs, lessons, hobbies, and/or interests, find out the cost at the new location. Also, think about whether the new location will force a change of lifestyle. For example, you may have to drive to work at the new location; you now commute using public transportation. Will you need a car?

Companies deal with cost differentials in different ways. Large companies with operations throughout the U.S. often have different salary structures for the different regions in which they do business. If the move is believed to be permanent, the company will likely build the cost of living right into your salary. By the way, if you work and live in a high cost-of-living area, and you are thinking of moving to another company in a lower cost part of the country, I have seen a few companies offer the same salary and try to call it "more," but I have never seen any company offer less. Cost-of-living wages seem to blend permanently into your market worth.

If the move is not permanent, be sure the company makes up the difference for the cost-of-living differences so you can continue to enjoy the same standard of living you had prior to the move.

I have just a couple more warnings, comments, and suggestions as you consider a move either as a current employee or new hire. Most companies provide miscellaneous expense and moving allowances, covering incidentals such as school physicals, fees for various services (e.g., utility charges and installation), and so on. You are generally allotted about one month of salary for these items. But make certain that you won't have exceptional expenses that will increase your costs beyond the typical limits: e.g., legal fees, state licensing fees, etc.

Moving expenses cover "standard" items. Most people, however, accumulate nonstandard things that require special handling during moves: pets, pianos, boats, cars, and artwork, for example. Again, anticipate your needs and bring them to the attention of your employer. Otherwise, you may end up paying to go to a place where you don't really want to go anyway and have less money to spend and save once you get there.

Finally, costs involved in housing are substantial. Your goal should be to obtain a house of equivalent size, in an equivalent neighborhood, with equivalent monthly expense. It would be difficult to argue for more, if not at your own expense. Your negotiations with your employer should center upon need, not greed. Most employers are remarkably flexible with respect to relocation and it is an area where open and candid communication will get you what you need (minimum economic and transitional discomfort) and what the company needs (a satisfied employee who is willing to move to a new location).

Chapter 8

Cha-Ching:
The Sound of Incentives

One of the fastest growing trends in compensation is the rise of something called "variable pay." As the name suggests, variable pay is pay that varies over time according to certain conditions. Those conditions are typically individual and/or group performance. The better you or the company perform, the more you make.

"Variable pay" is often used synonymously with "incentive" or "bonus." Unlike annual merit increases that we discussed earlier in the book, the cash you receive from variable pay programs does not get added into your base salary. You get your money, the clock is reset, and you begin all over again.

About one-third of all companies have some form of variable pay program. If your company has one (and some have more than one), you are fortunate indeed. The reason is simple: These babies are meant to pay out. A bonus plan without a bonus payout is like having a ticket to a closed Broadway show. There isn't much sense in having an incentive plan that never incents.

This chapter will take you through the ins and outs of incentive plans. I'll briefly lay some conceptual framework and describe how, in broad terms, companies approach incentives. Then I'll give you information on what these programs look like and how much you can expect to receive from these plans.

The Purpose of Incentives

Imagine this. You are on a diet. You are a sucker for sweets—any kind of sweets—chocolates, cookies, candies, you name it. I'll give you $100 if you go one month without one sweet. I shouldn't have to give you anything. Too much of these things is bad for your health and you'll look better if you lose the weight.

One night you are all alone and there before you is a batch of freshly baked cookies and an open box of your favorite chocolates (How did they get there!?). In the quiet of the night, do you take a nibble or two?

Or consider this. You have just stopped smoking once and for all. The habit is behind you and your lungs begin to regain some of their natural color. The prospect of a longer life lies ahead. I shouldn't have to, but I'll give you $100 if you don't smoke this month.

One day, after a particularly difficult day at work, you begin the long drive home. The highways are filled. Music is playing on the radio. Suddenly, you remember there is a half pack of cigarettes in the glove compartment of your car (How did it get there!?). It will be a while before you get home. Do you crack the window open and smoke just one or two?

If you have ever embarked on a program of behavior change, you know how hard it can be. I can assure you that the furthest thing from your mind at these moments of truth is the $100 reward—as you stare at the warm cookies or imagine the feel of a cigarette in your hand. Many things control behavior other than money at any given moment. Yet the carrot and stick of money is often the first and only motivational tool of choice used by companies.

Consultants and companies have various degrees of appreciation for the intricacies of behavior. Unfortunately, most take what I would describe as the "Three Stooges approach" to behavior management and change. Do you remember the Three Stooges as plumbers? They first attach a pipe to a leaky faucet and when that pipe begins to leak they attach a pipe to it and so on. Soon they have pipes running everywhere and they still have the leak.

Some companies think that they can control behavior—and, worse, that it is desirable to do so. Like laying in pipes, they try to stop or reroute behavior at every turn. This is the perfect way to squelch creativity and critical corporate adaptations to changing business conditions. Behavior can be controlled but only at very high social and economic costs. To control behavior, it always has to be watched and punished or rewarded at levels that make any form of deviance unthinkable. And, in the end, the company just gets what it wants—nothing more. If you have ever worked for such a company you understand how desire for absolute control is counterproductive.

The most important (nontrivial) behaviors in a company are those that are hard to control and for which the momentary value of money is negligible; when dealing with a belligerent customer, when trying to get a product specification just right (versus close enough), when handling an urgent request for immediate shipment, when making a modification to machinery when needed, and so on. Before you make your choice, do you reflect on the bonus plan? I don't think so. Your decision is out of view and, in the scheme of things, the money doesn't matter. Only the moment matters.

The best incentive plans are those that encourage:

(1) internalization of values
(2) self-regulation of behavior

They let you know what is important and get you pointed in the right direction. The rest is up to you. It's the only way you can make a difference and the only way for a company to succeed: when you, acting at your discretion within the broad corporate boundaries that have been set, do work that is satisfying to you and beneficial to the company.

There are several types of variable compensation plans. Out there, somewhere, is the plan for you. The following list does not exhaust the possibilities of variable pay, but it includes the ones most commonly used. Our discussion, therefore, will focus on these:

- current profit sharing: You get a cut of the profits according to an established formula.
- gain sharing: If you and your fellow employees can lower costs and/or increase productivity, you share the gains with the company.
- individual incentive: You receive a bonus based on your individual

performance. (Note: sometimes professionals make a big deal of distinguishing the words *bonus* and *incentive* and, true enough, they are different words but there is seldom a distinction in practice.)

- instant incentive: You get a cash award "on the spot" for a particular achievement.
- organization-wide bonus: You receive a bonus (with other members of the organization) based on organizational performance, as variously measured.
- recognition awards: You receive a cash or noncash award based on noteworthy behaviors and accomplishments; because these awards are often noncash awards, they are sometimes discussed separately from "variable compensation"—but there is nowhere else in this book to discuss employee recognition programs so I thought this would be a good place.
- small group (team) incentives: You receive an award based on the performance or achievement of the group to which you belong; this chapter is not the best place to discuss small group awards—small group awards will be discussed in Chapter 10.

The Anatomy of a Bonus

There are certain terms and processes associated with variable compensation plans with which you need to be familiar. There's nothing terribly complicated here but it will enable you to ask such discerning questions as:

- "What's the target?" and
- "What's the upside potential?"

You will amaze your friends and impress your company. In describing the terminology of bonuses, we'll use a standard-looking individual bonus plan as an illustration.

Bonus amounts are generally expressed as a percent of base salary. A minority of companies express bonuses as a percent of the salary midpoint. With the latter approach, everyone within a particular grade is treated alike and bonuses are not subject to one's station in life, so to speak.

In either case, the bonus payout goal, as expressed as a percentage, is known as the "target." For example, your bonus target may be 10% of your base salary. If you earn $50,000, your target bonus is $5,000. This is the amount you would receive for meeting planned performance goals.

In order to collect your target, you'll have to earn it. You can either earn it through your individual efforts and performance or through the efforts and performance of a group (e.g., team, business unit, corporation) to which you belong, or some combination of these. Indeed, companies routinely contemplate how heavily to weight award criteria between individual performance and group performance (e.g., company, division, etc.) when determining payouts. There is no formulaic answer to this but, in general, the higher in the organization you go, the more encompassing the level of performance measurement until you reach the limiting case of the chief executive officer where corporate-wide performance alone matters.

Your actual award will depend on the level of performance. The better the performance, the greater the reward. Generally, there is a minimum expectation, or a "threshold," that will generate a minimum bonus—anything below that threshold yields $0. A normal, minimum bonus would be one-half of your target bonus. There is also a bonus maximum for performances that exceed expectations. Bonus maximums are often two times the target.

An example of a simple, traditional individual bonus plan is illustrated in Chart 8A. The objectives are weighted, rated, and summarized. The summary score maps directly onto the bonus. This "mapping" can occur in two ways.

First, the performance criteria can act as "cliffs." The performance and payout brackets are discrete so that you have to reach the next performance plateau to receive the next highest bonus. For example, let's suppose your performance is scored as a 3.60. Even though you are above the minimum of the "meets all expectations" bracket, you'll receive 100% of your target bonus and no more.

On the other hand, the performance and bonus scalings can be assumed to be continuous so that the higher your performance, the higher your bonus. Assume again that your rating of performance is 3.60. Through algebraic manipulations, it can be shown that your target bonus would equal 140% of your target award. If, again, your target bonus is 20% of a $50,000 base salary, then your award would be as follows: $1.40 \times .2 \times \$50,000$, or $14,000.

You have probably realized by now that the size of your bonus potential

CHART 8A.   SAMPLE INDIVIDUAL BONUS PLAN

Weight	Objective	Rating (1-5) (1=poor, 5=great)
.50	Make all deliveries on schedule	4
.25	Receive customer satisfaction ratings of 95% (or higher)	3
.15	Record and forward all paperwork on time	3
.10	Be clean, thrifty, and brave	4

Total Weighted Average=3.60

Bonus Pay-outs

	Meets some expectations	Meets most expectations	Meets all expectations	Exceeds most expectations	Far exceeds all expectations
score	2.25	2.50	3.00	3.75	4.50
bonus (% of target)	50%	75%	100%	150%	200%

(below 2.25, bonus = 0%)

is interesting, but how hard you have to work to get it is equally interesting. A large bonus that is easy to get and a large bonus that is hard to get are two very different bonuses. A small bonus that is hard to get would be considered corporate hazing.

Setting performance goals is tough. It is difficult to manage that delicate balance between "too hard" and "too easy." You, of course, are instrumental in establishing your own performance goals and may be in a position to provide input on group or corporate goals. If it turns out that you set your goals far too low and believe you have unfairly profited, get over it. It happens. Shake your head and every chance you get mutter to anyone who will listen: "We've got to do better next year."

One way to do better is to wait until the end of the year to set your goals.

That way you'll know what you have already done. No joking. Some companies with incentive plans are forced at the end of the year to make "discretionary" bonus decisions because no one took the time to establish performance goals at the start of the year.

My suggestion to you, once again, is to be honest. A company may be forced to give bonuses to people for borderline accomplishments. But companies aren't blind. They do recognize what they are paying for, especially when they have to pay it. So ensuring yourself a higher bonus by pretending that your performance goals are truly strenuous, might be a neat short-term strategy but it won't get you ahead over the long haul.

You don't have to set impossible goals either. Just reasonable ones. Achievable individual performance goals are important because many companies "double dip." They use the same performance goals to allocate bonuses *and* merit increases. So there is a lot riding on a single set of goals. There is often overlap among compensation programs such that one set of performance criteria pops up in different places and is used to simultaneously reward employees.

How Your Company Views Your Bonus

Companies give considerable thought to their compensation philosophy, which most often involves deciding how to divide up employees' total annual cash compensation between base salary and bonus. Most companies want to end up paying competitively on total cash compensation, but they get there in different ways.

Essentially, there are two main philosophical choices, although there are many variations. First, a company can set the pay structure (i.e., the mid-points) for base salaries at average levels compared to other companies and pay additionally for the bonuses. Together, the base salary plus bonus is equivalent to what other companies pay in total cash on average. This is the customary approach and is labeled "Method 1" in Chart 8B.

The second method is one in which the company sets the base salary structure below average and uses larger bonus amounts to move you past average in total cash compensation. This is "Method 2" in the illustration. The company figures that if it is going to ask you to take a little less in base salary than you could get elsewhere, there should be something in it for you, such as greater earnings potential.

Frugal, cost-conscious companies may try to pay a base salary below av-

Chart 8B. Basic Compensation Philosophies

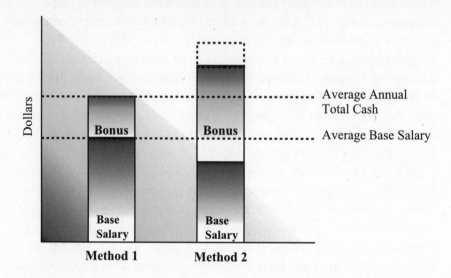

erage and a bonus that will just get you back to average total cash if you make your bonus. This is not a great deal for you: Financially troubled companies may resort to this strategy. It may be better than the alternative, though—losing one's job. Emerging, or risk-oriented, companies like Method 2 as normally practiced. Sometimes they will make the bonus portion much larger—represented by the dotted lines in the illustration. If you help the company to succeed, you win big time. If not . . . well, it was worth taking the chance.

Companies don't have to exclusively use one method versus another. They can use one philosophy for one set of employees and another method for another. They typically don't do this, but they could and some do. I have seen companies use Method 1 for employees lower in the organization who count on the cash flow from their base salaries for sustenance but gradually shift to Method 2 for employees higher in the organization. The reasoning would be as follows: Employees higher in the organization have salaries great enough to sustain their needs (so it's okay to offer a little less in base salary) and have a more direct effect on company performance and profitability (so it's okay to offer a little more in bonus).

All else being equal, companies may lean toward one pay philosophy as opposed to another. You now at least know what the main choices are and can inquire about the philosophical stance of your own or of a prospective company. By the way, "all else" may not be equal with companies that hold these different philosophies. Lurking behind these philosophies may be very distinct attitudes toward employees. You should explore this possibility. For example, Method 1 companies may like to "take care of its employees," and therefore, tend to be paternalistic and risk averse. Method 2 companies may breed a high-performance, "put up or shut up" culture. It's wise, as an employee, to recognize the attitude your company holds toward its people so that you can know just what to expect.

Incentive Plan Particulars

For the remainder of this chapter, we'll focus on four questions:

(1) *Why* do companies use variable pay programs?
(2) *Who* is eligible for these programs?
(3) *What* are the programs and how do they work?
(4) *How much* money can you expect from these programs?

Why

Variable pay programs began to gain prominence during the last recession. Cash-strapped companies could ill afford additional fixed expenses such as base salaries and associated benefits costs (certain benefits are linked to salaries). To help ease the financial pain, variable pay plans that compensate employees only when there are earnings to distribute caught on. Thus, financial necessity is one reason for the growth of variable plans.

The philosophical undercurrent of financial necessity is "pay for performance." This is a phrase you probably hear quite a bit these days and a second major reason that companies have resorted to variable compensation. Not many people actually know what pay for performance means. Even within the same company, if you asked 100 people about the meaning of "pay for performance," you would get ten different definitions.

Pay for performance means that your company is willing to give you greater compensation if certain conditions are met:

(1) The company makes money, and/or
(2) You had demonstrable effect on important end results.

In essence, pay for performance means that the company will reserve a pool of money (usually from profits) and give it to those, individually or as a group, who contributed to the company's success. Fortunately for you, a company doesn't necessarily have to make money nor do you necessarily have to produce results to get extra compensation, but you get the idea.

Over time, the added compensation becomes enculturated. Employees expect and count on the extra cash. Many employees plan their consumption according to the bonus schedule. I just spoke with an employee who is planning on getting central air this year with his year-end bonus. He doesn't know, by the way, how the company is performing—he just knows he will probably get his bonus.

There is considerable anguish during off years, however, when bonuses are not paid. This is the way incentive plans are designed to work— sometimes you win and sometimes you lose. But during those down years Human Resources hears a lot of grumbling and complaining. Social theorists who study revolutions call it the "J" curve of rising and falling expectations. To get the picture, you have to mentally rotate the "J" counter-clockwise until the straight portion is on an incline pointing upward to the right and the curved part is pointing downward. With good times, people expect more and more and when there is a sudden drop in what's delivered, they get so ticked off that they sometimes overthrow governments. Remotely aware of social theory and very aware of employee dissatisfaction, companies often scale back their performance expectations or revise their variable compensation plans so that these plans end up delivering the goods and employees don't storm the palace gates.

To review, cost reduction and paying for performance are two reasons companies introduce variable compensation plans. A third, often cited reason is to "get employees to think like owners." Profit-sharing, gain-sharing and various bonus programs try to get employees focused on various aspects of the business and aligned with the key objectives of the business. I've been an owner; I've met many owners. It isn't that hard. Just get yourself a set of golf clubs and learn to say, "No, that's too expensive," and you will have nearly mastered the thought processes of an owner.

There are many other reasons companies give for moving toward variable pay, such as to encourage teamwork, facilitate organizational change, increase productivity, etc.

Who

Variable pay is all around us. These days, there is something for everybody and enough to go around.

Perhaps the most noteworthy trend is that variable pay programs traditionally reserved for "management" are now being introduced to all ranks of employees. Stock options (discussed in the next chapter) and bonus plans, once the sacrosanct privilege of a few, are now extended to many. For example, more and more employees are being included in the traditional company bonus plan that used to be reserved for people earning roughly $70,000 or more.

This trend is attributable to a couple of factors. First, small, start-up companies (especially in the high tech industry) started giving everyone stock options instead of big base salaries and that didn't seem to do any harm. Second, companies began asking more from their employees and have been encouraging more employee involvement in the business—sharing some of the profits and equity seems like a good idea under the circumstances. Third, it's been a good economic run for companies these past several years and the good times are trickling down (as well as up). It will be interesting to see if these programs endure during the next business down cycle.

For the most part, there are not many distinctions among industries or size of company with regard to the variable pay plans that are offered. You can find just about anything anywhere with a few exceptions. Bonuses, for example, are rare in nonprofit organizations and health care. Nonprofits have to be careful that the money they take in is used for its nonprofit purposes or for the benefit of its members; if bonuses are paid, the argument has to be made that these don't interfere with its primary mission and, ideally, help the organization to advance its nonprofit interests.

Organizations such as those in health care that provide public goods also offer fewer bonuses. Again, bonuses may be offered but they should be held out in a way that would not disincent employees (or contractual providers) from providing essential services (e.g., providing expensive but important diagnostics or treatments). Bonus plans should not be used to regulate public policy—and, mostly, they don't.

Manufacturing companies are most likely to use gain sharing where operating costs (e.g., labor) and the value of production are important measures of success. You tend not to see profit-sharing plans in regulated or quasi-regulated industries such as utilities and banking. Profit sharing is more prevalent where the company has greater control of its pricing of products and services. Small group and team awards are obviously more prevalent in larger companies where there are more people to form groups.

If you look at the list of types of variable pay plans presented earlier and reflect upon each, you can probably figure out which ones make the most sense for your organization. You may even be surprised to learn that your company has a plan that you didn't know about. I was recently speaking with a group of employees who didn't know that their company had a formal employee recognition program with substantial awards attached!

Companies don't always do as good a job as they should in publicizing their various compensation programs and employees don't always do a good job in reading corporate newsletters and memoranda. One of the things you should do, then, is find out what programs are available to you and what the requirements are for awards. You, too, may be surprised.

If you are comparing jobs between companies (or even between divisions of the same company), be sure to include variable pay in your calculations. I would advise that you not use the maximum amount you can receive as the basis for your decision. Companies like to be optimistic when they are trying to lure you away from your current employer by using the highest figures possible, or by saying things like, "This is the target bonus, but *you'll* get more." It is also easy for you to assume that you will earn the maximums on everything. These plans are not designed to pay everyone the maximum. If everyone got the maximum, a lot of people would rightly be asking if the requirements for the awards were too low.

I suggest you ask companies about the history of their various plans— of the actual average payout (expressed as a percent of base salary over the last three years). Averaging payouts over the past three years should give you an idea of what to expect. If a plan is new or has been substantially revised, a conservative rule of thumb is to use one-half the target award as an index of your prospects. Target awards are often set so that about one-half of the eligible employees reach or exceed those levels; the other half do not. Multiplying the target award by one-half takes into account the fact that it is not entirely certain you will receive the whole thing and, therefore, it is advisable to discount it a little.

What

In this section, we'll take a closer look at a few of the more common types of variable compensation plans. Keep in mind that there are hundreds of variations to a given type of plan but each plan has a basic underlying structure.

The Garden Variety Plan—Organization-wide Bonuses. The grid in Chart 8C illustrates a simple, common annual bonus plan in which all employees are eligible to participate—making it an organization-wide plan. By the way, I'm all for simple. Some people, consultants included, can get real enthralled with numbers and develop masterfully complex, financially intricate bonuses that no one really understands. This proves what I have always suspected. It is easier to get numbers to do what you want than it is people. You can make numbers do all sorts of fancy things but these plans are supposed to be about people, not accounting ingenuity.

Anyway, back to the chart. There are several features to this plan. First, there are measurements. Often, one axis is a financial measure and the other is a strategic measure. In this case, net income is the financial measure and percent of revenues from new products is the strategic measure. This company naturally wants to make money but it wants to make it in a particular way—by focusing its efforts to grow through commercially viable, new products.

CHART 8C. SAMPLE BONUS PAY-OUT GRID

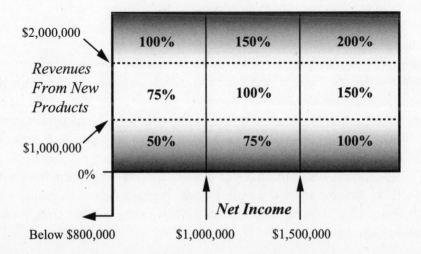

Including non–bottom line measures (e.g., strategic measures such as a market share, number of product sales per client, customer satisfaction ratings, etc.) in bonus plans is a new development and is due largely to influential articles by D. Norton and R. Kaplan in the *Harvard Business Review* on the topic of "balanced scorecards." You now hear lots of discussions of scorecards in company hallways. How the times have changed—people huddled around the water cooler discussing in hushed tones . . . balanced scorecards. In essence, anything is ultimately game as a measure as long as it is consistent with the directions and objectives of the business. Most boards and senior managers no longer feel constrained to limit performance measures to financial indicators of success.

The measures in the chart carry the same weight. The percentages in the grid move at the same rate, whether you move across or up. It is sometimes desirable to weight certain measures more than others, in which case a company may want to attach higher percentages to one axis than to the other. Increasing net income, for example, may lead to higher payouts relative to increases in revenues from new products.

Second, the percentages in the chart are references to your target bonus. For instance, "100%" means 100% of your target bonus: if your target bonus amount is 10%, your bonus payout would be 100% × 10%, or simply 10%.

The chart also shows that you can earn a range of bonus extending from 50% of your target bonus to 200% of your target bonus. You can also get 0% of your target bonus if you don't make it onto the chart at all—we'll get to that in a moment. The 50%–200% range is customary but 50%–150% and 50%–300% are commonly used as well, depending on how conservative or aggressive your company chooses to be.

There are a few conditions that may change what you actually receive as a bonus. This is the third thing I want to talk with you about. To get onto the grid or payout chart, the company has to meet certain minimum performance standards. These minimums are known as performance thresholds as we mentioned earlier. They are generally set at 80% to 85% of the goal needed to meet target. For example, a minimum of $1 million in net income is needed to reach the middle three vertical cells in the chart; $800,000, or 80% of $1 million, is required to get onto the grid.

Two other possible preconditions of payment do not appear in the chart at all. The first condition is a performance "trigger." That is, to qualify for a bonus at all, certain basic conditions may have to be satisfied first. These can be such things as:

- The company must remain number one or two in market share.
- Customer satisfaction levels must be at 95% or higher.

The other precondition is how an employee performs on an individual basis. Sometimes group variable plans have "individual modifiers" which are used to adjust each person's bonus payout by his or her unique contributions. Typical modifiers look like the individual performance measures presented earlier in Chart 8A. If you meet your objectives, you get your bonus as determined through the grid in Chart 8C. However, your bonus amount can change if you fail to meet, or if you exceed, your personal objectives.

For example, suppose your target bonus is 20% of a base salary of $80,000. Further suppose that you earn 150% of that bonus on the basis of group performance but that your individual performance falls "below expectations." You should calculate your actual bonus as follows: .20 (your target bonus) $\times$ 1.50 (your group award) $\times$ .75 (your individual award). This equals 22.5% of your base salary or $18,000. Not bad, eh? Think of what you could buy with $18,000!

As you might imagine, as "hard" as the personal objectives might be, most people do pretty well on these. Again, telling someone that he or she didn't perform to expectations isn't the forte of many company managers. As a consequence, some companies place limitations on how much they are willing to pay out in bonus awards (e.g., 5% of net income) lest the awards get too high. Some make the individual objectives piece a "zero-sum game." If someone is rated at "above expectations," someone else has to be rated "below expectations" so that the collective evaluation will equal a bonus modifier of 100%.

Piecework. We have already looked at how a typical individual bonus plan works through our discussion in the section "The Anatomy of a Bonus." There are other types of individual incentive plans, most notably piecework.

There are plenty of jobs where people fasten, punch, weld, type, attach, drill, screw, bend, process, etc., all day long. These employees may take great pride in their precision and speed. You may be one of those employees.

If you are very good at what you do, and better than most, which bonus arrangement would you prefer: one in which everyone gets the same based on collective performance or one that would award each person for his or her individual performance? You'd probably want the latter, which would directly reward you for your contributions. On the other hand, equal rewards means the best people should share their "equity" (i.e., the benefits of their special skills and talents) with others. Under this scenario, the possibility of free-ridership exists. A free-rider, as the label suggests, is someone who purposely does not fully participate in the work being done, knowing that he or she will capitalize on the abilities of others.

Piece-rate systems are individual incentive plans that reward you directly for your output. They do not enjoy a good reputation or widespread acceptance because of associations with Dickensian sweatshops where men, women, and children slaved away for twelve hours a day for barely a living wage and no health or pension benefits.

Well-designed piece-rate systems can work. First, they do not make all of your pay contingent on your output. The company provides a reasonable salary base and rewards you additionally for your performance. Second, piece rates should be set at levels that are attainable; you don't want to participate in a system that extracts blood from a turnip because guess who's the turnip?

You may also want to second-guess plans that deliver the money but destroy your quality of work life in other ways. For example, you might not appreciate someone standing behind you with a clipboard and stopwatch all day, observing your every movement: If constant counting and monitoring come with the plan, you might not be so keen on it. Also, if the piece-rate plan focuses attention on individual production to the exclusion of any meaningful collaboration and help among workers, then you may feel you are giving up too many other things that make the workplace appealing to you in exchange for money. Piece-rate plans can work to your financial benefit, but you have to be careful that you not lose out in other ways.

Current Profit Sharing. Profit-sharing plans allow employees to participate in, you guessed it, the profitability of the business. Companies with cash profit-sharing plans generally hold out an extra 2.5% to 7.5% of base salary in bonus to you.

You know that "profit" is what you have left over after your expenses, but there are a couple of definitions of "profit" used in these plans of which you should be aware. First, some companies have profit thresholds. That is, profits don't count until the company has made a certain amount of money first. Second, profit can refer to the year-end results from all sources (including what the company invests, buys, and sells) or just to profits from its continuing operations—its businesses. Companies with a lot of cash can usually do pretty well just through investments.

From your point of view, "first dollar" plans (plans that pay out from the first dollar of profit) that include all possible sources of revenue in the profit equation are almost always sure to generate some bonus amount. Give someone (or something) a couple hundred million dollars and they can usually make something happen.

Suppose you start a roadside fruit stand for the summer and you hire three eager high school students to pick and sell berries. They are awakened at five o'clock each morning by a cannon ("the bird bang") that keeps the birds off of the crops. They rise, play baseball till about 7:00 A.M., have breakfast, and get pickin'. This is bringing back memories.

The threesome are paid $75, $50, and $25 (based on experience levels) for the summer plus the first 10% of all profits that the honest farmer says he's made. There is a $100 profit so there is $10 to be split among the high-schoolers. The money could be split equally ($3.33 each), and some companies do that. But most companies and consultants would argue that equal amounts would not be equivalently motivating to employees who are paid different amounts: the same flat amount to higher-paid employees, for example, would be a lower percentage of their base pay than that paid to lower-paid employees and not equivalently motivating—in theory, at least. Therefore, most companies opt for constant percentages among employees.

To return to our three friends, they have earned $10 profit on a total payroll of $150 or 6.67% of total salaries ($10 ÷ $150). Multiply each salary by 6.67% to obtain each person's share of the profits:

BASE SALARY	×	6.67% PAYOUT
$25		$1.67
$50		$3.33
$75		$5.00
		$10.00

The high-schoolers got their summer salaries plus a nice, extra-cool bonus, plus all they could eat.

To give you an idea of the power you have over profits, picture this. You are walking along a railroad track. You stop, chest puffed out, shoulders back. You draw in a deep breath, you extend your arms in front of you and stagger your legs, one in front of the other. You tilt your head ever so slightly as you brace to stop an oncoming train. Moments later, you are peeled from the tracks. There are just some things beyond your power.

Most profit-sharing plans let you "walk on the tracks." You get paid but have no influence on what you get paid for. Over time, most employees find that it is more prudent to hop on the train and go along for the ride. The company ends up going where the train would have gone anyway.

Trains can be stopped, slowed, or diverted if you know how to do it. Similarly, in order to effect profits, you have to know three things:

- the mechanics of the business—how money is made
- what you can do as a part of your job to help
- ongoing feedback about how the company is performing

If your company just wants to be nice and share its profits with you, that's great. But if it wants you to help generate the profits, then you will have to know how to do it and how you are doing. Companies that take the time to teach you about the fundamentals of the business and who are willing to share intimate financial results with you are most likely practicing "open book management." Open book management is a process that "opens the books" and entrusts the guts of the business to the people who are doing the work. For you to be an effective participant in a profit-sharing plan, it is important that the company provide you with adequate tools and information. You should insist upon it.

Gain sharing. Gain sharing is a method of rewarding employees for increases in productivity: Gains in productivity are shared between the employee and the company. You may hear gain sharing referenced by a particular brand of gain sharing such as Scanlon, Rucker, or Improshare plans. Regardless of the specific type of plan, all gain-sharing plans adhere to a basic formula that compares inputs to outputs over time, where

inputs = costs associated with production (most notably labor costs),
            and
outputs = units produced, sales, etc.

If, over time, employees can produce more for less, the plan will pay out.

Unlike other variable compensation plans that are largely management inventions, gain sharing is a grassroots phenomenon. The concept originated with Joseph Scanlon, a steelworker and president of the local union at Empire Steel and Tin Plate Company. In order to save jobs due to the threat of plant closure, Scanlon persuaded management to try to improve productivity by sharing gains with the workers.

Although you might run across gain sharing anywhere, it is still most often used in manufacturing. Let's look at a simple plan, some of the guiding premises of these plans and, finally, a few of the plan components of which you should be aware.

You own a chain of cookie stores with a total of 100 employees paying $2,000,000 in annualized salaries. We could use a paper mill or steel reroller plant or any other business where something is produced to illustrate the basic principles, but let's stick with cookies. You study your costs and profits over time and find that, on average, your labor makes up 30% of your net sales (total revenues minus the cost of goods sold).

You challenge your workforce. If they can find ways to increase net sales and/or reduce labor costs so that the labor-to-sales ratio declines (from 30%), you'd be willing to share the gains with your employees 50-50. During the first quarter of this challenge, your employees eliminate overtime through scheduling innovations and locate a less expensive vendor for the same ingredients. Your labor costs average $550,000 for the quarter and your net sales are $2 million. This is a 27.5% labor-to-net-sales ratio. The employees win! The company wins, too. This is the beauty of gain sharing.

One common way to calculate the bonus pool for employees is as follows: Subtract the actual labor costs from the allowable labor costs and multiply that amount by employees' share of the pool. Allowable labor costs are the costs it normally takes to produce the desired outcomes—in this case, net sales. If the standard labor-to-profit ratio is 30% and net profits for the quarter are $2 million, then allowable costs are .30 × $2 million, or $600,000. So the quarterly results look like this:

$600,000	allowable costs
$550,000	actual costs
$50,000	quarterly gain
× 50%	employees' share of gain
$25,000	employees' pool of dollars

This generates a pool of $25,000 to be shared among the 100 employees in the plan. There are two ways of doing this. One way is to just divide the pool up by the number of employees: $250 each. Many companies do that. The other way is to give employees an equal percent of base pay as the gain-share bonus. In this case, the percent is the same but the amounts will vary.

The formula for determining the maximum percent that can be allocated to each person from the bonus pool is as follows:

$$\frac{\text{total bonus pool}}{\text{total annualized base salaries}}$$

In the example, each person would get a bonus of 1.25% of his or her base pay *for this quarter* ($25,000 ÷ $2,000,000). Someone making an annual income of $20,000 would get $250 for the quarter whereas someone making an annual income of $50,000 would get $625. At this pace, employees would end up with an additional 5% in compensation by the end of the year, which is about average for these types of plans. Most of the time, a company will not pay out all of the earned bonus at the time it is earned; a small portion will be reserved and paid during periods when there is little or no bonus award earned. This makes something available to employees most of the time, and evens out bonus payments throughout the life of the plan.

Gain-sharing plans and measures can get terribly complex. I have found that an intelligent and enlightened chief financial officer can keep these plans from going too far afield. For these plans to be effective, they have to be connected to key business objectives. They also have to involve employees in the process; fundamentally, gain sharing is about involving employees more intimately in the business.

Because a fundamental part of gain sharing is employee involvement, when these plans are developed, you may be asked to . . . well . . . to get involved. I want you to be prepared for the "kickoff" gain-sharing meeting, so here are a few decisions that have to be made or issues that will have to be considered:

- How you will be measured: We've already talked about this but there is one issue that comes up, and there are enough mouth-gaping, glassy-eyed people looking at each other when it does that it just has to be mentioned. Sometimes you can create a measure that produces "gains" but no profits and you will have to decide whether or not payments should be made under such a condition.
- Frequency of measurement/payouts: Whereas monthly measures and payouts are the most common, the measurement period can

range from weekly to yearly. It depends on what makes the most sense to the business.

• Payout caps: Sometimes performance can be real, real good and the question will surface, "Should the payout also be real, real good?" Some companies believe that results that challenge reason cannot be due solely to human effort—and probably weren't. Therefore, some companies, and just *some,* put caps on what can be earned during a given measurement period.

• Sharing arrangements: The most common split of gains I have seen is 25% for you and 75% for the company although I have seen it as low as 15%/85% and as high as 50%/50%. The split doesn't matter much in itself. You have to anticipate how much you will be splitting as well—the size of the pie is as important as the size of the slice. And it doesn't have to be either-or. Payouts can be arranged so that as the pie gets bigger, your slice gets bigger.

• The standard or comparison ratio: Gains are based on change and change implies a comparison between current performance and something else. One basis for comparison is against historical standards, as was done in our example. The other comparison is against a goal that employees and the company set. In either case, there will come a time when the entire plan has to be rethought because there will be no more gains to be had. The limits of your efforts will have been reached.

Instant, Lightning, or Spot Awards. These are awards given out to employees throughout the year for their special achievements and contributions. They are mostly awarded to individuals, but they can be given to groups as well when it is not easy to disentangle the individual's work from that of others. Many companies have themes for which they are willing to hand out money such as superior service, quality improvement, cost savings, and the like.

These are terrific awards, first, because they are immediate and, second, because they can be quite lucrative. These awards are given when you have performed or completed noteworthy work so you and everybody else knows what you did and why you are receiving the award.

Companies who offer these awards reserve about 1% of their payroll to give away during the course of the year. Further, companies fully intend to give these awards to roughly one-fourth of the employees who are eligible. In addition to that, you can receive more than one award in a year.

One percent of payroll is quite a bit of money. Hypothetically, let's say you belong to a 2,500-employee company with a 100-million-dollar payroll (the average salary is $40,000). One percent of $100 million is $1 million and 25% of the 2,500 employees, the number targeted to receive awards, is 625. The approximate amount to be allocated among potential winners is $1,600 per person, or about 4% of base salaries on average (i.e., $1,600 divided by the average salary of $40,000). The company may not give out all of the money or it may decide to spread it around to more people, but the prospects of substantial sums of money going to qualified high performers are quite good. For the high performer, these awards will add 2% to 4% to your annual compensation in addition to your normal merit adjustment (your annual increase).

If your company does it right, a usual award will be between $250 and $1,000 for a particular achievement. Companies like to keep the size of cash awards at fairly modest levels to maintain law and order: Huge awards to a few people have a strange way of arousing the greed and avarice gene. It is not unusual, however, for super performers to bag two or three of these things in the course of a year. It adds up.

Noncash Recognition Programs—Trinkets and More Put succinctly, the objectives of employee recognition programs are to motivate and direct behavior in desirable ways, often utilizing reward mechanisms other than "traditional" cash compensation. The behavioral goal underlying these programs is straightforward—to increase the incidence of desirable behaviors through nontraditional means. Personally, outside of sales contests, I have seldom seen employees get too charged up over these programs.

- Employees grow tired of the "certificate" and "plaque" corporate mind-set that appears to many to be shallow attempts at manipulation.
- The value of the awards is suspect. They are frequently too small to be actively sought by employees and awarded too privately to convey any useful corporate purposes. The claim that these programs change behavior is highly questionable.
- Certain recognition awards are often inappropriate for the effort required. Movie tickets can be an appropriate "thanks" for staying late to finish a project but not for implementing a new quality control process. It's not just that the award is too small; it's the wrong one.

Effective employee recognition programs are ones that are corporate-wide celebrations: They are "grand productions" that recognize the many talents of *all* of the people acting in harmony. By way of analogy, these programs are like the Academy Awards. Winning an award should produce teary-eyed blabberings about family, friends, and company. Indeed, the most successful programs I have seen are those with multiple award categories and subcategories. These categories recognize special talents (e.g., best spreadsheet design), special roles (e.g., best manager), realization of corporate ideals (e.g., quality), best performances (e.g., most sales), etc. The best noncash programs I've seen are:

- Symbolic: The program should represent the "spirit" of the company in name, style, and substance. For example, if globalism is important, it could be an international program with an international flavor. If personal expression is important, the company could incorporate a category that recognizes personal achievements outside of work.
- Inclusive: The very worst thing a company can do is to create a special program for the "little people." A company depends on everyone, and everyone should be included. The program should have motivational value to an executive as well as to the receptionist (e.g., include a category such as executive of the year). If this tenet cannot be adhered to, the program will often be perceived as insignificant.
- Big: If the program is to influence behavior, it must have "pull power." The program has to be on a scale that attracts attention and bestows honor. You have to want to win. The award has to be coveted.
- Public: There should obviously be a celebration for award winners, but the various achievements should be publicized in other ways as well. For example, training materials could incorporate samples of what the best employees do and company newsletters should report on special accomplishments of employees. There are many ways to enshrine employee achievements.

Having said all of that, don't be deterred by a demeaning and offensive program. The awards are still offered to people who excel in ways that are of value to the company. It's far better to get an award (or other form of recognition) than to not get one. Then it is important to showcase your awards. I discover two things about you when I see certificates plastered all over your wall. First, I see that you are a superior performer and, second, that you take great pride in your work. Every time someone walks by your office, including your boss, he or she is reminded of these two facts. So, rather than reject or shred a worthless piece of paper (the award certificate) from a truly thankless employer, earn the award and display it. Believe me, you'll go a lot further. Displaying your honors is one important way that you can take an intangible (your capabilities) and make it real for others.

How Much

Now for the part you've all been waiting for. The question of questions: How much? First, know that not all companies offer bonuses to its employees. But, again, the trend is clearly in the direction of more variable pay. If there is a mantra in compensation circles it is "variable . . . variable . . . variable."

Second, there is a relationship between bonus amounts and base salaries. The more you make in base, the more you get in bonus. Chart 8D shows customary bonus amounts associated with various base salary levels. So, for example, if your base salary is $100,000, your target bonus, expressed as a percentage of your base salary, will be between 15% and 20%. That is, if you earn $100,000 you can expect between 15% and 20% in variable compensation from a bonus-paying company.

If you want a nice, easy shorthand way to calculate what your target bonus should be, multiply your current base salary by the magic number .00015 (±2.5%) and, presto, there's your answer. For instance, if you are

CHART 8D. TYPICAL BONUS AMOUNTS

Base Salary	Target Bonus
$25,000	2%–5%
$50,000	5%–10%
$75,000	10%–15%
$100,000	15%–20%
$150,000	20%–30%
$200,000	30%–40%
$300,000	40%–60%
$500,000	60%–100%
(or greater)	

currently earning $45,000 in base salary and want to know how much in variable pay to expect from a bonus-paying company, your answer is $45,000 times .00015 or about 6.75% (±2.5%, or around 4% to 9%).

The rationale behind progressively higher bonuses for progressively higher salaries is the belief that a greater proportion of an employee's total cash compensation should be "at risk" the greater the employee's responsibilities (i.e., the higher in the organization he or she is) and accountability for end results.

In the jargon of compensation practice, the ability to see and control important end results is called "line of sight." It is assumed the higher in the organization you go, the better the line of sight. This is a huge assumption. Some managers, for example, wouldn't recognize a customer if they tripped over one. Even so, the more the company counts on an employee to "deliver the goods," the more that company is willing to reward that person for a job well done and to penalize him/her for a job not well done (by holding back the bonus amount).

Notice that this view of "risk" is a little curious but one to which you should grow accustomed. The usual formula for risk is: The higher the risk, the higher the potential reward, where risk is defined as a probability of losing something of value. Most people are willing to assume greater risk only when the potential gains are greater.

Under most corporate arrangements, however, there is no risk of losing anything. You just don't get as much. With this scenario, the risk/reward formula is reversed—the greater the reward, the greater the risk. This is good news for you. Most plans offer you upside potential and "soft landings." Companies don't do this because they are dumb and "don't know no better." Believe it or not, they do it because they really don't want to harm employees financially.

Calculating Your Worth in Total Cash

In earlier chapters, you were given various opportunities to estimate your worth in terms of base salary. Here's what I'd like you to do next: Take the estimate of your base salary you feel is the best, or take an average of all of them, and add in the bonus amount that is appropriate for the salary using the information from this section. This will give you an idea of your worth in terms of your total, annual cash compensation. Be sure to bracket this amount, using typical bonus maximums and minimums. For example, let's say you figure you are worth $60,000 in base salary and using the formula presented in this chapter (.00015 times your salary) worth another $5,400 (9% of your base salary) in bonus from a bonus-paying company. So, on average, you would earn $65,400 in total cash compensation. Assuming that you will earn anywhere from one-half (4.5%) to two times (18%) your expected bonus amount, your total worth in total cash is between $62,700 and $70,800.

I hope you now have a good idea how variable pay works. Plans that you encounter in your workplace will be customized to your company but will have the same basic structure as all types of variable pay:

(1) Something of value to the company is identified (individual behaviors, corporate performance, etc.).
(2) Something of value is measured.
(3) The measurement is compared to some expectation or standard.
(4) The degree to which expectations/standards are met produces bonus payments.

As I mentioned previously, more and bigger bonuses go to employees higher in the organization. However, interestingly, bonus plans themselves can affect how high you go. Some management-level bonus plans function as social clubs. To get in, you need to be someone with whom the current members wouldn't mind having lunch. I can always tell at what grade level a management bonus begins because there is always an unusual amount of people "waiting to get in." If you look at where employees are distributed in the company by grade level, there is always a spike in the number of employees right around the bonus gateway.

You now know most of the rules of the game surrounding bonuses. If your company doesn't have bonuses, you can help your cause by voicing your support for variable compensation and by talking it up with your managers, on company surveys, etc. "Pay for performance" is sweet music to companies.

As bonuses are planned for introduction into your company, many companies will want to exclude variable compensation from defined benefit and defined contribution calculations (i.e., retirement benefits) and not make provisions for increased disability payments in case of sickness or injury. Two bonuses of the exact same amount offered by two companies will have *dramatic* differences on your long-term earnings if one gets included in your benefits calculations and the other does not. Ask if the bonus gets included in benefits calculations.

All companies will tell you that certain things—good corporate citizenship and community relations, United Way campaigns, and keeping the office plants alive—are terribly important, and to someone they are. But they are not the most important things to companies. When you are in a bonus plan, *be sure to organize your activities around it.* The bonus plan itself will tell you which behaviors the company most esteems. Those are the behaviors that you should perform. Don't be severely sidetracked by things that have to get done but that go unrewarded.

Chapter 9

The Thrill of Ownership

Imagine you are a big fat cow grazing on a lush green patch of pasture. Occasionally you lift your head, look around to see the other cattle grazing alongside you, and think how lucky you are to have such a wonderful farmer-owner who treats you so well. After all, you could belong to a farmer who would graze you outside this pasture—on the other side of the fence where the terrain isn't as hospitable to your king-size (or queen-size) diet.

However, you begin to wonder if this good life can last forever. Is it right for this many cattle to be grazing on such a small plot of land? Will you consume more than the earth can replenish? You think that perhaps it would be more responsible if, on occasion, you jumped the fence and grazed on the stubble of grass on the other side just long enough to give your own pasture land time to grow in again. But if you did that and none of the other cattle did, you'd suffer and get all skinny while the other cows get fatter. And the problem wouldn't be solved. So you stay and munch on, hoping there will always be grass.

This story describes what is known as the "commons" problem. The dilemma originated in old New England towns where farmers would use the thick grass in the town's commons to graze their cattle. The farmer that did this had a competitive advantage because he could fatten up his cows more on this rich land, and increase the value of his cattle. But once one farmer did it, they all did it.

The problem then becomes how do you stop before you destroy the very land that is supporting you? It makes no sense for a single farmer to move his cattle off the land to less wholesome grounds because that would put him at a disadvantage. Either they all must move in concert, or not at all.

The commons problem illustrates a situation where collective behavior and individual choice collide. The usual solution to these types of situations is the big "R": Regulation. If people can't regulate themselves, someone else will do it for them. A government agency, for example, steps in and says things like:

- You can only graze on the green at certain times and under certain conditions.
- You can only consume a certain amount of grass from the green—you have to pay extra for more.
- You can only eat 1.5 times what the average cow on the other side of the fence consumes, and so on.

You are now caught up with what is going on in executive compensation. There are a lot of cattle grazing on the green. Is it wrong? Probably, in a collective sense. In an individual sense, with some egregious exceptions such as Michael Ovitz's $100 million take from a brief stint at Disney, it has all of the hallmarks of rationality.

The Internal Revenue Service says that the following factors should be considered when setting compensation:

- The compensation of others with comparable responsibilities/ duties or who render similar services within like enterprises (usually similar types of companies of similar size and complexity, operating in common geographic regions)
- The circumstances of similar companies when the compensation is paid (this can be interpreted very broadly: as companies with comparable profit margins, growth rates, etc.)

There is a lot of leeway in these criteria and a lot of room for shenanigans; even something as seemingly straightforward as type of company is open for interpretation. I recently asked a group of people what company they would compare Kodak with and got a variety of answers ranging from high tech to manufacturing. Basically, as long as a company pays what everyone else is paying, everything is fine. And the rising tide will lift all boats.

Compensation committees of boards doggedly adhere to the criteria above. They insist upon objectivity, analytical completeness, and fairness. Consultants who routinely work with these people earn their keep. So it does take a lot of hard work before everyone agrees to rich compensation packages for the executives.

Rules and Regulations

Meanwhile, on the regulation front, a couple of things have taken place over the past few years. Unless the business community can limit executive feeding on the green, I would expect more regulations to emerge at business's first sign of political weakness—during a recession.

The Million-Dollar Salary Cap

Believe it or not, as of 1993 the five highest-paid executives of a company can't make more than $1 million as a legitimate expense for doing business, according to Section 162(m) of the Internal Revenue Code. Amounts over that are not deductible by the company. OOoo! Ouch! Yes, but that cap doesn't include stock options approved by shareholders, performance-based bonuses, and who really cares anyway!? Every year there are more executives whose salaries exceed $1 million. If it's between getting or keeping a good executive, the loss of a minor deduction is a very small price to pay. If you are ever so lucky to bump up against the one-million-dollar cap in corporate America, fear not.

Compensation Multiples

In a survey conducted in 1991 by *Industry Week* (April 15, 1991, p. 16), 60% of *Industry Week* readers who responded to the survey believed CEO pay should be limited as a multiple of employees' salaries. Indeed, such discussions periodically and ever so briefly echo through Congress.

Some companies such as Ben & Jerry's Ice Cream and Herman Miller, Inc., have had self-imposed caps on executive compensation. Management guru Peter Drucker has suggested that the ratio of the highest to lowest paid worker should be no greater than 20:1 (*BusinessWeek,* May 6, 1991, p. 93). Currently among major corporations, the ratio is more like 30:1 for base salaries and 60:1 for total cash compensation (base salary plus bonus) between the salaries of the lowest paid and that of the chief executive officer.

Self-interested capitalism, however, runs rampant in the corridors of business. Holding someone else back is not as important as employees getting ahead. I've found that if presented with the option of personal pay advancement and pay limitations on others, employees will uniformly pick the former. Furthermore, employees tend to be extremely fair-minded toward executives despite executives' lavish compensation packages. It's not what executives make that matters: It's what everyone gets in return.

Golden Parachutes

Golden parachutes are severance packages for executives that are triggered when the company they manage changes hands. Change of control generally occurs when there is a 20%–40% change in voting power (according to stock ownership) and/or a change in a majority of the board's membership. Golden parachutes provide a safety net for executives who must objectively size up offers that may be in the best interest of shareholders but not in their own personal interests. As a way of negating natural self-interest and of ensuring some management continuity in the event of a possible acquisition, executives are given lucrative contracts that offer some peace of mind.

During the 1980s there were "excessive" and disturbing severance arrangements popularized by William Agee's severance upon the sale of Bendix. Congress tried to curb abuses (under Section 280[g] of the Internal Revenue code), setting a limit to severance arrangements at 2.99 times the average W-2 earnings over the previous five years without a penalty tax being invoked. Therefore, an employee whose average compensation during the five years preceding change in control is $500,000 would receive a $1.5 million payoff, I mean payout, either as a lump sum or in installments.

The law appears to have had the effect of *raising* the standard severance package to the allowable limits and beyond (some companies exceed the limits and pay the 20% excise tax on the excess). Gold has turned to platinum. In essence, the law legitimized severance packages and now just about everyone has to have one for just about any imaginable reason. Even blatant failure can give rise to substantial paydays. Some of this may be at-tributable to lack of power or lack of guts in the boardroom: It seems we can't tell someone he's not cutting it without handing him a check.

You should investigate "tin parachutes" for yourself if you are not one of the very top executives in your company. Tin parachutes usually provide salary and benefits continuation for about a year if you are terminated with-out cause within two to three years of the change in control. You are most likely to find tin parachutes in industries where there is quite a bit of merger and acquisition activity and there is a need to retain critical talent through-out the ranks. Banking, consumer goods, health care, and pharmaceuticals are the best bets these days.

You will also want to do what the executives do. First of all, you don't have to be terminated to collect. You can quit if you are not treated well: Your compensation and your responsibilities are reduced; your office is smaller; you have to travel farther to work. Second, make sure you will receive a pro-rata share of your annual bonus. And, third, don't leave your stock options behind. If your company is taken over, it is nice to have a provision in your severance contract that accelerates vesting of all stock options. This is like in the westerns when the poker player lays four aces, extends both arms across the table, and rakes it in, laughing: "Thank you, gentlemen."

In the right doses, parachutes are good ideas. If you join a company that has the potential of being acquired—and more are—you will want to pro-tect the assets that have been promised to you. You can partly do this through change in control agreements. You don't have to be a big shot to ask for one. There is no cost to the company to back up its assurances with a signed piece of paper.

As a general rule, you will want to know all of the "What happens if . . . ?" with regard to your various incentives. What happens if you leave the company voluntarily, you lose your job through downsizing, you are fired, the company is taken over, you are demoted, you switch divi-sions, etc.?

FASB and Nonqualified Stock Options

Since stock options are the most likely form of long-term incentive you will encounter in the workplace, I will have much more to say about these momentarily. They have been likened to legalized embezzlement and the greatest social welfare program in the history of mankind. With such strong language and emotion surrounding them, you know they have to be good.

(If you don't know what stock options are, you might want to skip to the next section of this chapter, Types of Long-Term Incentives, for a review before reading on).

Over the past several years, the Financial Accounting Standards Board (FASB) studied stock options and grew quite partial to a recommendation that surely would have limited stock options—had the recommendation not been vigorously fought by corporate America and rejected. Actually it was modified; a compromise position was reached.

The thing that makes stock options attractive to companies is how they are treated for tax purposes. A company can give these things away (with shareholder approval) and when the options are exercised and gains are realized, the company gets a tax deduction for the size of the gains. That helps the company lower its taxes. But unlike the salaries companies pay, with options there is no charge to earnings that reduces profits. There is no expense for stock options that goes on the books.

FASB argued that options have value when granted, that there should be a charge to earnings, and those charges should appear on companies' annual financial statements. That never happened. But, starting in 1996, companies have had to provide a footnote in their statements that explains what would have happened had they had to include options as an expense in their financial statements. Aren't compromises great!?

Chart 9A lists the companies and industries that would have taken the biggest hits to earnings if they had to account for their option grants and those that claimed the largest tax deductions from options. These companies aren't diabolical or bad. I am providing you with this list because these companies offer the most options. From your point of view, these are good companies because these are places where you would most likely be a recipient of these potentially lucrative programs. You can get very, very wealthy with stock options: You can quit your job and blow glass on a Pacific island, as I know one employee did.

Stock options often really do cost a company money and shareholders do vote extravagant plans down. When options are granted and exercised, there is more stock in circulation that dilutes, or lowers, the per share price of the stock. More shares mean the value of each share goes down. To prevent existing shareholders (who paid for their stock) from being adversely affected, a company will often buy back shares at market value in order to keep the number of outstanding shares relatively constant. If you have a right to buy a share of stock from your company for $10 that is currently valued by the open market at $25, the company collects $10 for the pur-

Chart 9A. Representative Companies and Industries with Large Reductions in Earnings and Large Deductions Due to Stock Options

Companies		Industries (in order from more to less)
Alcoa	J.P. Morgan	Investment banking and brokerage
Amgen	Microsoft	
Armco	Morgan Stanley	Insurance brokers
Ascend Communications	Netscape	Hotels and motels
Avery Dennison	PepsiCo	Money-center banks
Bristol-Myers Squibb	Raytheon	Entertainment
Cascade Communications	Republic Industries	Specialized services
Cisco Systems	Reynolds Metals	Computer software and services
Compaq	Seagram	
CUC International	Sun Microsystems	Building materials
Genentech	Travelers	Computer systems
Georgia-Pacific	3Com	Home building
Gillette	United HealthCare	Long distance communications
Inland Steel	Unocal	Airlines
Intel	USAirways	
MCI Communications	Westinghouse Electric	
	Walt Disney	

Sources: *BusinessWeek*, April 21, 1997, p. 62; *Wall Street Journal*, June 26, 1997, p. C1; *Wall Street Journal*, May 13, 1997, p. A1; *New York Times*, May 30, 1997, p. F1.

chase of its stock from you but has to pay $25 to get it back. A total of $170 billion worth of stock was bought back in 1996 (*Wall Street Journal,* April 14, 1997, A1). Even after deductions and all of the financial rigmarole, that deal usually costs the company money—the real kind, hard cash.

Controversy aside, stock options are great ways for smaller companies to level the compensation playing field. Many companies can't pay the salaries that will attract top talent but they can offer lots of stock in exchange. If you get in on a good thing early, you can do very well for yourself. In making the decision to join a small or start-up company, however, you will want to weigh the long-term prospects of the company. Ten thousand options may sound like a lot, but multiplied by $0 . . .

Types of Long-Term Incentives

When I ask employees what they would like to know about long-term incentives (i.e., incentives measured and paid over a period of greater than one year), the nearly universal response is, "What are they?" In effect, employees want to know what they are missing out on and if there might be a way to experience these moneymaking delicacies for themselves.

Working for a publicly traded company definitely gives you an advantage because the most ubiquitous form of long-term incentive, stock, is available to you. There are alternatives to stock, of course, but it is stock appreciation that can make you rich. Just ask the Microsoft millionaires of Puget Sound.

Let's look at the most often used forms of long-term incentives.

Nonqualified Stock Options

Overview. About 5 million people now have stock options in the U.S. Large companies now reserve 5%–10% of their stock for options and 10% to 15% of employees in large public companies are now eligible for options.

More and more companies are adopting broad-based option plans. One recent estimate is that about two thousand companies now widely distribute options to employees (*BusinessWeek,* July 22, 1996, p. 80). I find the logic of these plans to be far-fetched (stock ownership creates a greater personal investment in the company which yields better corporate results) but, hey, who cares? They do make you an owner, temporarily. Broad stock ownership also tacitly recognizes that everyone in the company has a hand in making the company successful. In theory, they will also get you to think smarter and work harder. One thing it gets you to do is look closer at the financial section of the newspaper to see how your company's stock is performing.

Traditionally reserved for the corporate elite, stock options are coming at you.

The Basics. In general, options give you the right to buy or sell stock at a certain price within a given time period. With nonqualified stock options, you are given the right to purchase your company's stock at the current market price of the stock after a certain period time has elapsed (usually at least a year). So, after one year, if the stock price of your company has increased, you are in the money because you can buy the stock for less and sell it for more. Most of the time you will not be able to cash in on all of your options at one time; many companies have "ratable" vesting schedules that permits you to exercise a certain percent of options after one year, a certain percent after two years, and so on. On the other hand, companies that have "cliff" vesting will allow you to exercise all of your options at one time, but you usually have to wait longer to do it (three to five years).

Chart 9B provides a mini-dictionary of options language and shows you how they work. Suppose you are designated as a key employee and receive, at the discretion of your company's management, nonqualified stock options. Further, let's say you earn $60,000 in base salary and get awarded 300 stock options. If your company's stock is currently trading at $10 per share, your options are equivalent to 5% of your base salary, when the options are valued at their face value (300 shares times $10 per share equals $3,000).

You now have the right to purchase those 300 shares at $10 per share. If the stock price of your company goes up, you make money. For example, let's say that two years have passed. Your company's stock price is now $25 per share. Guess what? You've made money. You've made $15 per share, or $4,500.

CHART 9B. OPTIONS BASICS

The Present

Current Stock Price = $10

You are *granted* 300 options, which gives you the right to purchase 300 shares of stock at a future date.

The *exercise price* = the current market value of the stock (the exercise price is the price at which you can buy the 300 shares of stock; this price can be set anywhere but is usually the price of the stock on the day it is granted).

Before you can exercise your options, the options must *vest*, meaning that you will have to hold on to them for a specified period of time (usually at least a year).

The Future

Current Stock Price = $25

You *exercise* options by purchasing the stock for: 300 times $10 = $3,000.

You then sell the stock for: 300 times $25 = $7,500.

Your *gain* is the difference between the purchase and sale prices; $7,500 minus $3,000 = $4,500; you are liable for taxes on the gain.

Keep in mind that you are dealing with stock. Stock can go up or down in value. So, if you are reserving your options for a specific purpose, such as college education, you'll have to think about the best time to exercise your options and take your gains. I have known several employees who held on to their options until they needed them just to find the stock price precipitously fall before they exercised. Don't let the event for which you are saving drive your decision about when to exercise your options. You may want to think about converting your stock portfolio well in advance of a specific need.

When you "exercise" your options, you will be taxed on the gain ($4,500 in the example, above). You will be taxed when you purchase your shares, not when they are sold. "Buy and hold" strategies in which you exercise your options but retain the stock will require you to have money to pay for the stock and the tax liability. As a consequence, most employees including executives buy and sell in one swift and effortless motion.

Cashing in Your Options. Your human resources department can tell you how to purchase and dispose of your stock. There are a couple of ways. The "cashless" exercise is the easiest, most convenient way to convert your options to cash. Most companies have relationships with brokers who can get the job done faster for you than using your own broker. Essentially, the broker is giving you a short-term loan to cover the cost of the options while the underlying stock is being sold.

In addition to cashless exercises, you can also exercise with stock that you already own either by converting that stock to cash and using the proceeds for the exercise or by a "stock-for-stock swap": trading shares that you own for the options.

Suppose you have the right to purchase 100 shares of stock at $10 each. Also assume that the stock is currently worth $20 and that you own 50 shares. Your company may allow you to use the $1,000 of stock you already own to exercise the options at $1,000. The exchange of 50 shares of stock for a new set of 50 shares is tax free. The additional 50 shares you now own, worth $1,000, is taxable to you. You can redeem some of your shares to pay the tax.

On occasion, companies provide employees (executives mostly) with "tandem stock appreciation rights/options rights." A stock appreciation right (SAR) entitles an employee to receive the appreciation value of a specified number of shares of company common stock over a specified time period. If the right is granted when the stock is worth $10 per share and, following a holding period of two years, for example, increases in worth to $20, the employee is owed $10 per share. No cash is required.

A tandem right means that you can exercise either one SAR or one stock option. The exercise of one cancels one of the other. Companies sometimes offer enough SARs to pay for the options. Again, suppose you have options on 100 shares of stock that are exercisable at $10 per share and that the current stock price is $20. You have a gain of $1,000 minus taxes owed. You can exercise 70 SARs and get $700 from your company (70 SARs times the $10 per share gain). This will cancel 70 of your options. You have 30 options remaining. You can use $300 (of the $700) to purchase the options and reserve $400 for taxes.

If you are thinking of cashing in on your options because you need the money, many brokerage companies now have various loan programs that use the options as collateral. So you don't necessarily have to exercise your options to pry some value from them. Just make sure you know what you are getting into if you take out a loan. Some loan programs are based on "margin" that allows you to borrow up to 50% of your investment portfolio, including options. If you are maxed out on your loan and the value of your options declines, you may have to come up with more money to cover the loan.

Immediately cashing in on options violates what a lot of boards think executives should do: namely, own company stock outright. After all, if the board wants executives to work on investors' behalf, executives should be investors in the true sense of the word: with their own money.

To encourage employees to purchase and hold company stock, companies sometimes offer employees something called "reload" options as an incentive to hold on to stock they purchase. Reload options are options that are replenished upon exercise if the exercise is made with previously owned shares of stock. So if you buy and hold stock and use it to pay the exercise price of options, you'll get more options equivalent to the number of shares used in the exercise. This feature encourages employees to hold some of the stock they purchase so it can be used to buy more options.

In contrast to this desire to have employees hold on to stock, a newly revised Securities rule (16b-3) makes it easier to rid oneself of stock options. The revised rule allows stock options to be transferred. This doesn't mean company plans will allow it but transfers of options to family members will definitely rise. Passing options between family members makes it easier for wealthy individuals to avoid or defer estate taxes (which are 55% of the estate above a unified tax credit of $625,000—which will increase annually through the year 2006). There will undoubtedly be a blunder or two where companies will find they have new, major shareholders (e.g., somebody's spouse) that they would prefer not to have, but the new transfer rules will give you greater ability to manage your finances and greater certainty that your economic wishes will be carried out, postmortem.

The Amount of Options. There is a familiar pattern to the amount of stock options you can expect to receive *if* your company offers them and *if* you are included in the plan. These amounts are given in Chart 9C. The percentages indicate the face value of the options at the time of grant expressed as a percent of your salary. For example, if you make $50,000 within a company whose stock price is $40 per share, and are granted options equivalent to 20% of your base salary ($10,000), you would receive 250 options ($10,000 ÷ $40). The more you make, the more you get. This is why promotions and earning more money is always highly desirable. Because you will be in line to get more in other ways.

This brings us to one of the great circularities of compensation. People who are judged to be of value are paid more. However, people who are paid more are often judged to be of greater value. And, hence, the more they should be paid. Think about it. If you don't know what something is worth—a piece of jewelry, for example—you will judge its worth by the price tag. Pricier pieces of jewelry must be of greater worth, else why the steep price? This principle, by the way, is not lost on roadside jewelry stands.

CHART 9C. FACE VALUE OF STOCK OPTIONS AS PERCENT OF BASE SALARY

Base Salary	Percent of Base Salary
$25,000	5%–10%
$50,000	20%–25%
$75,000	30%–40%
$100,000	50%–60%
$150,000	85%–100%
$200,000	115%–130%
$300,000	185%–200%
$400,000	240%–260%
$500,000	300%–350%
$750,000	400%–500%

The same principle applies to you. If you can get your price up, you will be perceived to be of greater value, if not in the company for which you currently work, then someplace else. As in a jewelry store, some expert somewhere has appraised your value and metaphorically hung a sign around your neck advertising your worth. This becomes the opening bid for all future transactions.

The Real Worth of Your Options. Although you can't take your options the day you get them and cash them in, they are nevertheless worth something the day you get them. They probably *will be worth* something, and that has value. If you are really interested in knowing what value your options have on the day you get them, you can apply a complex model, known as "Black-Scholes," that puts a price on your options. In 1997, Robert Merton and Myron Scholes won the Nobel prize in economics for their remarkable work, which, believe it or not, is actually economically useful. They took much of the guesswork out of options pricing, which subsequently led to the growth of the global options markets.

Most people aren't really interested in how to account for options using sophisticated pricing techniques. But it will come in handy if you ever have to prepare a financial report or proxy statement. There is an easier way to estimate the worth of your options, if you really must know. Look back and see how your company's stock performed during each possible five-year period, beginning ten years ago. Average the annual returns for those periods. You don't have to do anything fancy: Just look at how much the stock price has increased over the five years (as a percentage) and divide by 5. That should give you an idea of how your company's stock performs over time. The past is a pretty good predictor of the future.

Suppose your stock averages a 9% increase per year and that the current price per share of stock is $25. This is the price at which you are granted company shares and the price at which you can purchase your company's stock five years from now. At a 9% annual increase rate, in five years your stock should be worth $38.50. That's a gain of $13.50 per share. If you were originally granted 100 shares, you will make $1,350. To get an approximation of the real value of your options today as they sit idle, you have to discount the potential gain by a projected rate of return. That rate is determined by the risk you have assumed through the investment. You can calculate a risk factor by taking the rate of return for a safe investment such as a five-year Treasury bond (reflecting the period of your option; assume the current return is 6%) and adding a 6% equity risk factor (equity investments have no guarantees that you will make money or recover your principal and 6% represents the standard added risk). If you have a fancy calculator, the discounting is straightforward. If you do it by hand, divide the $1,350 by the risk factor (1.12, or 12%), five times. You should get $766 as the present value of your options.

The lowest value your options can have at the time of grant is the difference between the money you would have to invest in a risk-free financial instrument to produce the face value of your options at the underlying stock price (over a period in which you expect to hold the stock), and the face value of the options. For instance, at 6% interest over five years, you would need $1,868 to purchase an asset worth $2,500 (the face value of your options). The difference between $1,868 (the hypothetical purchase price) and $2,500 (the face value of your options) is the minimum value of your options ($632). This is all a bit tricky but the more comfortable you feel in the world of options, the better off you will be.

Special Kinds of Nonqualified Stock Options. Options breed people I call "cyclical geniuses." These are the executives who do well for a few years (in terms of stock price) and then do poorly for a few years. The company's stock basically tracks the fortunes of the overall business and economic climates. How can a person do so well for a few years and then do not-so-well? Because he or she ain't driving.

There is a lot that goes into a stock price: business, economic, and psychological factors all influence stock price. To prove a company's management and employees are truly responsible for their company's success, it would be nice to see that the stock price has beaten the upswing in the general market or the average returns of a peer group of companies before anybody collected anything. Such options instruments exist. They are called *index options* and *premium options*.

Index options tie the exercise price of options to a particular rate of return such as the return on government securities (T-bills). Unless your company's stock can better the return on a risk-free instrument, no one gets anything. Premium options have a fixed exercise price above the current market value. For instance, if I know that over time the average five-year return of a peer group of companies has been 60%, I may be inclined to set the exercise price of the options to 60% above the current price. Despite the fact that this is quite easy to do, only about 5% of companies offer premium options and never as high as 60% above market price. Twenty-five percent is more like it. Further, a company that offers premium options usually offers more of the regular variety of options to offset gains that employees may have to forgo because of the premium pricing.

These varieties of options make considerable sense. It is best for everyone, however, that we not do the sensible thing.

Incentive Stock Options

There is another type of stock option that currently is not widely used. These are virtually the same as nonqualified stock options except: (a) You are taxed when the shares acquired *are sold,* (b) you are taxed at capital gains rates, and (c) if certain guidelines are adhered to, the company does not get a deduction.

It's really the capital gains part that nixed these things; because ordinary and capital gains rates have been for many years the same, there haven't been monumental advantages to the employee (and a host of restrictions), so most companies didn't bother. But since the reduction in capital gains has brought the rates once again to 20%, expect to see a resurgence of interest in Incentive Stock Options. "Why is this so?" you may ask. Because highly paid executives will really want them in order to reduce their taxes.

There are two restrictions, however, that will keep incentive stock options from sweeping the countryside. The first is the holding period: in order to qualify for the lower capital gains tax treatment, you have to hold the shares at least one year from the date of exercise or two years from the date of grant. That's not too bad. The tax savings may be worth the wait.

The second restriction, however, may negate the tax savings altogether. Many highly paid executives are subject to an alternative minimum tax which is a special tax that tries to keep wealthy individuals and corporations from avoiding taxes. The practical effect is that you may end up having to pay ordinary tax rates on the "bargain element," or gains, of your incentive stock options.

Restricted Stock

Restricted stock is the grant of company stock subject to certain restrictions. The main restriction is usually the passage of time. Certain performance conditions can be attached as well but this is less common. Restricted stock is often referred to as a "warm body" award. As long as you are still breathing after at least a year, you will make money.

If a company really wanted employees to think like owners, it would make employees pay for the stock. Fortunately for you, that isn't done too often. As a consequence, this is as close as you can get to a corporate gift. Unlike stock options whose value resides in the appreciation in the stock price, restricted stock carries the full value of the stock plus any appreciation. Because of the greater value of restricted stock versus stock options, when both are granted to employees they are usually given in about a 3-to-1 ratio: 3 options for every share of restricted stock.

Restricted stock provides a powerful incentive for employees to stick around until the time restrictions lapse and they can collect. You may be seeing more of these throughout your company as companies struggle to keep good people put. When the restrictions lapse, you will incur a tax based on the current market value of the stock. If you are given 100 shares of restricted stock worth $10 at the time of grant and two years later the stock "vests" (e.g., you have fulfilled your service requirement) at $20 per share, you will have taxable income of $2,000 (the original grant plus the appreciation).

There is a special provision in the tax code (Section 83[b]) that allows you to be taxed on the award at the time of grant (for the amount taxable) and again when the stock is sold. This allows you to break up your tax liability and gives you greater control over when you will be taxed on stock appreciation. Be warned, however, if you make this election and end up forfeiting the stock because you leave the company before you meet your service requirement, for example, the IRS will not give you your money back. So you end up paying tax on something you never received.

Phantom Stock

Sometimes nonstock companies, privately held companies whose stock is illiquid (not traded), or divisions of large companies that have no stock of their own want to offer select employees something like stock. These companies can offer employees phantom stock.

It's a pretty good bet that you won't run into this stuff in your lifetime, but you might if you are a key employee of a family-owned business but not a member of the family or an executive for a large division of a major corporation. In the former case, the company wants to retain your talents and treat you as a member of the family (but not really); in the latter case, the company wants to make you directly responsible for the increase in value of the division and give you something tangible to show for it (and is willing to tolerate the administration and accounting hassles that can accompany these plans). To give the semblance of something tangible, companies can print fake stock certificates so you can have a pile of something that is worth more than other piles you've encountered in the past.

The trick with phantom stock is figuring out what a share of stock is worth. There are many ways of doing this. Some of these are costly and time consuming (i.e., involve business valuations) and/or involve a number of assumptions to be made.

One of the easiest, most straightforward approaches is based on assumptions made about the Price-Earnings (PE) ratio for your industry group. For purposes of illustration, let's say that the average stock-price–to–earnings-per-share ratio (i.e., stock price ÷ [net income/number of shares outstanding]) is 12 for the industry to which your company belongs. Let's further assume that each share of phantom stock is to be initially valued at $1. If your company's current net income is $1,500,000, it can be shown that there are 18,007,202 mythical shares of stock outstanding (1 ÷ [$1,500,000/18,007,202] = a PE ratio of 12—rounded to the nearest whole number).

Your company reserves 5% of these shares for its phantom-stock plan and allocates 2,000 to you as a key employee. Five years later, the company's net earnings are now $7,800,000. This means, given all of our assumptions, the phantom-stock price is $5.20 per share.

$$\frac{\text{Stock Price}}{7,800,000/18,007,202} = 12$$

You can solve for the stock price of $5.20 by algebraically rearranging the formula above. The stock price is equal to 12 times 7,800,000/18,007,202. Since you own 2,000 shares, you have made $10,400. Since shares vest over time (meaning you can cash in portions of the phantom shares at specified times), you have probably been collecting pieces of this $10,400 over the five-year time period.

Most companies will settle any gains in phantom shares with cash. Large companies, however, sometimes exchange the phantom shares with real stock. In either case, you are generally taxed when you are in "constructive receipt" of payment—that is, when you can elect to receive payment in cash or stock.

Performance Shares

These are grants of actual or phantom shares of stock. The value of each share is tied to the value of a share of company stock, whereas the number of shares earned depends on the attainment of goals. The total amount you can earn, then, depends on at least two factors: (1) how well your company's stock performs and (2) how well you and your colleagues perform on some other organizational measurements, usually over a three-to-five-year time period.

For instance, suppose your company's stock is $40 per share today and you are a part of a group that has the following performance objective over the next three years:

PERFORMANCE OBJECTIVE NET INCOME FROM OPERATIONS	NUMBER OF SHARES EARNED
$1,000,000	25
$1,500,000	60
$2,000,000 (target objective)	100
$2,500,000	200
$3,000,000	400

If you hit your target on your objective, you will be awarded 100 shares at the going market price. If the stock has risen to $75 per share, you earn $7,500 (100 × $75). Whether you are paid in cash or stock, you will have a tax liability upon payout.

Companies have different philosophies regarding how often to run these programs. Most companies start a new plan every year or two so that after the term of the first plan expires, employees will continue to have a chance for pay outs every year or so. A few companies run these plans in discrete cycles with no plan overlaps.

Performance Unit Plans

Performance unit plans are like extended bonus plans (over a three-to-five-year time frame). Typically, an employee can earn a certain number of units of a given value (or, alternatively, a given number of units of variable value). The number of units can change depending on the performance achieved during a specified period. At the end of the period, the units vest and the employee receives his or her payout in cash or stock. The total value of the units is taxable as ordinary income when the award becomes payable.

For example, assume that each performance unit has a fixed value equal to the current stock price ($80). Over a three-year period, you can earn performance units according to the following performance schedule:

3-YEAR REVENUE GROWTH	PERFORMANCE UNITS EARNED	AMOUNT EARNED
15%	0	$0
20%	50	$4,000
25%	150	$12,000
30%	300	$24,000
35%	500	$40,000

If your company manages revenue growth of 25% over the three years, you can collect and cash in on 150 units worth $12,000 (150 × $80).

You can see why this is like a bonus plan. Basically, to use the example, the company is saying, "If you can help us get to 25% revenue growth, we'll pay you $12,000 extra." The assignment of units merely serves as a counter much like the clickers that track distance when you walk; it's a nice way of registering how much progress you have made and how far you still have to go.

Compensation Profiles

We have now examined three major components of compensation: base salary, short-term awards (bonuses), and long-term compensation. There are particular ways that these components fit together to form your total compensation package based on your level in the organization. Thus, your level in your organization not only determines how much in total you are compensated, *but the way you are paid* as well.

Chart 9D shows how compensation is usually carved up. See how your own compensation fits the patterns presented.

In looking at the chart, notice that as base salaries get larger, they make up less of the total compensation. That is mainly because the total compensation is likewise expanding at a very rapid rate. It is primarily the addition of more long-term incentives that makes base salaries proportionately less a part of the total picture.

In general, the lower your base salary, the more your base salary constitutes your total compensation. Chart 9E shows sample total compensation configurations at four salary levels. The pies in Chart 9E are differently sized to remind you that there are pies you can place on grandma's windowsill and pies you need a front-end loader to move.

This chart gives you a rough idea of what to expect in terms of total

CHART 9D. TOTAL COMPENSATION PROFILES

Compensation Percentages

Salary Level	Base Salary	Annual Bonus	Long-Term Incentives
$20,000	95%	5%	0%
$60,000	85%	10%	5%
$100,000	80%	15%	5%
$150,000	70%	20%	10%
$200,000	60%	20%	20%
$250,000	50%	25%	25%
$300,000	45%	25%	30%
$400,000	40%	25%	35%
$500,000 (or greater)	35%	25%	40%

compensation given a particular base salary. It also illustrates why it's good to work for companies that pay bonuses and offer employees long-term incentives such as stock options. They help to expand your compensation—if they weren't offered, the void would not be completely filled by a larger base salary unless the company absolutely had to because of tough competition for labor. If you work in a job that pays $60,000 within a company that pays a bonus plus offers stock options to key employees, you will earn $5,000–$10,000 more per year on average than someone in the same job within a company that doesn't have all of the compensation frills. Bonuses are good. Long-term incentives are good.

CHART 9E. SAMPLE COMPENSATION PROFILES

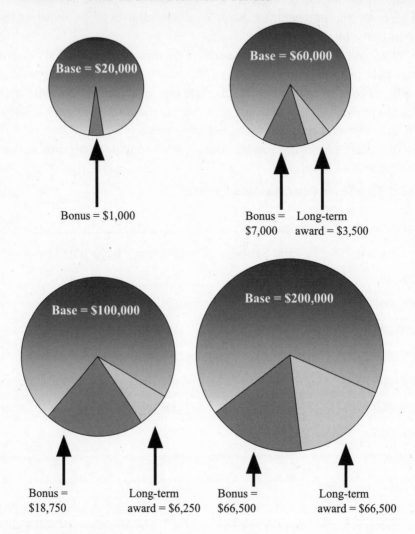

About "Value Added"

If you read through this chapter, you should have a pretty good understanding of what's going on in executive compensation; and the good news for you is that the wealth is being spread around more. You should be able to talk the talk with one exception—Economic Value Added (a trademarked concept of Stern Stewart). It, as well as a host of similar concepts from companies such as Boston Consulting Group, McKinsey, Braxton Associates, and Holt Value Associates, are all the rage.

Most long-term incentive plans are based on stock price appreciation,

CHART 9F. SAMPLE CALCULATION OF ECONOMIC VALUE ADDED

Company Y $(000)

1. Economic Capital =
   shareholders equity   5,799
   + goodwill written off   1,521
   + capitalized cumulative
      unusual loss   930
   + deferred tax   405
   + minority interests   2,352
   + total debt   4,415
                                   15,422

2. Net Operating Profit After Tax (NOPAT) =
   operating profit   3,406
   + interest expense   689
   − unusual gain   68
   − taxes   978
                                   3,049

3. Weighted Average Cost of Capital (WACC) =
cost of equity (this is calculated
using something called a Capital
Asset Pricing Model)   20.4%

cost of debt (the average interest
rate a company pays)   10.7%

WACC =   17.5%
(weighting in this example reflects greater equity than debt)

4. EVA = NOPAT − (capital × WACC)
   = 3,049 − (15,422 × 17.5%) =   350
(A positive result here represents "value added")

Source. *The Economist*, August 2, 1997. p.54.
Used with the permission of Stern Stewart.

total shareholder return (stock appreciation plus dividends), earnings per share, and return on equity. Economic Value Added is much less frequently used in both short- and long-term plans, but much discussed. Generally,

EVA looks at whether or not the returns a company is getting (as measured by net operating profit) is worth the risk and investment. The basic notion behind most EVA-like yardsticks is straightforward: A company creates value to the extent that the return on its capital (debt and equity) exceeds the rate investors could earn by investing in other securities of equivalent risk. In a sense, the measure forces management to look at itself the way an investor, who can place his or her money anywhere, does. What executives generally discover is that there is good reason why the stock price is high or low.

Chart 9F provides a sample calculation. These measures are surrounded by a religious zeal and aura by the companies that embrace them. They are surely better than traditional accounting measures but undeserving of the faith. My big problem with measures that are touted as management devices is that it is easy for management to lose the distinction between the measure and what it represents: The measure becomes an end in itself.

Take a thermometer. The temperature reading can change in two ways. The weather can change. Or, I can put a match under it. Too many managers "heat the thermometer." They take actions that directly affect the measure without substantively changing the nature of things. Nothing really changes except the measure, and it changes falsely.

There are no cookbook answers to management. Good managers look at the gauges of their success but are not governed by them. Besides, to say all that is needed to be successful is to use capital efficiently is to say a mouthful. As Albert Einstein once said, "Not everything that can be counted counts, and not everything that counts can be counted."

Chapter 10

Employee Contracts, Team Pay, Overtime, and Other Compensation Issues

We have covered a lot of territory in this book but believe it or not we still have two major trends to cover related to your compensation. These are team-based pay and the use of various employment agreements that can affect your livelihood after you leave your current employer.

There also are a couple of other issues that we need to address before concluding our discussion of compensation, such as overtime pay and pay equity. Without further ado, let us begin.

More Major Trends in the Workplace

Employment Contracts

The workplace is starting to look like the movie studios of the '30s and '40s and like professional baseball before free agency. These were the days when the mobility of talent was restricted by contract. In essence, preventing the free movement of people (along with their knowledge and abilities) from employer to employer aids a company's competitive position by stabilizing its talent pool while containing salaries. Entertainers and sports stars, for example, earn much more today, correcting for inflation, than they did years ago when they were unable to sell their services to the highest bidder.

Three types of agreements are becoming more commonplace. These are:

(1) Nonsolicitation agreements: These prohibit you from soliciting business from a former employer's clients or from recruiting employees away from a former employer.

(2) Nondisclosure agreements: These "confidentiality agreements" prohibit you from revealing trade secrets or other proprietary information such as customer lists, pricing strategies, and manufacturing processes to outsiders during or after your employment; even without your signature on a piece of paper, employers have legal recourse for the unauthorized use of proprietary information through the Uniform Trade Secrets Act, adopted by forty-two states.

(3) Noncompete agreements: These agreements, also known as restrictive covenants, noncompetition agreements, and covenants not to compete, prohibit you from working for a competitor usually for six months to two years regardless of the circumstances surrounding your separation—voluntary or not.

The meteoric rise of postemployment agreements is born of employers' natural fears of losing their trade secrets, special processes, unique methods, formulas, etc., as well as their customers and clients to the competition. Low unemployment, wider intracompany distribution of sensitive information, and a general shift from a product-based to a knowledge-based economy have made these various defensive arrangements both more fashionable and more vital.

As a general rule of thumb, ask your personal attorney to review any contract that you are asked to sign. Treat these contracts like any other by having a professional review them. Your attorney will be familiar with the state laws germane to these agreements and will be able to comment on the reasonableness of the contract and to offer valuable suggestions on how the agreement may be modified to limit your personal exposure and maximize your potential job mobility.

You should generally expect some "consideration" in exchange for signing a contract that places restrictions upon you. These considerations may include sign-on bonuses, salary increases, promotions, or stock options.

Bear in mind that these various agreements may have "payback" or "bad boy" clauses. For example, noncompete agreements may be inserted into a stock option plan with the caveat that if the noncompete agreement is violated, past gains on options (for a specified period of time) must be forked over and current unexercised options will be forfeited. Similarly, agreements may stipulate that sign-on bonuses and other recruiting costs (such as relocation) must be repaid if you leave the company before a certain time.

Nonsolicitation and nondisclosure agreements have become staples of employment, conveying a reasonable expectation of employers that you won't use information and relationships to which you are entrusted against them. It's the growing use of noncompete clauses that is raising the hair on people's backs. Once reserved for executives, the rank and file—ranging from engineers, to sales personnel, to telemarketers, to hair replacement technicians—are being asked to sign these things.

Noncompete clauses place restrictions on where and with whom you can work after separating from your current employer. The term of the agreement depends on the facts and circumstances of the specific case. In general, noncompete clauses are in effect for a minimum of six months and a maximum of two years. Shorter-term noncompete agreements usually pertain to lower-level employees who generally aren't privy to the robust, juicy secrets of the upper echelon and in industries where today's secret quickly becomes old news (software development). These contracts also are often crafted in a way that trades time for geography: "You can't compete against us *anywhere* for six months" versus "You can't compete against us *here* for two years."

Some of these agreements will appear unreasonable to you. Most employees unhesitantly sign these contracts because they don't believe they will be relevant (because they will never leave) or enforceable (if they do leave)—and they probably won't be, but why not deal with the "reasonableness" issue in a forthright manner? While you're at it, make sure you document everyone's thinking behind the restrictions advocated; it may be helpful in proving or disproving how reasonable the restrictions really are at a later date to a higher authority.

If you are asked to sign a noncompete clause, one thing you will want is for the agreement to be applicable only if you leave your job voluntarily. To be fired and then told you can't get another job with a local competitor for two years seems a bit unfair: "We couldn't use you here, but just to make sure no one else makes the same mistake, we will enforce the noncompete clause you signed." In actuality, if you have signed a noncompete agreement and are terminated (or resign in lieu of termination), you can generally have the contract torn up in exchange for assurances that you will go away quietly and will not be heard from again (personally or through your attorney).

Another thing you will want is specificity. The most nebulous concept these days involves "competition." It's a word that is often very hard to define in an era of merging technologies. Therefore, rather than assume that every company is a potential competitor, name the companies that are. A recent, high-profile case shows how this can work. Mark Suwyn was an executive vice president at International Paper in White Plains, New York, where he signed a noncompete agreement that prohibited him from working with any competitor for eighteen months after leaving the company. But Suwyn attached a memo to the contract that said the company chairman agreed that he would only be restricted from working for a direct competitor such as "Georgia Pacific, Champion, or Weyerhaeuser." This subsequently allowed Suwyn to take over as chairman of Portland, Oregon–based Louisiana-Pacific (another forest products company) after separating from International Paper.

Team-Based Pay

Just as our schools once prepared us for yesterday's workplace by teaching us to work independently ("keep your eyes and your hands to yourself"), schools are now preparing youngsters for today's workplace through more group projects and more work in teams. Just about every company today will tell you that the one thing they need more of is "teamwork." In many instances coordinating and integrating work through the use of teams is a much more efficient way of getting things accomplished. Teams frequently yield higher productivity and higher quality—not always without considerable angst and the mutual derision of fellow team members. Companies also believe that teams serve as a better foundation for open communication and idea generation, an interesting but speculative thesis.

A lot of what gets said and written with respect to teams is gibberish and a lot of what gets done in the workplace is downright scary. Team formation often amounts to little more than rounding up the usual suspects and calling them a team. Kids on the playground give more thought to how to form teams. In work settings, there is much more confusion about what teams are and what makes them effective.

To give you a flavor for the complexities of teams, and how one team may differ from another, I asked thirty human resources professionals to assess how similar or different a number of intact groups are from one another. The results are displayed in Chart 10A.

CHART 10A: TYPES OF TEAMS AND THEIR DIFFERENCES

Dimension 1

Example Groups on Dimension

Examples on
  One Side of Dimension

Examples on
  Other Side of Dimension

Church members*	Orchestra*
Neighborhood residents	Cast in a play*
Parent-teachers association	Race car team
Roommates	Marching band
Condo association	Tag-team wrestlers
Members of a local union	Beauty contestants
Self-help group	Rock band
Pallbearers	
Family	

Differences Between Sets of Groups

- Membership is determined by factors outside members' control.
- Members have strong personal interests.
- Can't eliminate a member (but can isolate or ostracize).
- Have "organizers"
- Size of group is logistically determined.

- There are external reviews or criteria for success.
- Certain members stand out or are given special status.
- Actions are "choreographed" or synchronized.
- Members are inseparable—win or lose, succeed or fail as a group; mutually dependent.
- There is a lead person or director.
- There are rules or standards that define permissible activity.
- Group entry requires a test or set of qualifications.
- Size of the group is functionally determined.

* Most representative of set; listing of differences is not exhaustive.

At a glance, it is easy to see that there is no one type of team. There are many types of teams that vary on a continuum along several dimensions. There are vast differences in how members are recruited and selected; group membership is maintained; member performance is assessed; mem-

Dimension 2

Example Groups on Dimension

Examples on *One Side of Dimension*	Examples on *Other Side of Dimension*
Sewing circle*	Posse*
Sailing crew*	Road crew
Golf foursome*	Flight crew
Investment club*	Migrant workers
Volleyball team	Human resources department
Baseball team	Coal miners
Aerobics class	
Gymnastics team	

Differences Between Sets of Groups

- High status
- Group identity and distinctiveness
- Individual contribution to a group result (called upon to play a certain role)
- Coordinated action (lateral processes).
- Events surround the group (e.g., dinners, spectators, socials).
- Unpredictable outcomes
- Recreational/fun
- Group usually remains intact over longer periods of time.
- A member can play a variety of roles.

- Guided by work processes (actions are calibrated to something external to the group—e.g., special dress, uniforms, defined roles and procedures).
- Outcomes are predictable (if procedures are followed).
- Impermanence (easy to replace members).
- Low status
- Involves work/labor
- Group dissolves when the "project" is completed.
- A member generally provides a specific service.

*Most representative of set.

bers are supervised; members are eliminated from the group; membership lengths of term are established; members relate to one another; members execute their work effectively; and so on. Teams shouldn't just happen. All of the above concern decisions that must be made as teams are formed.

Three general observations may be made with regard to teams and pay:

(1) Even though the idea of teams connotes a "oneness," having a common stake in some enterprise doesn't mean that everyone

Dimension 3

Example Groups on Dimension

Examples on *One Side of Dimension*	Examples on *Other Side of Dimension*
Family*	Platoon*
Beauty contestants*	Blue Angels
College class*	Board of directors
Chat room*	Math team
Hospice patients*	Firemen
Commune*	House Ways and Means Committee
Religious cult*	Physician's office
Gang members	Bucket brigade
	Members of local chamber
	Lifeguards

Differences Between Sets of Groups

- Emotional ties and connectedness.
- No specific objectives (range of activities and obligations).
- Identity with group persists, even when member is no longer an active part of it (e.g., former beauty contestant).

- Specific objectives
- Common interests and belief systems
- Coalesce at a given time
- Can't withdraw from the group when in action—(otherwise, members may not want to participate; formal means of withdrawal).

*Most representative of set.

should be paid the same, and paying everyone the same won't lead to better outcomes—a baseball team or an orchestra doesn't pay a flat fee for their talent nor would doing so necessarily result in a championship or world-class music. As long as individuals' roles are different within the team, pay should be different.

(2) Many types of teams allow members to make differential contributions to end results. That is, certain members turn out to be more valuable than others. If the pay scheme doesn't recognize these differences (everyone gets the same bonus amount, for instance), then you may end up being the victim of "free ridership." This is when *you* do the work and someone else, who hasn't worked as hard, collects an equal reward.

(3) Some teams aren't really teams at all. They are gaggles of employees assembled in a common area. I refer to these arrange-

ments as "circular sweatshops" because often a company takes production workers (those who manufacture units, process claims, etc.), seats them in a common area (circles are fashionable), measures them on total production by adding up what each person produces individually, and calls them a team. In addition to forty lashes from a supervisor, employees are asked to whip each other into shape as well.

If your pay is distinguishable, your compensation should be distinguished.

Most types of teams in organizations are defined by (1) the goal of the team, (2) its anticipated duration, and (3) the level of involvement required (i.e., part-time or full-time). Ad hoc teams have very specific goals and short time frames and require part-time involvement. On the other hand, product/service/process work teams tend to have broad objectives (e.g., improve service), an ongoing existence, and a full-time, dedicated staff. Project or task teams are somewhere in between.

Chart 10B shows that the more general the goals, the longer the time frame, and the deeper and longer your time commitment to a team, the more

CHART 10B. TEAM PAY

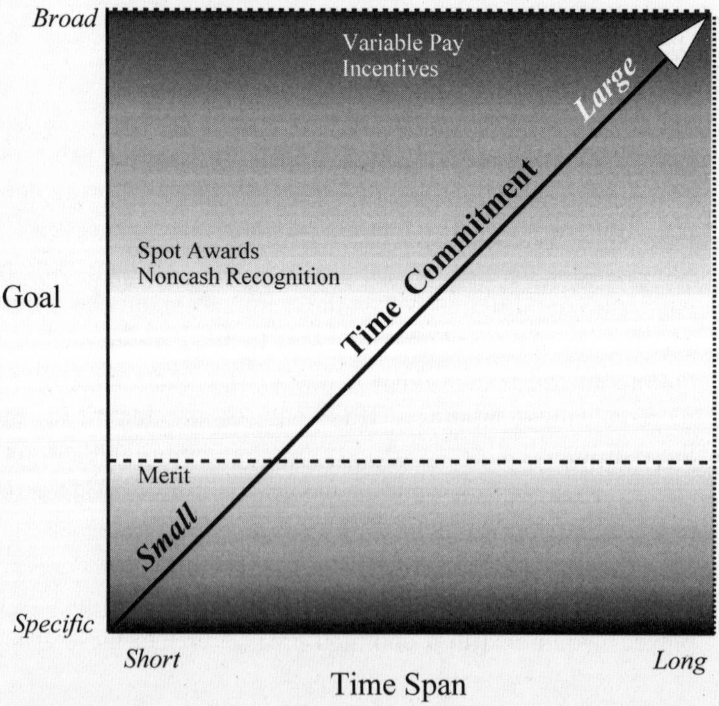

money you will receive through your participation. Permanent, intact, full-time teams (work groups) with a broad ongoing mission and purpose are generally provided with cash incentives (for companies that offer bonuses), much like the awards we discussed in Chapter 8. These awards generally allow team members to share the results of their endeavors when they meet important financial and nonfinancial goals. Sometimes award amounts to group members are modified by each person's individual performance.

Project teams are most often given noncash recognition and special one-time (spot) awards for the successful completion of a project. Finally, there are usually no special rewards for members of short-lived groups that convene on a part-time basis. Maybe they get a thank-you. Maybe.

For more permanent types of teams, a company often wants employees to learn different skills and different jobs within the team. A given team member, then, can play a variety of team roles and can fill in whenever and wherever needed. It's like having a utility infielder or a handyman. This can make the team more flexible and adaptive to changing conditions and needs. It also makes it easier for the company to maintain the right skill mix among team members.

Job rotation and skill-based/knowledge-based pay, then, are sometimes used with teams to encourage workers to develop new skills. With job rotation, in essence, you swap jobs with another person until you have mastered the new set of duties. This job exchange is generally supplemented by on-the-job training.

Skill-based systems reward members for the acquisition of new skills. Sometimes this means earning a certification (given by the company or an external agency) and sometimes it means just showing you can do something that you couldn't do before. In either case, teams provide a great forum for expanding your horizons and learning new skills. You increase your worth with the company's blessing and may even get paid en route to making yourself more valuable.

I will caution you, however, that companies have become increasingly suspicious of rewarding employees for skill acquisition without getting something in return. Wanting a tangible result in exchange for anything has become a corporate reflex. To be fair to companies, programs that rewarded every little skill have often encouraged feeding frenzies in which employees swarmed to skill development like fish to bread. Companies, as a rule, no longer reward employees for every little skill that they may develop.

Other Matters You Should Know About

Overtime

The rules of overtime pay (as well as minimum wage, child labor, and equal pay) are governed by the Fair Labor Standards Act (FLSA) and, for a seemingly straightforward topic, are complex. If you have questions about overtime pay, consult your in-house corporate attorney as a start. You also can call the Department of Labor; there are regional offices that you can contact. I don't want to build your expectations up too high, but when I have had questions, I have always been successful in finding the right person with whom to speak, and that person has been both knowledgeable and polite.

If you are a part of the "nonexempt" workforce, that means that you are not exempt from the overtime rules of FLSA. That is, the rules apply to you and you must receive overtime pay if certain conditions are met. Just because companies call you "nonexempt" or "exempt," however, doesn't necessarily mean that you are. Companies are careful when making these determinations but they are not always right. Now that I think about it, they are not always that careful either. For example, companies have been known to erroneously classify jobs as exempt and end up having to pay back wages for overtime when the error is discovered (i.e., when it is determined that the jobs are really nonexempt and the overtime pay was due all along).

So, if you are a part of the nonexempt workforce and are truly nonexempt, you must receive overtime pay of:

(1) one and one-half times your regular rate of pay,
(2) above 40 hours worked per week (where a week is 7 consecutive calendar days).

The overtime does not have to be paid to you during the week in which it is earned; it is typically incorporated into your usual paycheck that covers the week in which you put in overtime.

Your "regular rate" of pay is determined in a variety of ways depending on how you are paid (hourly, semimonthly, commissions) but all of the methods are designed to figure out what you earn during a work week, and dividing that number by the hours worked to arrive at an hourly rate. What makes this calculation interesting is knowing what gets included in your earnings in determining your regular rate and what does not. Certain types of bonuses must get included in your regular rate calculations. This means that overtime has to be paid on not just your base salary, but you should receive time and a half on your base salary plus bonus. I have seen several employers forget this little fact and retrospectively have to pay back wages. There are most likely employers who still inadvertently overlook certain bonuses in their calculations of overtime.

As an informed employee, you will want to know what counts toward your regular rate, in general. Bonuses based on the following criteria result in a proportionate increase in your overtime pay because they are included in your regular rate:

- accuracy of work
- attendance
- cooperation and courtesy
- efficiency
- length of service
- number of overtime hours worked
- production of either individuals or groups
- quality of work

Any bonuses promised at the time of hire must also be included in the regular rate.

Purely discretionary bonuses do not have to be figured into your regular rate. Discretionary bonuses are those whose payment and payment amounts are solely exercised by the employer where the employer's discretion exists throughout the period covered by the bonus. In appearance, these look and feel a lot like gifts to good, cheerful citizens of the company.

Percentage-of-wage bonuses also do not have to be included in the regular rate as long as the bonuses are based on an employee's total earnings—straight time plus overtime. It doesn't matter what type of bonus it is as long as bonus amounts are allocated on a percentage basis (e.g., certain employee groups get bonuses of x%, other groups get y%, etc.). This rule isn't really an exclusion: Since the bonus is based on total earnings, the overtime worked gets figured into the bonus actually paid.

Certain groups of employees, such as police and firefighters, as well as those who work within hospitals or nursing homes, have their own special overtime rules with which you should become familiar—if you are one of those employees. In addition, although an employer doesn't have to pay an "exempt" employee for overtime, some do. I see this occurring less and less as competition among businesses has become more fierce. I used to see this practice most often in "monopolistic" companies (i.e., those with domestic market share of at least 80%) whose employees were accustomed to "cruising"—putting in their hours, collecting their money, and going home. Anyone who ever had to put in extra time over a threshold of hours above the customary work week (usually five hours above normal working hours) would receive time and a half.

Equal Pay

The Equal Pay Act of 1963 (EPA) is an amendment to the FLSA that says that women who perform substantially the same work as men under similar conditions should be paid no differently from men. It not only pertains to nonexempt employees, but to exempt executive, administrative, and professional employees. State and local government workers are also subject to equal pay laws. In general, women in the workforce earn 75¢ to every dollar earned by men. This represents a substantial increase from just 1980 when the wage differential was around 62¢ to 65¢ on the dollar.

These figures don't necessarily suggest bias: just differences. There may be good reasons why the differences exist. For example, more women may be in lower-paying jobs than men. They may enter the workforce at lower levels, not advance as quickly, and their careers may stall following life events such as childbirth or tending to a sick parent. So the distribution of jobholders of men and women may be like that shown in Chart 10C.

This, of course, raises other possibilities for bias; namely, that women aren't being hired into companies at as high a position as they should, moving up as quickly as they should, or advancing to the level they should before bumping their heads on the "glass ceiling." To overcome this glass ceiling, women often find better opportunities working for a company headed by a woman or a company that has a good representation of women on the board of directors (although gender bias may appear even in these kinds of companies). I have included a list of some of the most powerful women in corporate America as well as major companies with a healthy number of women on the board in Chart 10D.

While there may be reasonable explanations for the differences in the wages of men and women in the country as a whole, on a company-by-company basis there shouldn't be any substantive difference between the pay of men and women doing approximately the same work. If there is, the rate of pay of the disadvantaged group must be increased to match the pay levels of the higher-paid group.

In looking out to make sure you are being treated fairly, you should know that "equality of jobs" is shown if the work performed involves *all* of the following:

(1) equal skill
(2) equal effort, and
(3) equal responsibility
(4) executed under similar conditions

Chart 10C. Distribution of Men and Women in the Workplace

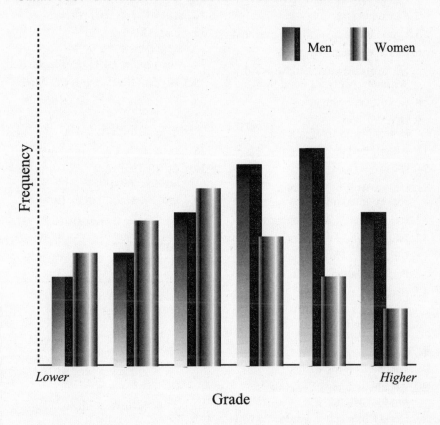

Equal skill. This is demonstrated when jobs require approximately the same level of ability, education, experience, training, and such. There may be trade-offs among these factors such that lesser education may be offset by more experience.

CHART 10D: WOMEN OF INFLUENCE/ COMPANIES WITH WOMEN BOARD MEMBERS

Top Women-Owned and/or -Run Businesses

1. Martha Ingram, Ingram Industries
2. Loida Nicolas Lewis,
   TLC Beatrice International
3. Marian Ilitch,
   Little Ceasar Enterprises
4. Maggie Hardy Magerko,
   84 Lumber
5. Lynda Resnick, Roll International
6. Linda Wachner, Warnaco
7. Liz Minyard/Gretchen Minyard
   Williams, Minyard Food Stores
8. Gay Love, Printpack
9. Donna Karan,
   Donna Karan International
10. Ardath Rodale, Rodale Press
11. Christine Liang, ASI
12. Donna Wolf Steigerwaldt,
    Jockey International
13. Helen Copley, The Copley Press
14. Jenny Craig, Jenny Craig
15. Irma Elder, Troy Motors
16. Patricia Gallup, PC Connection
17. Barbara Levy Kipper,
    Chas. Levy Company
18. Jane O'Dell, Westfall-O'Dell
    Transportation Services
19. Ellen Gordon,
    Tootsie Roll Industries
20. Annabelle Lundy Fetterman,
    Lundy Packing
21. Doris Christopher, Pampered Chef
22. Gertrude Boyle,
    Columbia Sportswear
23. Ebba Hoffman,
    Smead Manufacturing
24. Rachelle Friedman, J&R Music
    and Computer World

25. Kathy Prasnicki Lehne,
    Sun Coast Resources
26. Jill Barad, Mattel
27. Carol Bartz, Autodesk
28. Sally Crawford, Healthsource
29. Estee Lauder, Estee Lauder
30. Ngaire Cuneo, Conseco
31. Jane Hirsh, Copley Pharmaceutical
32. Nancy Pedot, Gymboree
33. Sharon Mates,
    North American Vaccine
34. Amy Lipton, CUC International
35. Charlotte Beers, Ogilvy & Mather
36. Jane Thompson, Sears Roebuck
37. Lois Juliber,
    Colgate-North America
38. Dorrit Bern, Charming Shoppes
39. Christie Hefner,
    Playboy Enterprises
40. Carol St. Mark, Pitney Bowes

Sources: *Working Women*, October 1997, pp. 34–68; *Working Woman*, January 1997, pp. 26–30.

Companies With 4 or More Women on the Board

Avon Products

Aetna

Fannie Mae

Gannett

Golden West Financial

Hasbro

Principal Financial

TIAA/CREF

Source: *The New York Times*, Wednesday, October 1, 1997, p. D11.

Equal Effort. This element of the job is demonstrated by the amount of physical and mental exertion *routinely* needed for the work. It does not necessarily involve the most or highest physical or mental exertion, if that exertion is used infrequently. Moreover, the elements of effort, physical and mental exertion, are additive. The measure of effort is the sum total of these elements.

Equal Responsibility. Responsibility is concerned with the amount of an employee's accountability. When you think of a job's "importance," you are usually thinking about the amount of responsibility contained in that job. There are certain things that can give you greater responsibility:

- being accountable for important end results related to revenues, quality, innovation, etc.
- being at risk of incurring financial loss if one's duties are not performed well.

This is not an exhaustive list but it should give you an idea of what may give one job more responsibility than another.

Working Conditions. Two jobs may be equivalent on all of the dimensions discussed above but still be considered "unequal" because they are performed under dissimilar conditions. Conditions can vary in different ways. First, the general surroundings where a job is performed may differ significantly. If the types of experiences (due to heat, air quality, spatial arrangements, etc.) you encounter in your work setting differ in frequency and/or magnitude from those encountered by someone else in the same job, the jobs will be considered unequal. Conversely, similar surroundings imply similar working conditions.

Certain environments may also present different physical hazards in both frequency and severity. Two jobs that are presented with different hazards are unequal. On the other hand, if two jobs are performed under substantially the same level of hazardous conditions, the jobs will be considered equal if all else about the job is approximately equal.

Equality of work does not necessarily imply equality in pay. Differences in pay may legitimately exist on the basis of seniority, merit, and "incentive system." Incentive systems within the provisions of FLSA are systems that link employees' earnings to the quality or quantity of production. If there are substantial differences in the pay between men and women who occupy the same jobs, and if these differences cannot be explained by factors such as merit, the company has a problem.

When pay equity studies are conducted, the news is seldom good for women. Women who perform work equal to that of men, in general, earn less than men after correcting for possible non–gender-related influences on pay such as merit and time in the job. I have rarely seen women earn more than 90¢ on the dollar to men in studies that have been carefully conducted and statistically controlled. The one exception I have seen involves jobs that call for heavy doses of math/physics. Mathematics seems to be a great equalizer in pay for women.

Most illegitimate differences in pay between men and women can be traced to the first day of work. Women are usually hired at lower rates of pay. I have heard intriguing corporate discussions on companies' social responsibility toward women and starting salaries. If a woman will accept less for similar work than a man, should the company pay less? Is it the social responsibility of the company to pay it or does it make good business sense not to? A woman's willingness to accept less pay upon hire for the same work performed by men is not mentioned by FLSA as a factor that can be used to justify differences in wages.

Don't count on the mere existence of the Equal Pay Act to help you out, though. Companies don't look very hard at pay inequities between men and women. It's a little like peeking in one of your children's closets—you don't usually do it because you are afraid of what you will find.

There are many reasons why a woman may be offered less money than a man for equal work at the time of hire. The theory that I believe has the most merit, however, is the one that says that most hiring supervisors and managers are men and that this fact may make negotiations and settlements more difficult for women. My suggestion? Be firm, be diplomatic, and use the negotiation strategies we discussed earlier in this book. There is no reason why, through sound negotiation tactics, you can't get your starting salary to a more deserving level.

Setting Your Sights

Now that we've walked through the components that all factor into your compensation package at work, I hope you realize two things:

(1) A good part of your recognized worth depends on making a best case for yourself. Companies often don't know what you are worth to them, whether you are a newly hired employee or have been with the company for some time.

To use an analogy, they know what a Mercedes is worth and they know what a Civic is worth—they can look the values up in a guide—but they don't know which one you are until you either tell them what you have "sold for" in the past or what you are willing to accept for your services in the present.

You have to prove which "model" you are. If you leave it to someone else to decide what you are worth, you better have a generous manager. Otherwise, not much will happen.

(2) Your worth is relative. It depends on the job and your skills but also on the time and the place. Two people with the same job descriptions, with the same talents, who work in two different companies of the exact same size can earn significantly different amounts of money. That is because, at the time, the one company may need the person more and will value his or her skills more highly.

We've talked about this in earlier chapters. Let me ask you, "How much is an apple worth?" Two apples that come from the same tree are worth different amounts to a person who is starving and to one who is satiated or who finds fruit distasteful. Similarly, companies that have greater need for a given set of skills will pay a higher price. The recommendation that follows is straightforward: Search for the company that needs your skills the most.

There is only one thing left for you to do. It's time to set a goal for yourself. You know how much you currently make; but where do you want to be? Specify what you realistically believe you should be earning based on what you have learned from this book—based on what you are worth.

And don't stop with naming a goal. You have to formulate a plan as well. What will you do differently that will help you to achieve your goal? Go ahead and develop a detailed strategy in which you describe the specific steps you will take to reach your goals and how you will overcome certain obstacles you foresee along the way. Set your goal, develop a plan, decide how you will deal with potential barriers, and get going.

You should now see the world of compensation as the pros do. Your eyesight might even be better. When you come right down to it, compensation is not that mysterious after all. A company has to pay you something and it tries to pay you what *it thinks* you are worth. It's your job to convince your company that you are worth more and not less, that you are an investment and not a cost, that you are an asset and not a liability, and that you are like a coveted, rare bottle of wine that gets better and more valuable with age.

Chapter 11

Don't Forget Your Benefits

Many employees think of benefits as lists of goodies they get in addition to their pay; they are often considered to be secondary concerns or extras. I want you to think of benefits, however, for what they really are: important complements to your earnings. Benefits represent sizable corporate investments in you. On average, companies spend about $15,000 per employee on benefits (see *ACA News,* June 1997, p. 9), which is equivalent to roughly 30%–40% of your cash compensation.

Benefits can protect your earnings or enhance your earnings in a variety of ways. In one way or another, benefits either help you to keep what you've got or help you to accumulate more. In other words, benefits help you to meet your financial needs at different periods of your life. If you didn't receive benefits from your employer—such as disability or retirement benefits—you'd have to find a way of fulfilling all of your financial needs on your own, using your personal income and savings as the means.

The types of financial needs that benefits can help you with can be classified according to the matrix found in Chart 11A. You can have short-term and long-term (or indefinite) needs. You have needs to protect or replace your income and needs to accumulate wealth through savings.

There is some overlap in benefits programs among the cells in the chart

CHART 11A. MATRIX OF FINANCIAL NEEDS

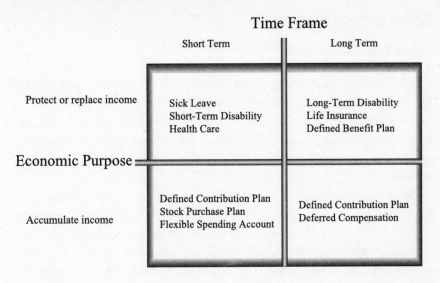

Time Frame

	Short Term	Long Term
Protect or replace income	Sick Leave Short-Term Disability Health Care	Long-Term Disability Life Insurance Defined Benefit Plan
Accumulate income	Defined Contribution Plan Stock Purchase Plan Flexible Spending Account	Defined Contribution Plan Deferred Compensation

Economic Purpose

because a given benefit can fulfill multiple objectives: Certain features of certain benefits allow them to fulfill more than one financial need over the course of your employment tenure. It is important to use your employer's benefits programs wisely in association with benefits you may purchase outside of your employer in order to prevent gaps or shortfalls in coverages and to preserve, as best as possible, your quality of life.

A financial planner, or a professional who serves that role for you, such as your accountant or brother-in-law, can help you to maximize your benefits dollars and minimize your risks from the vicissitudes of life. Most people plan on an "as is" basis, forgetting that life sometimes throws some curves. What if you die or become disabled? What if you face a major (and expensive) health problem? What if you lose or change jobs? Will your income and savings be preserved under these conditions? You see, benefits can help you to maintain your income and savings, and to enhance your lifestyle if you are smart about it. The first smart thing you can do is this: Don't ask your brother-in-law for advice.

Benefits Programs

Short-Term Protection

Sick Leave and Short-Term Disability. Companies will generally pay you for days you are unable to work due to injury or sickness. These plans will pay you all or a portion of your salary for a specified period of time, usually around twenty-six weeks. If you are still unable to work at that time, your benefit is extended but covered under the provisions of long-term disability.

Many companies have "waiting periods" for coverage, meaning that upon hire, you'll have to wait a certain period of time before you become eligible for benefits. At least half of all companies you come across that offer salary continuance for sickness or injury will make you wait at least one month and sometimes as long as six months before coverage begins. That means, aside from the few sick days you will be permitted by your employer at full pay, you will have to foot the bill for longer incidences of absence during the early months of your employment. If you can't afford to do that, and you are insurable, insurance companies have "bridge" policies that will enable you to insure your risk on a short-term basis—until you are eligible for your employer's program.

The extent of your coverage mostly will depend upon your years of service. In general, either the length of your coverage and/or the magnitude of your coverage increases with the number of years you spend with your employer. With long service records (e.g., twenty years or longer), you often will reach twenty-six weeks of leave at full pay. Until that time, you will receive a combination of full and partial pay for a period of time (e.g., twenty-six weeks).

Partial pay is usually 60%–66⅓% of your usual income. Most people can get by on reduced income for thirteen to twenty-six weeks because their cost of living, without work, won't be as great. They won't be getting out much or entertaining; they won't have transportation costs associated with commuting; they won't have much need to buy lunches or new clothes, etc.

Health Care. The one surefire way to have your income ravaged is to need health insurance and not have it. I have spoken with hundreds of employers about their health care benefits for employees and there is near uniform agreement that employees underappreciate the value of this benefit and do *not* use it responsibly. Their concern is understandable when you consider that group health coverage costs roughly between $5,000 and $7,500 in premiums per family per year ($1,500 to $2,500 per employee per year). It would cost you more to find a comparable benefit on your own; employers work hard to find the highest quality of health care at the best price. Really.

Let's begin our excursion into health care with a quick review of the alphabet soup of health care:

- Traditional Indemnity (or fee-for-service) Plan: This is the type of plan everyone used to have. You go to any doctor and any hospital and pay a fee for the services rendered; you pay a deductible and usually 20% of charges thereafter.
- Health Maintenance Organization (HMO): From a network of doctors, you select a primary care physician who oversees your care including referrals to specialists within the network.
- Point of Service Plan (POS): You have access to an established network of physicians, but, for a price, can go outside of the network; sometimes you can go outside the network at your own choosing and sometimes you must get a referral from an in-network physician.
- Preferred Provider Organization (PPO): Again, this is a network of doctors who perform services for plan members at a discounted rate; you can generally see any doctor within the plan at your own discretion.

The latter three types of plans are part of the "managed care" landscape. Don't expect this landscape to change any time soon; managed care has become increasingly entrenched. By now you've heard the joke about the managed care doctor who died and went to heaven but was only allowed to stay twenty-four hours. I'll not betray my biases on health care; I will say, however, that it remains a system in disrepair—something you may already know.

I have provided a taxonomy of managed care plans in Chart 11B. The taxonomy is based on the way employees generally experience managed care. There is a network of doctors. Either there is a "gatekeeper" primary care physician (a PCP: a doctor you must see before seeing specialists within the network) or there isn't; and either you can go outside the network or you can't. Many companies will give you a choice among these types of plans. The ability to go outside the network and to sidestep a primary care physician will cost you more money if you make these elections.

CHART 11B. TYPES OF MANAGED CARE PLANS

Network Conditions

	Can't Go Outside Network	Can Go Outside of Network
Gatekeeper	Traditional HMO	Point of Service
No Gatekeeper	Preferred Provider Organization	Point of Service

Gatekeeper Conditions

Employees are usually interested in three items related to health care: cost, coverage and choice—"the three C's." One of the most pervasive trends in health care has been for employers to shift more of the premium costs to employees. A majority of employers now expect employees to contribute to health care premiums, usually between 15% and 25% of the total cost. Cost shifting from employer to employee has been most pronounced among smaller companies, those with fewer than 200 employees. At the same time, employees in small establishments are *not* getting the other two "C's" discussed below. Cost shifting also has been more pronounced in the retail and service industries, and less pronounced in high technology and manufacturing.

Overall, whereas health care used to be free to about 3 out of 4 workers in companies of 100 or more workers in 1980, today it's free to only about 1 in 3 (*Wall Street Journal,* October 24, 1997, p. R9). In addition, to contain costs, companies have been increasing deductibles (the part you pay for medical expenses before an insurer begins to share the burden) in plans where they are applicable. Deductibles that became as low as $100 as a corporate norm have sprung back up to $200 to $500. This is reasonable given that the fundamental purpose of health care coverage is to protect you from financial ruin in the event of a catastrophic illness.

The issue of choice of doctor remains one of the biggest to employees. If you have developed a trusting relationship with your physician, you won't want to give it up easily. Several types of medical plans, such as indemnity plans, allow you to see whatever physician you like. Others require that you see a doctor within the insurer's network of physicians. Some plans allow you to go outside the network to the doctor of your choice for an extra charge.

With respect to coverages, in addition to the typical hospital and medical coverages, most employees look for the extras that can make a big financial difference. Does your plan include the following?

- Dental
- Prescription
- Preventive care
- Vision

These add-ons can save you a bundle. All of these, especially preventive care, have become prevalent through managed care plans. Unfortunately, the recently enacted Mental Health Parity Act will not substantially improve your mental health benefits—loopholes and possible employer exemptions will assure the second-class status of these benefits.

"Portability" rules that took effect in 1998 make it easier to move from company to company without fear of losing coverage due to uninsurability. You should be familiar with these new regulations. In general, an employee who switches from one company to another cannot be denied coverage. You may still have to wait until preexisting conditions are covered, but that wait will be shorter with the new laws (the maximum wait is one year). The period of time you were covered for a health condition under your old plan can be used to decrease your wait under the new plan. Also, since 1985 under "COBRA" rules, you have been allowed to extend health care coverage for eighteen months at the group rates plus 2% after you leave an employer. If you will be without employer-sponsored health coverage for a brief period of time (i.e., you are in between employment gigs), you may consider this option.

Finally, a healthy number of employers still offer retiree medical coverage, though the numbers are waning. If you are lucky enough to get in while the getting is good, more power to you. You'll have the benefit of good coverage at a time in your life when you will need it the most.

Long-Term Protection—Income Replacement

If you have sick leave, salary continuation, and health care plans, your income should be fairly well protected in the short-term. But you will also have to protect your income in the long run.

Long-Term Disability. But what if you have an illness or injury that keeps you away from work for an extended period of time (over a year)? What then? You will need to have your income replaced while you are out of work. That is the role of long-term disability, a much underappreciated benefit since most people believe they will never need it. Most people are right. But it comes in handy when you do need it: It's the way to pay the bills and keep the house. These plans usually pick up where short-term coverages (e.g., sick leave plans) end, after about three months and will pay 60–66⅓% of your income for a specific period of time. These plans can be a little tricky so here are some things you should think about:

(1) What is your company's definition of disability? Some companies have very stringent definitions that basically say as long as you can work at anything, you are not disabled. Some companies have definitions of disability that are more favorable to you: As long as you can't perform activities for which you are suitably trained, you are "disabled."

(2) Does the disability coverage amount include bonus payments in the calculations? If you have grown accustomed to living on the "extras" of compensation such as bonuses and those bonuses aren't factored into your disability payments, you may have a shortfall on your living expenses. Some companies will allow you to purchase extra coverage.

(3) How long does the coverage last? It would be nice if coverage lasted to your age sixty-five; payments then would continue under rules governing disability through Social Security. Nevertheless, some plans have shorter durations in which benefits are paid (five years would not be out of the ordinary).

Life Insurance. Life insurance is a great product. If your spouse is dependent on your retirement benefit when you get older but you die young, how will those retirement benefits be funded? Life insurance. If you are busy saving for a child's education but you die before you've saved enough, how will your children go to college? Life insurance. If your income is needed to pay the mortgage and your income vanishes with your death, how will the bills you leave behind get paid? Life insurance.

Life insurance is an amazingly flexible product that can make sure your wishes are carried out after you're gone—both your short- and long-term wishes. The purpose of life insurance is to (a) settle your estate and (b) fund financial goals such as education for young children. Unfortunately, many people never think about how much life insurance they will have to have in order to attend to all of their postmortem needs.

Most employers offer employees group term life insurance for one to two times their salary. Some minimum amounts are often extended to members of the employee's family. These coverages are generally employer paid. Sometimes you will be given the option of paying for extra coverages for yourself and other family members.

The questions you should ask yourself with respect to life insurance are:

(1) Can you obtain all the coverage you need from your employer, or do you need to supplement your coverage on your own?
(2) Will you be able to obtain the coverage you need if conditions change; if you change jobs or decide to work for yourself, will you be insurable?

A financial planner can help you decide how much coverage you need and how to prevent lapses or holes in coverage.

Defined Benefit Plans. Long-term disability plans replace your income over a prolonged period due to sickness or illness. Defined benefit plans, or pension plans, replace your income over a prolonged period of time when you retire.

There are two major types of "retirement" plans: defined benefit (pension) and defined contribution plans; there also are certain types of plans where this distinction is blurred. Defined benefit plans provide a fixed benefit amount upon retirement, and the company makes actuarially determined contributions in your behalf (most pension plans are employer paid) to make sure you get what you are owed when it is due. Because these plans obligate companies to make regular and substantial contributions to your account, their enthusiasm for these plans has declined over the past fifteen years. I never hear an employer wanting to introduce such a plan anymore.

"Old" companies, like transportation and utilities, "well-to-do" companies like petroleum companies, and government are most likely to have pension plans.

For defined benefit plans, years of service and your average earnings over the last three to five years before retirement are important. This is a big reason to get your income up as high as it can go: It will affect your income in your retirement. It also says that while job hopping has some advantages, helping you in retirement isn't one of them. To avoid a meager retirement, you need a good retirement income. Social Security helps a little but not much. Here's a prediction. If you accumulate a certain amount of wealth in your lifetime, don't count on seeing a Social Security benefit. You need good corporate retirement benefits and/or you need to save as well.

One more thing. Pension calculations at retirement are sometimes incorrect. When there are errors, they are usually underestimates. In a recent study, the Pension Benefits Guaranty Corp. showed that 8.2% of employees who took pension benefits in lump sums were underpaid. Of these, one in three were underpaid by at least 10% (*USA Today,* June 16, 1997, p. 1A). There is nothing intentional here. It happens because of the types of data mistakes that are made. There is a simple remedy. Make sure the information being used to compute your retirement income is correct. There are three areas where mistakes are most likely to be made:

(1) the interest rate used in calculations
(2) the employee's age
(3) the number of years an employee has worked

Short Term—Accumulate Income

Defined Contribution Plans. This is the other major type of retirement plan. Unlike defined benefit plans in which payments are made to get you to a particular retirement income level (ideal for older workers who don't have much time to save), defined contribution plans take in money and, over time, accumulate in value (ideal for younger employees who have longer to save). There are several types of defined contribution plans that allow you to save good sums of money over the long run with the help of your employer and the Internal Revenue Service. Most of these plans are intended to supplement your retirement income, but vesting rules and certain plan provisions make it possible to get at your money sooner.

The basics of these plans are easy: save, invest, and wait. The sooner you begin to save, the better off you will be. Did you know that if you saved $2,000 for five years during your twenties (and then stopped saving) you'd still have more money in retirement (at 7% interest) than waiting the five years and saving $2,000 *every year* to your retirement? Start now! That is the way defined contribution plans work: You put money into a plan to the extent permissible and let time and the financial markets do their work. Over time, you'll have quite a nest egg and quite possibly be a millionaire. You would be surprised just how many "defined contribution millionaires" there are. For example, of the 870,000 retirement accounts managed by T. Rowe Price, over 300 are for more than $1 million (*Wall Street Journal,* July 7, 1997, p. A1).

The most common versions of defined contribution plans are 401(k), profit sharing, and money purchase plans, with 401(k) plans the most ubiquitous of the bunch. If a 401(k) plan substantially invests its assets (your money) into your company's stock, it may qualify as an Employee Stock Ownership Plan. The parallel defined contribution plans for nonprofit organizations and government entities are 403(b) and Section 457 plans (deferred compensation), respectively.

You, and often your employer, contribute to these plans on a pretax basis. That means you don't pay tax on a part of your income; the tax is deferred until you take your money out. If you contribute $10,000 to a plan (which is the most you can contribute to a 401(k) plan during 1998, although most companies set lower limits) and 25% of your income normally goes to taxes, the government is loaning you $2,500 (25% of the $10,000) to invest in your future.

Also, companies will often contribute to your plan or make matching contributions (of a certain amount, such as 50¢ for every dollar you contribute) to your plan in your behalf. This is income, folks! You just can't put it in your pocket immediately. But you can do everything else with it—you can look at it (on paper) and count it. Companies want you to participate in these plans. Your executives want you to participate in these plans; the amount that higher-paid employees can contribute depends on how much non–highly paid employees contribute. Nevertheless, whereas two out of three highly compensated employees who are eligible for defined contribution plans such as 401(k)s, contribute, only about one in three eligible, non–highly compensated employees contribute.

The companies with the best 401(k) plans are AlliedSignal, Chrysler,

Citibank, DuPont, and Ford (*USA Today,* November 24, 1997, p. 3B). Three key components of these plans make one plan better than another:

(1) your company allows higher employee contributions so you can defer and invest as much as the IRS will permit

(2) your company matches contributions—50 cents on the dollar would be normal and a dollar for dollar match would be great

(3) your company keeps the match in effect for a higher percentage of your contribution—it would be typical for your company to match the first 6% of your pay, above that would be gravy

One thing that can be worrisome in these plans, and especially in the kindred 403(b) and Section 457 plans for nonprofits and municipalities, is the fees attached to them. These include management investment fees, marketing and advertising expense fees (12b-1 fees), and for insurance products, mortality expense charges. Most companies perform due diligence in plan selection in an attempt to get you the plan with the highest returns at the lowest costs. But don't be oblivious to what's going on around you. A 1% difference in fees, all else being equal, is money out of your pocket in retirement. Take the time to educate yourself on the fee structure and returns of your plan; these are publicized in the prospectuses associated with your plan's investment choices.

If you are young and not worried about retirement, start worrying. Government safety nets may be way gone by the time you reach retirement age (these are insufficient now anyway). If your cash flow allows, you should take full advantage of these plans. One piece of advice routinely given by benefits managers with whom I spoke with regard to these plans was: "Start early and contribute as much as you can." A recent study by the accounting firm, KPMG, showed non–highly compensated employees contribute about 2% less of their income to these plans than highly compensated employees (*Wall Street Journal,* August 21, 1997, p. C1).

The money you put into a plan is always yours, whether or not you choose to stay with your employer. The amount the company puts in is subject to "vesting" schedules, usually linked to your time of service. Most employees "vest" with five years of service or less.

Most plans allow loans and withdrawals. Withdrawals may be subject to penalties, so be careful. It's the loan feature that makes these plans short-term savings vehicles. They are not the best short-term vehicles because it will cost you money to use the money from these plans. But the loans are low interest and if you have big expenses coming like a college education, they may be better than the alternatives.

These plans also generally offer you a number of investment options, typically in various types of mutual funds. There is a range of options with which you are presented: high growth stocks, blue chip stocks, bond funds, balanced (stock and bond) portfolios, and money market funds. If you have time on your side (ten years or more), go for the stocks. They generally outperform other investments over the long run. Thirty-year-old employees think they are being safe when they invest half of their money in bonds and half in stock. Do you know what a 2% difference per annum investment return makes over a thirty-five-year period, assuming $2,000 is invested per year? Over $425,000! That's the difference between an average performing stock portfolio and an average performing bond portfolio. Many investment advisers suggest putting your money in stock in your younger years and, as you approach retirement, gradually moving money over to more stable investments.

One common problem with your investment options may be lack of diversification. Mutual funds offer diversification within investment categories (e.g., growth stocks) by investing assets in many companies across industries. But some companies invest more than 50% of all of your money in your company's stock. I have included a list of prominent companies that heavily invest defined contribution dollars in its own stock in Chart 11C.

Some companies make investments in your own company the only investment option. These plans usually allow you to diversify into other investments as you approach retirement (usually by age fifty-five). The problem, of course, with these plans and another specific type of plan that makes you a company owner (an Employee Stock Ownership Plan), ready or not, is that it puts a lot of your eggs in one corporate basket. If the basket doesn't remain solvent—a viable economic entity—you lose. I suggest you write to the head of your benefits program if you want greater investment options.

There is another side to lack of diversification. If you work for the right company, you'll do much better than the market in general. You'll do better than you could ever dream of doing.

Stock Purchase Plans. When I asked benefits consultants and benefits managers what employees should look for in a benefits program, a number of them zeroed in on this benefit—stock purchase plans.

Stock purchase plans, although not pervasive in corporate America, are

Chart 11C. Companies Heavily Invested in Their Own Stock

Banc One

Bell Atlantic

Cooper Tire & Rubber

Walt Disney

FMC

Ford Motor

McDonald's

Pacific Gas & Electric

Reynolds Metals

Rockwell International

William Wrigley

Weyerhaeuser

Note: The companies listed have more than 50% of their 401(k)
or profit-sharing assets invested in their own stock.

Source: *The Wall Street Journal*, July, 15, 1996, p. C1.

straightforward (most plans are subject to the qualifying rules of Section 423 of the Internal Revenue Code). These plans enable you to purchase your employer's stock at a discount through payroll deduction. Typically, you purchase the shares during a "purchase period" (often three months or one year). The shares are normally purchased at a 10% to 15% discount based upon the stock price at the beginning or at the end of the purchase period, or the lower of the two. This is a great return on your investment! Furthermore, you are not taxed on your purchase until you dispose of the stock—an event which you now control.

Flexible Spending Accounts. Flexible spending accounts allow you to pay for unreimbursed medical expenses (typically any item that the IRS would consider to be tax deductible, such as co-payments, glasses, dental care, prescription drugs, crutches, etc.) and child care costs with "pretax" dollars. The medical and child care accounts are generally financed with your money through salary deduction. Companies generally allow you to reserve up to $5,000 for each account on a use-it-or-lose-it basis.

If you have estimated, for example, that you will have unreimbursed medical expenses of $5,000 and child care expenses of $5,000, without flexible spending it will cost you the $10,000. With flexible spending, it costs $10,000 minus your tax savings because this money isn't taxable. If you pay 25% of your income in taxes, you will save $2,500! This isn't paper money. It's real money that is now yours courtesy of our government.

Most major employers offer flexible spending accounts. They are not that costly to set up or that expensive to administer. The cost is small, the benefit to you is great. If you don't have one where you are, why don't you volunteer to run a task force to investigate starting one at your company? There are plenty of benefits professionals around who have this benefit who would be willing to share their expertise and experience with you.

Long Term—Income Accumulation

We have already discussed how a lifetime of savings in plans such as 401(k)s can make you very wealthy later in life. Deferred compensation plans, generally available only to the upper crust, can help you quite a lot as well.

Deferred Compensation. This is one of my favorites. Nonqualified deferred compensation is an amazingly flexible pay delivery mechanism that can be good for companies and good for employees. ("Nonqualified" means these plans, if structured properly, are *not* subject to most ERISA guidelines—the Employee Retirement Income Security Act). Unfortunately, none of us is likely to be a part of one in our lifetime; they are mostly confined to executives, although they may be used for a select group of management or highly compensated employees.

My purpose, then, is to acquaint you with deferred compensation so that you know it exists and to teach you a few good words to use in the corporate hallway. There are two general varieties of deferred compensation. First, there are "top-hat" or "nonqualified salary reduction" plans that allow executives to postpone receipt of a portion of their income such as salary and bonus. The traditional reason for doing this was to give executives a means of shifting income to a period in their life (retirement) when they will need it more and be taxed less. The primary question for those who have an option of deferring portions of their salary and/or bonus is, "Does it make sense to do so?" One argument is to *not* defer but to pay taxes on your income at ordinary tax rates and invest what you could have deferred in long-term securities; under present tax laws, the gains from these securities will eventually be taxed at the lower 20% capital gains rate. This strategy says, then, "Pay your dues now so you can benefit later."

Of course, this strategy hinges on two crucial facts: that you will actually invest your "leftover" money, and that years from now the government will still allow the beneficial tax treatment of this money. For many employees, deferral of income may still make economic sense even though the money will eventually be taxed at a higher rate. The reason involves the magic of deferral which permits your money to grow unencumbered by taxes. If the investment returns are large enough and the deferral period long enough, this might be the most advantageous approach.

The second type of deferred compensation arrangement is known as a "salary continuation plan" of which the most prominent versions are Retirement Benefit Restoration Plans and SERPs (Supplemental Executive Retirement Plans). I told you you'd learn some good jargon!

Because executives make so much money, there has to be a way to pay them more. This is one way. Actually, there are restrictions to how much money executives are able to save for retirement through *qualified* plans. In order to preserve the same lifestyle in retirement that you enjoy while working, a certain percent of your working income must be replaced in retirement. Depending on your lifestyle, the ratio can vary but 75% would be a good starting estimate. This percentage represents how much money you'll need in retirement compared to your income as you approach retirement. There are many ways of setting these plans up, but the premise is the same: to provide added compensation to executives in retirement to make up for money they are unable to receive through traditional retirement plans because of limits imposed by our government.

One curiosity of these plans is that they are typically "unfunded." That means that your company is making a *promise* to pay you in the future; any money it chooses to save is not being specifically saved in your behalf. The money remains at the fingertips of the general creditors of the company. That means that in the event of a change for the worse in your company's fortune, everyone will start diving for the money and poor little you will be way back at the end of the line. If you think your company will be solvent a few years from now, don't worry about it. (Some companies will purchase surety bonds to protect the promise to pay in case the employer defaults.)

But buying protection against declining corporate fortunes won't help you in other ways; and we all know that promises can be broken. Company promises can be broken in two ways:

- change of heart ("Sorry, I changed my mind.")
- change in control ("Sorry, it's not my promise to keep anymore.")

What kind of world is this? Because rabbis understand the foibles of man, a rabbi came up with the idea of creating an irrevocable trust that will protect your assets in case of change of heart and change in control. You guessed it; this trust is called a Rabbi Trust. When the assets of deferred compensation plans are stored in this trust, you will have protection from management's change of heart or from the company's change in control.

That's all you need to know for now. If you are ever fortunate enough to be included in one of these plans that's terrific because it means one of two things: (a) you are making a lot of money and/or (b) your company really wants to make sure you stay with them. Not bad either way.

Other Benefits

Vacation and Holidays. My family has had the pleasure of sponsoring foreign students in our home over the years. At the conclusion of their stay, I invariably ask, "So, what did you think of the United States?" After a year of living together, our guests no longer feel compelled to beat around the bush: "You people are maniacs!" They are alluding to the alarming lack of time off from work as well as robust work days that leave little room for good, old-fashioned socializing.

The table in Chart 11D speaks to our guests' points of reference when it comes to vacation. The U.S. gives new employees two weeks vacation when they start and adds one week to that for about every five years of service. In addition, Americans get eleven holidays, on average. Three of those days are usually "floaters." These are days that you can use to celebrate or observe occasions or events that are special to you.

One emerging trend is to create a pool of days (vacation plus holidays plus sick days) and throw them into a bucket. With the exception of nationally observed holidays, you can use any of these days for whatever reason you want. The problem for you is that this doesn't expand how much time you have off. It just says the company no longer cares how you spend your time. In fact, you can now tend to elderly parents, sick children, and everything else going on in your life by using your vacation days. Companies want to discourage the "call in sick at the last minute" routine.

CHART 11D. VACATION DAYS

Country	Days off for employees on the job one year
Austria	30 days
Brazil	30 days
Finland	25 days
Norway	25 days
Sweden	25 days
Germany	24 days
Britain	22 days
Australia	20 days
Netherlands	20 days
Switzerland	20 days
Colombia	15 days
Canada	10 days
Japan	10 days
United States	10 days
Mexico	6 days

Source: *New York Times*, May 11, 1997, F12.

General Trends

Recently, a group of human resource and employee benefits professionals listed the ten most significant employee benefits innovations over the past ten years (*Human Resource Executive,* May 6, 1997, p. 48). They are:

- managed care: Less than half of all employees have the old indemnity plans that were standard ten years ago.
- wellness and health promotion: This includes health screening, lifestyle classes, and fitness centers.
- flexible spending accounts: Enables employees to be proactive in dealing with medical and child care costs by reserving funds for these expenses on a pretax basis.

- employee assistance programs: counseling and referral services for mental health related issues (including substance abuse)
- casual dress: Since IBM went casual, so has everyone else; be aware, however, that those knit blends that conform to your body's curves and shape aren't as useful for covering flaws as your wool suit!
- retirement cash balances: the rise of defined contribution (or hybrid defined contribution/defined benefit plans) that offer a myriad of investment options
- domestic partner benefits: Employees in higher education and in the public sector lead the way; these benefits generally extend health care benefits to unmarried partners regardless of the gender configuration.
- employee self-service: greater automation of benefits information and more ready access to your benefits information
- managed disability: Principles of managed care are being extended to disability (and worker's compensation) claims.
- Internet access: online benefits descriptions

Benefits trends to look for in the near future fall into three categories:

(1) better and more information/communication: Companies are trying to make learning about the benefits program as easy and as painless as possible for you. One of your responsibilities is to know what is available to you so you can take advantage.

(2) more choices: Lifestyle-oriented benefits, in particular, will continue to grow in popularity; these include child care, home purchase assistance, discounts to cultural programs, sabbaticals, etc.; also, there will be increased emphasis on letting employees pick and choose benefits from a menu of choices depending on an employee's unique needs.

(3) greater portability: An even more mobile workforce will want it to be as easy as possible to have continuity of benefits across companies.

Given that benefits account for such a large portion of your total remuneration and that they are so vital to your current and future welfare and lifestyle, take a hard, comparative look at the benefits program when you are making decisions about your job and career.

Chapter 12

Money Isn't Everything

What's the difference between a chain gang and a corporation? On a chain gang you get to work outside (*Fortune,* February 3, 1997, p. 113). What's the difference between a modern family and a corporation? Corporations still have picnics. Longer hours, hard work, declining time spent among family members: If you feel like you are working harder, longer, and for less, and feel your spare time being squeezed ever tighter, you are not alone. More people are pressed for time and find it difficult doing all but the essentials of life, such as eating and sleeping. A neighborly game of horseshoes in the backyard seems a relic of the past except in quaint little places where the present hasn't quite caught up.

In this chapter, we'll first explore some emerging trends in the workplace and what they might mean to your paycheck. Then we will review what people like yourself consider to be of value in the workplace besides money and how much those nonmonetary factors count toward your total "compensation." Finally, I'll ask you to weigh the "quantity" of your workplace (i.e., the compensation you receive) with the "quality" of your workplace (i.e., how much you enjoy being where you are, doing what you do). This will put you in a better position to balance what your mental wellbeing and continuing sanity are worth compared to how much you are paid.

How much in satisfaction are you willing to trade off for more money? Conversely, how much money are you willing to give up for a better place to work and a more fulfilling job?

What's Happening at Work

General Trends

There are many trends affecting the workplace, but two stand out:

- more women in the workplace and more dual-income families (driven by high divorce rates and the need for two paychecks, respectively)
- the rise of alternative work arrangements such as temporary services

Changing patterns of work have created all kinds of intrigue, finger-pointing, and accusations. Part-timers feel abused by full-timers; full-timers feel they have to pick up slack from uncommitted part-timers; younger male executives envy the pampered existence of a traditional lifestyle of older male executives—in nicely pressed white shirts; women think they are not given equal opportunity for pay or advancement; singles or childless couples believe they are asked to perform a disproportionate amount of work so those with family responsibilities can go home; marrieds with children believe they are competitively disadvantaged for lack of corporate face time due to family obligations; and on and on. You get the picture. The workplace is not as simple or predictable as it used to be.

There are elements of truth in all of this. Consider the fact that there are more women in the workforce now than in any other period in modern times. Fueled by both genuine and perceived need for two incomes, over 80% of married couples have both husband and wife in the workforce. This trend has created great pressure on family members to try to be at two places at one time. I know many employees who bring their work to swim meets, who dictate letters while on a treadmill, who bring their kids to work on weekends, who pay their bills on the commuter train, who study after the kids go to bed, who work through lunch, who leave voice-mail messages at night, who wake at 3:00 A.M. to start their day, etc.

The issue of family is an important one with big implications for pay. A recent study (reported in the March 1997 *Fortune*) found that husbands with nonworking spouses (versus husbands with working spouses) earn more—about 30% more—and are promoted more often. Nonworking spouses are able to manage the household and attend to social events (like throw a party) that can promote goodwill with the spouse's superiors and ultimately promote their spouse's careers. As a sociological observation on cultural transitions to fewer stay-at-home spouses, it seems safe to say that the party is a dying animal. Work parties have become brief assemblages of people making cameo appearances in between work and family.

Most working couples can attest to the fact that it takes money to make money. Sending both spouses to work adds to child care, transportation, clothing, and food expenses. The findings reported above suggest that you may not be gaining much economic ground given the additional costs of dual careers and the possible slowing of your salary because of the diversions associated with managing the household. But, then again, there are many reasons to work besides money.

Companies can help you and your family in a number of ways. Overall, they can display tolerance of people who have competing needs. It is one thing to hold back the pay and career progress of those who cannot devote all of their time and attention to work; it is quite another to punish them for having these needs.

Second, companies may specifically help you by providing the following:

- on-site child care assistance or back-up child care for emergencies
- elder-care assistance for aging parents and relatives,
- on-site summer camps
- valet services for dry cleaning, groceries, and gifts
- fitness centers
- paid and unpaid leaves of absence
- flexible hours and scheduling, including telecommuting

Some companies have even gone so far as to build public schools on their premises (e.g., American Bankers Insurance, see *Forbes,* November 18, 1996, p. 165) and to send a "concierge" to an employee's house to wait for a delivery or service hook-ups (e.g., cable, telephone). Increasingly, companies resemble the old city-state, fashionable in the early years of industrialization. Companies like Colt and Hershey built complexes where employees lived and worked. The workplace was the community and the community was the workplace.

I have provided a list of companies that are generally recognized as family-friendly in Chart 12A. They not only offer family-friendly programs but employees feel they are able to use the benefits without adverse consequences to their careers. This is an essential point to consider if you are looking for a family-friendly organization: Many companies tout their programs but either discourage their use or structure work in a way that use is nearly impossible. A company I recently visited talked about its wonderful flexible scheduling and telecommuting benefits. At the same

CHART 12A. BUSINESSWEEK'S 1996 TOP FAMILY-FRIENDLY COMPANIES

• DuPont
• Eddie Bauer
• Eli Lilly
• First Tennessee Bank
• Hewlett Packard
• Marriott International
• MBNA America Bank
• Merrill Lynch
• Motorola
• Unum Life Insurance

Source: *BusinessWeek*, September 16, 1996, pp. 74 ff.
Note: The companies above were determined to have the best programs that are readily and fearlessly used by employees.

time, the company wanted people on-site at particular times. Needless to say, this schizophrenic approach to "family-friendly" yielded very low usage rates.

Flexible scheduling options have been lifesavers for some and empty promises for others. There is an entire milieu of scheduling possibilities that is intended to help employees gain control over their time. One type of schedule allows employees to set their arrival and departure times within certain boundaries. For example, employees can arrive at any time between 7:00 A.M. and 9:00 A.M. and leave between 3:00 P.M. and 5:00 P.M. as long as an eight-hour day is worked. Most companies like to know when employees will be at work so they ask employees to declare the schedule that best fits their needs.

There has to be some give-and-take in this form of scheduling since everyone can't leave at 3:00 P.M. Someone has to stay to answer the phone. The best way this form of scheduling can work is to alternate times among you and your fellow employees rather than sticking the one person who has absolutely no personal life with the late shift.

Shortened work weeks are alternatives for some. Again, these schedules have to be coordinated among employees, but it gives you the opportunity to concentrate your work on three or four days, with the remaining time as free. Appointments, deliveries, and miscellaneous chores can be handled during the free day.

Under a split-shift arrangement, you work a set number of hours, take a few hours off, then work the remaining number of hours. It's like taking a siesta. The problem with this schedule is that companies often "invite" employees to work the time they are scheduled to be off. So this scheduling, in essence, becomes an unsplit, split shift.

The problem with flexible scheduling arrangements, in general, is that they often conflict with the needs of the business. Everyone's heart is in the right place but it is difficult to get all of the people in all of the right spots at the right times when employees are coming and going at different times. This is a way of saying that many companies advertise and promote flexible scheduling, but only a few pull it off. If you ask the company about the extent to which they actually practice what they preach—very few. Before you commit to an organization on the basis of its "scheduling flexibility," make sure you will really have the options suggested.

Alternative Job Arrangements

If you want flexibility in order to juggle your many responsibilities, you often have to rely on the actual configuration of the "job": where you work, who you work for, how many hours you work, and how you choose to spend your working time. In terms of quality of work life, the employees I spoke with over the past few years covet flexibility in their work regimen more than ever in order to manage some form of life outside of work.

Telecommuting. In this Age of Information, the leading contender of timesaving ideas is to skip the commute and work with your screaming kids, meter readers, home repair workers, phone and door-to-door solicitors, and jackhammering road crews right in the comfort of your own home. Despite the rhetoric, a tiny percentage of our population "telecommutes." Most of us still auto-commute, or train-commute, taxing our congested national infrastructure to the limits.

To understand how far we really are from a telecommunicating culture, here's a brief conversation I was recently party to:

EMPLOYEE: "I would like to work at home a day or two per week."
SUPERVISOR: "How will I know you're working?"
EMPLOYEE: "How do you know I'm working now?"
SUPERVISOR: "Why *not,* then!?"

Telecommunicating often doesn't work because of lack of trust between employees and supervisors and because, as a medium, a phone wire or cable still isn't as good as face-to-face contact. Telecommuting can also be isolating, reserved for those few who like being isolated. That's good news to the other employees of the company since they generally want people who like to be isolated, to be isolated.

Of course, you can always go "hoteling." This is when you don't work anywhere in particular but can drop by the "office" at designated times and it will be ready for you. Someone will put the picture of the wife and kids out on the desk and fix up the office as if they really cared you would be there. Since they really don't, you usually get a cubicle and a computer—just for you. Just for the time reserved.

Part-time. The big trend in alternative work arrangements is toward the use of part-timers. There is no universal definition for "part-time." Trivially, it refers to an employee of the company who works less than full-time. Often there are varieties of part-time within the same company. For example, some employees may work twenty hours per week and some may work thirty hours per week. Companies need part-timers to perform work that doesn't require an additional full-time employee. Job sharing arrangements are unique forms of part-time work in which two part-time employees fill one full-time equivalent position.

Part-time work can give you the time you need to pursue whatever it is you do in your free time while keeping you engaged in the workforce. Keeping your hand in the workplace is not a bad idea versus exiting for a couple of years (e.g., to raise children) and then making a "triumphant" return. Returns after prolonged absences are seldom triumphant. You will have been passed by by lesser mortals and there will be the pervasive assumption that your brain and/or physical capacities have shriveled during that time period. You will seriously consider starting your own business against the humiliating prospects of starting over.

There is one other reason companies like to use part-time employees and *this* you need to know. It's often cheaper for them. They will pay you an hourly rate commensurate with the salary grade, but often will give you fewer benefits or none at all. The most expensive benefits are the ones you should be most concerned about: retirement benefits, health insurance, and long-term disability. Not having these benefits, particularly health and disability coverage, can have catastrophic effect on your economic well-being in the event you are injured or sick and will be out of work for an extended period. Aside from the overuse of credit cards, lack of medical and disability coverages during emergencies are leading reasons why people file for personal bankruptcy. Finding a part-time job with these benefits is worth thousands of dollars per year to you, and much, much more if a need arises. Benefits are often "tiered" by the hours you work: you may get full coverages at 30 hours per week, some coverages at 25 hours per week, and none at all at 20 hours per week or less. It may be worth it to you to put in a few extra hours per week in order to receive the added benefits. Part-time work as a second job may also help with your Social Security benefits in retirement—if you don't earn the taxable maximum of $65,400 (in 1997) in your "day job."

Temporary Help. The average daily employment of temporary help is approaching 2.5 million people and is growing at an annual clip of about 5% to 10% (see *HR Magazine,* April 1997, p. 65). Temporary services have been around since the 1920s, originally furnishing clerical services to companies. Office/clerical work remains the most often filled job category for temporary services but the services are gradually expanding into production fields and professional-technical-managerial areas. The demographic profile of the typical temporary worker reflects these changes: Temporary workers are older and more educated than in the past.

If you are a temporary employee, you will likely work for a temporary service company such as Kelly Services, Manpower, or Olsten. When a company needs help in a particular area, it makes a specific request to the temporary service company, which then tries to find the best match among its available employees. The company would pay the agency for which you work a fee and your agency would then pay you for your services. You can usually pick and choose the assignment that best fits your needs and schedule so "temping" does offer some flexibility. More and more, however, temping is like a 35-to-40-hour-per-week job except you're not an employee of the company.

If you ask temporary workers what they want most, it's a traditional job. Companies understand this and dangle the fruit of permanent work in front of the temp in return for "commitment." There is a sunny side to this. Some companies reserve permanent full-time work for temps, and temping, then, becomes a way to showcase your skills and for you and the prospective employer to assess one another for compatibility before entering into a more permanent arrangement. It's the courtship before marriage.

Temping can be a great entrée to a company that would otherwise be difficult to get into. I have seen four-week trials turn into great permanent jobs for many temps over the years. To prevent misunderstandings, however, you should find out prior to accepting an assignment:

(1) if the company seeking your services reserves positions for temps, i.e., if permanent, full-time openings go to temps first
(2) the number of temps who have actually been hired full-time (of how many)
(3) whether the position in which you will be working will turn into full-time work *and* the time frame for this decision

There is a dark side to temping as well. First, companies sometimes use and abuse their temporaries who, after all, "aren't really their employees." Second, the prospect of future full-time employment is often a chimera. Known as the "gateway myth," companies often try to get you to perform unnatural acts of commitment in exchange for a possible full-time job. Third, the pay is up to 40% lower (see *USA Today,* April 11, 1997, B1) for the same work performed by a full-time employee, and there are seldom health and pension benefits. Temping is not the way to get paid what you are worth. Some of the larger temp agencies provide benefits but you have to work a certain number of hours to be eligible.

In other words, despite the mistreatment, low pay, and lack of benefits, temping can be a lot of fun. Actually, you should view temping as it was meant to be: as a *temporary* (short-term) assignment. Do not accept "permanent temping" as an option. This is where a company takes you on indefinitely *as a temp.* In that arrangement, everyone gets fat except you. The company gets a "discounted" worker, your service agency gets nice cash flow from fees, and you get: low pay, few (if any) benefits including paid sick time off, none of the corporate goodies (e.g., educational reimbursement) that are reserved for the full-time staff, and often second-class citizenship. Would you be party to such a one-sided relationship in any other arena of your life? No one is doing you any favors here.

Other Contingent Work Arrangements. There are three other prominent forms of contingent work. By far the largest is "independent contractor," a form of work that applies to 8 to 9 million Americans. About one-half of all self-employed have independent contractor status. Essentially, you work for yourself and contract out your services to others. You determine how, where, and with whom you choose to work. Many consultants, real estate agents, financial service representatives, home remodeling contractors, writers, software developers, etc., are independent contractors. Independent contractors are self-employed—a topic discussed earlier in this book.

The Worth of Happiness

Having briefly considered workforce trends, let's now turn our attention to the nature of work itself. In particular, let's explore what it is like to do your job: what you like and don't like about it. As we begin this adventure, you'll want to reflect upon your job and pay and repeatedly ask yourself, "Is it all worth it?"

What is happiness worth to you? How much money would you be willing to exchange for happiness, if you had to give up anything at all? There is a dynamic, give-and-take relationship between money and other items of value within the workplace. The more of these items you possess, the less important the money because you are prospering in other ways. On the other hand, the fewer of these items you have, the greater the importance of money. Ideally, you will be amply rewarded with money *and* job satisfaction.

Most people who leave companies say the reason for leaving is money. But it is almost always money *relative* to what they have to endure at work and compared to what they can earn elsewhere under different conditions. Increasingly, people are trading high pressure, high earning jobs for greater simplicity and lower pay. These trade-offs are occurring frequently enough that they have acquired labels: *voluntary simplicity* or *downshifting.* It is a version of Thoreau's "simplicity, simplicity, simplicity." But keep in mind that Thoreau was a wealthy business owner who, to my knowledge, never gave up his successful graphite manufacturing facility.

Although the desire to downshift has been largely a luxury for the privileged who can afford to live with the consequences, everyone can make lifestyle decisions that can remove stress from their lives. You can move to a job that demands fewer hours and that is located in a place where the lifestyle is more leisurely and less hectic. If you have ever lived in different parts of the country, you know that the local environment is infectious. There are healthy places, fun places, relaxed places, frenetic places, quiet places, etc. Chart 12B lists *Fortune*'s rankings of the top U.S. cities where it is easiest to combine work with quality of life.

You can also decrease your career expectations and decide you can ex-

CHART 12B. FORTUNE'S 1996 BEST CITIES FOR WORK AND FAMILY

- Seattle
- Denver
- Philadelphia
- Minneapolis
- Raleigh-Durham
- St. Louis
- Cincinnati
- Washington
- Pittsburgh
- Dallas–Fort Worth
- Atlanta
- Baltimore
- Boston
- Milwaukee
- Nashville

Source: *Fortune*, November 11, 1996, pp. 113 ff.

ist happily with fewer material possessions. If you can make do with less and, in good conscience, scale back your personal ambitions, perhaps you too can be a downshifter. It's worth considering. We'll discuss the trade-offs between satisfaction and money in the remaining sections of this book.

The Job Satisfaction Game

We are going to play a game that can help you decide what happiness is worth to you on your job. In that way, you can have a better idea of how much money you might be willing to give up or need to take in in exchange for increases or decreases in happiness. Here is how it works. I am going to give you twenty gold coins at the start of the game. Depending upon your answers to the questions in Chart 12C, you will either get to keep the coins or give them up to me. When the game is complete and all of the coins have been allocated, I'll tell you what to do next. For now, go ahead and answer all of the questions in Chart 12C. Then we'll discuss what lies behind the questions in the following sections.

There are a number of different factors that make a job satisfying or dissatisfying. Some of these factors have to do with the job itself, some with the boss, and some with social and environmental conditions surrounding the job. I call the various types of factors that lead to employee satisfaction or dissatisfaction "environments"; these various environments are discussed below.

Job Environment

There are several "satisfiers" specifically related to a job that can make the experience of work more fulfilling and you much happier. Research shows it, employees say it, everybody wants them. They are:

- challenge
- creativity
- growth
- meaningfulness
- responsibility
- variety

Challenge. If the job is too easy, it's boring. If you can do the work in your sleep, chances are that some days you will. There is nothing as unstimulating and as tiring as unchallenging work. That's right—*as tiring*. Overly simplistic work has the counterintuitive effect of lowering your work metabolism to near zero. Books on near-death experiences were probably written by employees in boring jobs.

CHART 12C. HOW SATISFYING IS YOUR JOB?

Instructions. Please read each question carefully and give your honest and frank opinion by circling the answer that best describes what you think. There are no right or wrong answers.

When you have finished, count up the number of gold coins you have retained and the number of gold coins you have given up.
If you answered "1" or "2" on any question, you will have to give up a coin.
If you answered "3" or "4" on any question, you get to keep a coin.

Satisfiers/Dissatisfiers	*Response Scale*
1. I feel challenged by my job.	*Highly disagree* 1 2 │ 3 4 *Highly agree*
2. I am able to be creative on my job.	*Highly disagree* 1 2 │ 3 4 *Highly agree*
3. My company encourages me to develop my skills.	*Highly disagree* 1 2 │ 3 4 *Highly agree*
4. I think what I do is meaningful.	*Highly disagree* 1 2 │ 3 4 *Highly agree*
5. I am able to think and act for myself.	*Highly disagree* 1 2 │ 3 4 *Highly agree*
6. My job has a lot of variety that is interesting to me.	*Highly disagree* 1 2 │ 3 4 *Highly agree*
7. I understand my role in the company and what I have to do.	*Highly disagree* 1 2 │ 3 4 *Highly agree*
8. My manager is honest, fair and trustworthy.	*Highly disagree* 1 2 │ 3 4 *Highly agree*
9. I feel that I am properly recognized for what I do.	*Highly disagree* 1 2 │ 3 4 *Highly agree*
10. My manager respects my needs and interests.	*Highly disagree* 1 2 │ 3 4 *Highly agree*
11. My manager sets and models high standards of excellence.	*Highly disagree* 1 2 │ 3 4 *Highly agree*
12. I would describe my work surroundings as neat and clean.	*Highly disagree* 1 2 │ 3 4 *Highly agree*
13. I work in a healthy and safe environment.	*Highly disagree* 1 2 │ 3 4 *Highly agree*
14. I feel secure at my company.	*Highly disagree* 1 2 │ 3 4 *Highly agree*
15. My job allows me to have a life outside of work, if I choose.	*Highly disagree* 1 2 │ 3 4 *Highly agree*
16. People are willing to help one another at work.	*Highly disagree* 1 2 │ 3 4 *Highly agree*
17. It is easy to make friends where I work.	*Highly disagree* 1 2 │ 3 4 *Highly agree*
18. I have a high-status job.	*Highly disagree* 1 2 │ 3 4 *Highly agree*
19. My job is fun. (*Note: This is worth 2 gold coins*).	*Highly disagree* 1 2 │ 3 4 *Highly agree*

TOTALS: Coins you give up____ ____Coins you keep

Read on in the book for a discussion of the various satisfiers/ dissatisfiers and what you might do better or differently on the job.

Many companies have some form of objective-setting process that allows you and your manager to establish goals for the year. These should be challenging. Many consultants make a good living giving talks on how to develop challenging goals that are specific, measurable, actionable (i.e., someone is responsible for the results), realistic, and time dependent (i.e., there is a due date). These are the infamous SMART goals. But I'll give you one subjective test of challenge that is all you will need. To know if a goal is truly challenging, ask yourself how you will feel if you reach the goal and how you will feel if you do not. There should be some emotional attachment to the outcomes. You should feel great if you make it and terribly disappointed if you do not.

For a goal to be challenging, there has to be some question of whether or not it can be achieved. It can't be a certainty. This means that you will have to muster resources or use skills that you didn't know you had or haven't previously exercised. It doesn't sound like it ought to be that tough to come up with a challenging goal, but for a lot of managers and employees it is. Many people get stuck on what they currently do on the job and so goals are just reiterations of job responsibilities. In other words, goals are often of the form: "Do what you always do." Ninety-nine percent of all goals out there do not require anyone to do anything differently or to stretch their capabilities. You might say they are "worthlessness added" goals.

Think about what is of value to your company and what excites you, and dream up a challenge that you can present to your manager. I have seen software developers take their dreams of new products through appropriate channels to the CEOs of their corporations. While you are at it, you might also want to consider the resources, time, and training you might need to fulfill your part of the bargain.

Creativity. There are many forms of creativity. It can be social, such as conceiving of a new way to organize a department. It can be technical, such as developing a new product specification. It can be operational, such as establishing new methods or procedures. The common theme is that you have made something either from scratch or, more typically, by combining thoughts and pieces of a puzzle in novel ways. Most people love to use their imaginations—it is the closest thing to play at work. It is a great feeling to say, "I did that!" assuming it is not in response to the question, *"Who* is responsible for this?" But you will have to speak up. Don't expect the weight of your creation or discovery to speak for itself. Many people probably set foot on America's shores before Columbus; but Columbus was the one who spoke up.

Does your job give you the opportunity to grow and learn or are you dying on the vine, gathering moss, stagnating, vegetating, hibernating, etc.?

You get the picture. I have seen employees mentally atrophy for lack of creative stimulation. If you are in a rut, the way out is not to dig deeper. First, try climbing out by having a frank discussion with your boss about how you might be able to solve a problem or address an organizational need if given the opportunity.

Second, you might discuss changing locations within, or outside, the company. Sometimes the ability to be innovative and to creatively flourish depends on the right set of conditions. Certain seeds (except bad ones) will do better under particular climatic and soil conditions. There is nothing problematic about the seed or the circumstances. They are just not right for each other. Similarly, some people may need the right corporate culture (e.g., inquisitive and experimenting) and to be surrounded by certain types of people. I have known many employees whose careers were at a standstill but who went on to thrive and excel at other companies. Some corporate grounds are more fertile to certain people than others.

Growth. Growth implies that you periodically undergo a transformation. You become different in some way by gleaning new insights, learning new techniques, acquiring more knowledge, becoming better at or gaining a new understanding of something, etc. This requires self-discipline and a dedication to your craft, vocation, or profession. Companies can make it easier for you through financial assistance and time off but in the end it is your commitment to your work that matters most.

The question for you is, "Does your company value growth and development?" There are a couple ways of knowing. First, does the company actively look for ways to deploy you in order to fully utilize or develop your skills? Second, does your company provide a logical career progression or does it pigeonhole you into a particular job? That is, does it give you room to grow? Third, does your company provide formal or on-the-job training? Fourth, does your company reward you for making significant developmental progress? One of the most enduring of human desires is to better oneself; it may be worth something to you to work for a company that cares about this.

Meaningfulness. This form of meaningfulness has nothing to do with the search for the meaning *of* life. It involves the less ambitious search for meaning *in* life. Unfortunately, there are no surveys or magazine rankings that will tell you what is meaningful and what isn't. It is entirely up to you. In organizations, meaning can simply involve being a part of something larger than oneself regardless of the specific purpose: manufacturing a better computer, selling more of a particular brand of cereal, providing higher quality customer service, landing an all-terrain walker on Mars, etc. It doesn't matter as long as the company can make everyone feel like valued members of a team—and be sincere about it. If that doesn't do the trick, there is a burgeoning number of "meaning" consultants who can help.

These consultants help companies find ways to incorporate employees' personal values and interests into the workplace. This is nothing new. For many years companies have tried to find ways to make work more meaningful for employees. Recently, however, it has become more fashionable. Sabbaticals, paid and unpaid time off for volunteerism, and company book clubs are all ways to enlarge a company's purposes to include your interests. Web Industries, for example, lets assembly line workers read thought-provoking books, while Autodesk lets employees bring their dogs to work.

For many employees, working for a cause that one is passionate about may be the way to meaning. You will not be lured into social services, for example, primarily by money. Working at a job with broader social aims— a cleaner environment, relief for the needy—is part of the reward.

Responsibility. There is nothing more frustrating than being powerless to affect important outcomes in your work environment. Is there? This is where you are not permitted to think one independent thought or to deviate a hair from a prescribed way of doing things without express permission from a superior, if then. The only thing worse is to think you have the authority to take action but are repeatedly countermanded by the very same supervisor who led you to believe you had the authority in the first place. This is the "not-like-that-you-idiot" approach to management. People like to have control and positive effect on what goes on around them. Fundamentally, being empowered means being trusted to make important decisions for which one is trained or experienced to make without incessant second-guessing, checking, and monitoring.

Keep in mind that "letting go" is extremely difficult for some people. It produces substantial anxiety in supervisors who want to know what's going on around them, lest their own supervisors let them know first. Keeping your supervisor informed is one way to ease his or her anxiety and to get the supervisor to progressively transfer responsibilities. Again, this is an area where you can be proactive. Think about the decisions you feel comfortable making and the responsibilities that you are prepared to assume, and make a pitch to your boss for greater accountability.

Variety. Variety refers to a healthy mix of job activities versus the dulling routine of the same thing day in, day out. A good job is like Thanksgiving dinner—lots of options and overindulgence. The principle is simple: Even the most succulent food loses its taste if that's all that's eaten. No matter how exciting a job, if you do the same thing over and over, your job will lose its appeal. Psychologists refer to this as "habituation."

Some jobs have variety because unexpected or unforseen events occur around them. You never know what will happen next and what you might have to do. As long as those events don't create too much stress, they can add color to a job. If your job doesn't have much built-in variety, you may have to create it. Most jobs can be expanded and spiced up at your discretion— even activities you perform every day. A telemarketer can experiment with different approaches to customers and scripts, an accountant can trial new software, etc. Most of the time, it's up to you.

The Management Environment

I have had the privilege of working with some of the best managers over the years, the kind of people who give management a good name and who you'd love to work for, versus those managers justifiably lampooned by the popular press and their very own employees. It is unfortunate that managers often don't realize the effect they have on someone else's quality of life. But if you have ever worked for a very good or very bad boss, you know. While there are differences in the dispositions and technical talents among managers, the best managers provide several key ingredients in the workplace.

Clarity and Direction. There's nothing quite like being at work and not entirely understanding why you are there. And if you feel that way, you're not alone. There are many employees who spend their days bewildered, asking themselves one of life's most fundamental questions, "What should I do today?" The extended coffee break emerges as a leading candidate for filling time.

If you don't know the answer to what you should or could be doing, it's partially your fault if you haven't tried to find out. But managers are to blame as well for either not understanding what has to be done or for failing to communicate it. The best managers let you know about three things:

- the major objectives of your group (e.g., department, function, and business)
- your role in meeting those objectives
- specific activities/tasks you have to perform to help meet the group's objectives

In other words, you know where you are going and how to get there. Good managers essentially provide good road maps where "destination" is clearly marked and alternative routes are displayed.

Honesty and Fairness. The heart of a good working relationship is one of those old-fashioned virtues: trust. Do you believe your boss would stab you in the back at the first opportunity? Does your boss take credit for the things you do? Do you believe what your boss tells you is the truth, rather than self-interested fabrications? If you asked your boss a straight question, would you get a straight answer? Does your boss treat everyone fairly or does he or she play favorites? Will your boss stand beside you when you need him or her to be there for you or will she or he slither away?

The answer to these questions should give you a pretty good idea of how your boss rates and what you must be experiencing in the workplace. Although relationships can spice up the workplace, working for someone who is dishonest, untrustworthy, and unfair is a nightmare.

Recognition. No matter how much of a self-starter you are, most of us sputter to a halt if not refreshed by an occasional thank-you. You can only go so far for so long before needing to be refueled by some form of recognition. Good bosses should be aware of your achievements and should periodically communicate appreciation for your efforts and contributions.

Why is this so tough? This is not unlike other relationships. When you do things on behalf of someone else, you expect some show of gratitude. If your manager thinks your paycheck is the only gratitude you need, you have a problem.

Spirituality. The best managers I have observed over the years have a spiritual quality. I don't mean that they are necessarily religious in a formal sense or that a religious person is necessarily spiritual. I mean that the best managers see the intangibles of work—they know that employees don't live by bread alone.

These managers are compassionate and respectful. They understand that employees have interests of their own, and are willing to listen to what those interests are. They see the individuality in people rather than seeing a homogeneous mass of "thems." This is in contrast to what one employee recently told me about her company: "If we were animals, the company would be fined for cruelty."

Indeed, having a boss who has no respect for you as a person, and no awareness of your interests and needs, is torture. Such a boss is bad news for you and bad news for the company.

Standards of Excellence. Working for good bosses isn't necessarily easy. I never said that! One of the great ironies of management is that although employees *like* bosses who are all warm and fuzzy as persons, they hate them as managers if they do not insist upon meeting high standards of excellence.

Good managers set high performance thresholds that they expect everyone to meet. They *expect* employees to scale to new heights. And because they expect it, more often than not, employees expect to succeed. There are few things as exhilarating and rewarding as feeling alive and successful. Demanding managers can help you feel both. On the other hand, easy, wishy-washy managers can help you to feel frustrated and defeated. You'd prefer the former kind of manager, wouldn't you?

Work Environment

Attractiveness. Take a look around your workplace. Is it dark, dirty, and dingy? Is it messy and unorganized? Is it cluttered and cramped? Does walking outside at the end of the day feel a little like *Escape from Alcatraz*?

The attractiveness of your surroundings has profound effects on your mood and work behavior. It rubs off on you. It is very hard to feel good and do a good job if all the "signals" around you convey sloppiness, incompleteness, and low quality. On the other hand, a neat, clean, and orderly environment can give you a sense of well-being, a greater sense of mastery and control, and the feeling that you are a valued employee. Speaking of environmental "signals," I once consulted to a company where the lights automatically went off at 5:00 P.M. "Good night, everybody."

Health and Safety. Some jobs may be hazardous to your health. Unless you have a perverse liking for high temperatures, sharp objects, and chemical waste, you won't find these jobs to be very attractive unless you are compensated for the exposure.

There are a number of things that can make a job unpleasant:

- loud noises (e.g., some types of machinery)
- heat and high temperatures (e.g., furnaces)
- bad odors (e.g., various types of mills)
- exposures to various hazards
  — sharp objects (e.g., meat packing)
  — heavy objects, equipment, machinery (e.g., construction)
  — chemical/radiation (e.g., waste treatment, disposal; energy)
  — fire/guns
- repetitive movements, confined movements, or awkward positions (e.g., assembly line work, data entry)
- physical exertion, (e.g., pulling, pushing, lifting)
- mental exertion, (e.g., work that requires high levels of concentration over extended periods, constant vigilance or repeated responses to problems or events largely outside one's control).

Call me particular, but I find that most people don't like these things.

Security. This has more to do with what's going on around you than what it looks like around you. Does the environment seem to be random and capricious? Might you lose your job through "downsizing" at a moment's notice? Will your department be "outsourced"? (Outsourcing is when another company performs the duties once done by your department; you are either transferred to the other company or let go.)

There is ample evidence that shows that high levels of anxiety disrupt job performance. The constant threat of losing one's job, and the loss of money and self-esteem associated with job loss, can be quite disturbing. Actually, it can be catastrophic given that loss of work sometimes leads to family break-ups, personal bankruptcy, and mental health problems such as substance abuse.

There is such a thing as psychic abuse, of which job insecurity is one form. How much is working under such pressures worth to you?

The Social Environment

There are a number of aspects to the social environment in which you work that can make a big difference in how satisfied you are. I discuss some of the more important "social" features, below, based on employee comments I've heard over the years.

Balance. Increasingly, employees are seeking greater balance between work and family or between work and leisure. We discussed this trend already. The question for you is, Are you able to find the "rewards" you seek outside of work, or does work have a stranglehold on your personal life?

You don't have play the part of unhappy community statesperson who sacrifices everything for work—unless you want to. It is possible to be dedicated to your craft or profession and to enjoy yourself. If you could step back and take an objective view of your life, can you imagine spending some of your time in other ways—more time with friends and family, guilt-free vacations, in pursuit of a special passion, a better diet, more exercise, etc.? You don't have to play the role of sufferer to prove your importance at work.

Often, being short of time is not your employer's fault. You don't take the time! I have seen companies *make* employees take their vacations, for example. Companies realize that you need balance in your life to be productive and that ideas germinate in unlikely places and at unlikely times. I recently saw a presentation with a novel design and layout. I asked the employee where he had gotten his ideas on the way he formatted the presentation. His answer: the Museum of Modern Art!

If you have tried to create or restore balance in your life and have failed because of that darn job, that probably cost you a gold coin in Chart 12C. Attaining balance is not easy and sometimes it's plain impossible. Many high-volume service-oriented companies and functions (e.g., amusements, customer service centers) control every minute of your time and a big chunk of your spare time by forcing you to work overtime or by calling you in to work on your "day off."

Cooperation. There are various degrees of cooperation but please don't look for the "work families" portrayed on television. The perfect combination of people who are never offended and who work in fun-loving harmony is rare. Cooperation means that you get along with your fellow employees in an atmosphere that is cordial, polite, and accommodating—not petty or mean-spirited.

It is possible to have a pleasant, cooperative social environment even when employees compete. Most work environments have elements of competition. Employees may compete for money, for recognition, for jobs, for choice projects, etc. Some people are better competitors than others and some companies may more purposely promote competition than others.

But competition can be constructive or destructive. I have seen the "carrot" of high rewards and promising career prospects dangled in front of ambitious employees lead to the sabotage of one another's work and of cutting corners to achieve results. At this stage, the competition is clearly unhealthy.

To assess whether the competition within your company has reached dangerous levels, ask yourself these questions:

- Do people try to look good by making others look bad?
- Do people try to throw up obstacles in front of other people's work?
- Are people quick to criticize or refute other people's accomplishments?

Friendliness. Friendliness concerns the extent to which you feel emotionally connected to the people with whom you work. You know; it's easy to make friends. There are people at work who you have over to the house or go out with after work.

So many times I've heard this employee lament: "If it weren't for the people, I'd be miserable." Having people around who you like can make a big difference in your attitude. They can support you when times are tough and inject a little humor and levity any time.

Having the right interpersonal chemistry at work is sometimes a matter of luck: The right people are at the right place at the right time. Sometimes certain kinds of people, people who share the same interests and who have similar belief systems, are attracted to the same kind of work. And sometimes the company actively looks for and selects people who are alike in many ways. Often companies develop a standard set of criteria that they believe will predict success on the job; they use those criteria to screen and select job candidates.

The Extra-Company Environment

There is one aspect to your job that you can do little about except to accept or reject the judgment rendered. That has to do with how much status your job has in the eyes of the general public. We are all status-conscious creatures and the work you perform is held at varying levels of esteem by others. You may have the self-confidence to fully enjoy what you do despite the opinions of others. You should.

However, many people are willing to take public accolades in lieu of cash. Often job prestige and money go hand in hand. More of one is related to more of the other. There are, nevertheless, noble professions such as academic jobs and public service positions in which the cash rewards are offset by the honor these positions bestow. The value the general community places on the job seems to be a kind of down payment for doing the work.

There is no foolproof "prestige" index that unequivocally measures the amount of prestige contained in a job. But you can probably guess with what prestige is associated: the big three of money, power, and knowledge. More of any of these things typically increases the perceived status of a position. Having a scarce and valuable skill or body of knowledge, having authority over others or being able to make decisions in others' behalf, having the business wherewithal or ability to attract lots of paying customers or spectators, etc., generally instills a sense of awe in all of us. Next time we are asked to pay for access to the special talents or services of these people, let's tell them that our public admiration should be payment enough.

Fun. This is a catchall category that sums up your experience in the workplace. Are you enjoying yourself?

I wish I had a dollar for every time a company said they would make work "fun." That would be compensation enough for me. "Having fun" vies with "People are our most important asset" as the corporation's top platitude. In between long hours, work force reductions, eroding advancement opportunities . . .

Are You Having Fun Yet?

The aim to have fun at work is laudable. At least it suggests that work shouldn't be that different from everything else you do in your life. Good companies have a way of bringing out and using the special talents of employees, including those related to hobbies and pastimes. Companies often try to extract these special qualities by creating stimulating, whimsical environments. I have seen companies mount musical instruments on the walls that employees can play as they pass down the halls; I have seen jigsaw puzzles laid out in public places to be jointly completed by employees; I have seen Research and Development laboratories set up tests and experiments open to others to work on. The goals are to provoke thought and to integrate work and play.

You ought to be thinking about what you truly love and how to incorporate those loves into your daily activities. If you think hard about it, you will be able to make connections between work and pleasures that on the surface may appear unrelated. Take a piece of paper and list your passions. Now think about the primary purposes of your job. Write one objective for yourself, consistent with your job role, that incorporates at least one of your passions into it. In addition, there is nothing stopping you from starting or joining a club at work with others who share your interests.

The Price of Satisfaction

To be sure, hard currency is important for much of our behavior, from what we buy at the store to whether we travel first class or coach. Economic realities inform many of our decisions. But it isn't everything and the proof is easy to find. I have been to companies that have abysmal jobs and working conditions. These are the jobs that you pray your own children will never have to do. When companies include these jobs in their internal transfer programs (so that employees can apply for open jobs throughout the company), the floodgates are opened. Employees in horrible, well-paying jobs will gladly take a "better" job elsewhere in the company, even if it pays less. Employees readily take *downward* job transfers that improve their total work life until the company tells them they can't do it anymore. Else no one would be left doing this other work for the price offered.

We all make trade-offs between our economic and psychological/physical well-being, and by reading through this chapter you are now closer to seeing what those trade-offs are and mean to you. In completing the questions in Chart 12C, you were able to earn, and were forced to give away, a certain number of gold coins.

Admittedly, there are some problems with the game that we are about to play. For one, there may be certain aspects of your job that you can't live without and, as such, you will attach greater importance to these aspects than to others. Not everything carries the same weight or has the same psychological value. I recently saw an employee reject a 25% pay increase at another company because the other company was "too structured" for him. It was worth 25% of his income to be left alone to do his own thing as he saw fit with little corporate intrusion.

Second, there may not be a price tag that can be readily placed on certain values that make you more or less satisfied on your job. I recently witnessed an employee return to her former employer after being away at a competitor for four months because she missed the camaraderie and friendship at the old place. This employee refused to negotiate—there wasn't anything the new company could do and no amount of money it could pay to keep her. This behavior seemed to be irrational and unpredictable from a purely economic point of view because there was no price tag that could be placed on the "sense of fellow-feeling." In actuality, the behavior might not be rational from a psychological point of view either—it seems a bit dependent to me. But anyway . . .

So the following pages look more like a science than they really are. But I didn't just make it up, either. Over the years, I have observed employees make trade-offs between money and various potential satisfiers at work and the trading range seems to be about ±20% of compensation. That is, employees tend to want approximately up to 20% more or less in pay, depending upon the psychological and environmental factors associated with the work for which they are educated and trained to perform. Thus, the ensuing "game" allows you to give or take up to 20% of your compensation in exchange for desirable or undesirable elements on your job. Like an old-fashioned scale that relied upon the balance of weights on each side, your goal is to find an equilibrium between the quality and satisfaction of your work life and what you are paid. Measuring how much gold you have accumulated (as an index of satisfaction) against how much you earn is a way to get you thinking about what matters least and most to you.

Having said all of that, now count up the number of gold coins in your possession. If you have all twenty, great! You are in the ideal job, from your point of view. If you had to give all twenty coins away, let's just say you are not in the ideal job. Most jobs, however, aren't all good or all bad. They have elements you like and those that you can easily do without. These types of jobs may be best described as "tolerable" (see Chart 12D).

Now let's say that each coin is worth 1% of your current compensation

CHART 12D.   YOUR JOB EXPERIENCE

Your Number of Gold Coins	Your Psychological Experience
+20	
+19	The Ideal Job —
+18	Did You Answer Truthfully?
+17	
+16	
+15	
+14	Pleasantly Tolerable —
+13	Not Perfect But Not Bad
+12	
+11	
+10	
+ 9	
+ 8	Unpleasantly Tolerable —
+ 7	Barely Bearable
+ 6	
+ 5	
+ 4	
+ 3	Do You Really Want to Do
+ 2	This Work?
+ 1	
+ 0	

(base salary plus any bonus you may receive). Chart 12E shows you what a fair exchange between material and psychological wealth might be if you were to change jobs (or if the job you are in were to change). If, in the new job, you believed you could gain five gold coins, for example, then you might be willing to take 5% *less* in pay (in actuality you'd probably take even less because most people wouldn't consider this an even trade—most people value their psychological health more than their material wealth).

On the other hand, if you were to move to a job where you expected five *fewer* gold coins, you would want more in pay to compensate you for the loss in some of the satisfying aspects of work. For example, you would want about 5% more in pay to compensate you for the loss of five gold coins. You

Chart 12E. Finding Balance Between Money and Happiness

If you could gain more coins from a job…	…you could take less money	If you would lose more coins from a job…	…you should want more money
+20 coins	-20 % in base salary	-20 coins	+20 % in base salary
+19 coins	-19 % in base salary	-19 coins	+19 % in base salary
+18 coins	-18 % in base salary	-18 coins	+18 % in base salary
+17 coins	-17 % in base salary	-17 coins	+17 % in base salary
+16 coins	-16 % in base salary	-16 coins	+16 % in base salary
+15 coins	-15 % in base salary	-15 coins	+15 % in base salary
+14 coins	-14 % in base salary	-14 coins	+14 % in base salary
+13 coins	-13 % in base salary	-13 coins	+13 % in base salary
+12 coins	-12 % in base salary	-12 coins	+12 % in base salary
+11 coins	-11 % in base salary	-11 coins	+11 % in base salary
+10 coins	-10 % in base salary	-10 coins	+10 % in base salary
+ 9 coins	- 9 % in base salary	- 9 coins	+ 9 % in base salary
+ 8 coins	- 8 % in base salary	- 8 coins	+ 8 % in base salary
+ 7 coins	- 7 % in base salary	- 7 coins	+ 7 % in base salary
+ 6 coins	- 6 % in base salary	- 6 coins	+ 6 % in base salary
+ 5 coins	- 5 % in base salary	- 5 coins	+ 5 % in base salary
+ 4 coins	- 4 % in base salary	- 4 coins	+ 4 % in base salary
+ 3 coins	- 3 % in base salary	- 3 coins	+ 3 % in base salary
+ 2 coins	- 2 % in base salary	- 2 coins	+ 2 % in base salary
+ 1 coins	- 1 % in base salary	- 1 coins	+ 1 % in base salary
+ 0 coins	- 0 % in base salary	- 0 coins	+ 0 % in base salary

…all else being equal

can never know for certain whether or not a job will have all of the elements in Chart 12C, but you can ask about these as a part of your job investigation and make a best guess.

Take an example. Suppose you are looking at a job in a different company. Further suppose that this other job is bigger than the one you have now—it would be about a one-grade jump for you. In calculating how much this other job is worth, you would need to consider the following:

- Value of the job promotion: estimate = +10% to +15% per grade (across companies)
- Nuisance or inconvenience factors (the psychological costs of terminating, of packing up, of becoming acquainted with your new job and new people, etc.): estimate = +5% to +10%

- Increases or decreases in total satisfaction (for purposes of this example, let's assume that you expected to collect 3 fewer coins in the new job): estimate = +3%

If you add this all up, you'll find that it will take from 18% to 28% more to get you to make the move. Again, you can't always know for sure how satisfying or dissatisfying a new job will be. You may want to play it safe and add in a +5% "uncertainty factor"—you'll need an extra 5% of your pay just to cover the risk of not knowing what you'll find in your new location.

You see how it works. Satisfaction is definitely worth something and this chapter is intended to help you think through what that is. Feel free to experiment. You might find that only five of the items in Chart 12C matter at all to you. Make each of those five items worth four gold coins (each worth 4% of your compensation) and see how your current job compares to another job you are thinking about. If you can gain in satisfaction, you can see how a lateral or downward move can sometimes make a lot of sense. But, again, there is nothing like loving what you do and getting paid a handsome sum for it.

I see a lot of inertia in the workplace. Employees who could have been contenders if only they had done something sooner. Don't become an embittered employee who complains daily about his or her fate but does nothing about it. I have never really understood the people who do this. Every time you think a negative thought about your job and your pay, I want you to take a positive step to correct it.

Are You Paid What You're Worth? has shown you that much of your compensation for your job lies in your hands, both in terms of tangible rewards (money, stock) and intangible rewards (job satisfaction). And more and more, this is precisely the way companies want it! They want proactive, vital employees who reflect upon such things as their development and contributions to their company and who take personal responsibility to enhance each. But don't stop there. That would be too abrupt an ending. A company has to pay you for the value you bring and, by this point, you should have good ideas on how to go about this.

Index